Purple Power

THE WORKING CLASS IN AMERICAN HISTORY

Editorial Advisors
James R. Barrett, Thavolia Glymph, Julie Greene, William P. Jones, and Nelson Lichtenstein

A list of books in the series appears at the end of this book.

Purple Power

The History and Global Impact of SEIU

Edited by
LUÍS LM AGUIAR and
JOSEPH A. MCCARTIN

1 2 3 4 5 C P 5 4 3 2 1
∞ This book is printed on acid-free paper.

The editors would like to thank the UBC Scholarly Publication Fund for financially supporting the publication of this book.

Library of Congress Cataloging-in-Publication Data
Names: Aguiar, Luis L. M., editor. | McCartin, Joseph Anthony, editor.
Title: Purple power : the history and global impact of SEIU / edited by Luís LM Aguiar and Joseph A. McCartin.
Description: [Urbana, IL] : [University of Illinois Press], [2023] | Series: The working class in American history | Includes bibliographical references and index.
Identifiers: LCCN 2022025030 (print) | LCCN 2022025031 (ebook) | ISBN 9780252044717 (cloth) | ISBN 9780252086809 (paperback) |ISBN 9780252053757 (ebook)
Subjects: LCSH: Service Employees International Union. | Service industries workers—Labor unions—History. | Social change—United States—History.
Classification: LCC HD6475.S45 P87 2023 (print) | LCC HD6475.S45 (ebook) | DDC 331.88/11000973—dc23/eng/20220622
LC record available at https://lccn.loc.gov/2022025030
LC ebook record available at https://lccn.loc.gov/2022025031

Contents

Acknowledgments

This book is a long time coming, not only for the lack of sustained and rigorous research solely dedicated to SEIU, but for the challenges it faced along the way—challenges that required perseverance from all involved. The contributors who have been with this project from the beginning know what we mean. Adrienne Eaton, more than anyone, knows what we mean. We thank her for continuing to support this book and advising Luís over the years. First of all, Luís wants to thank Dr. Lydia Savage, a pioneer in researching SEIU, for her hard work, under difficult circumstances, in supporting this volume from the beginning. He regrets that although Lydia's work has influenced many of the contributors to this volume, she could not be part of the final manuscript after having put so much work into ensuring it remained on the radar of the University of Illinois Press. He is also immensely grateful to Lydia as a model of altruism, professionalism, and solidarity. Second, Luís wants to thank all the contributors for staying with this project and keeping faith in (him and) the project's merit notwithstanding delays in bringing it to fruition. Thank you too to Tina Marten for reading most of the chapters herein and for making insightful observations and comments for their improvement. Allison Kooijman also read some of the chapters and offered suggestions for their improvement. Luís offers special thanks to his coeditor, Joe McCartin, for stepping in without hesitation and for injecting this book with the energy and momentum needed to bring it to completion. The many workers, activists, and union personnel interviewed for the various studies herein should also be thanked. This book would not exist without their time and cooperation and insight into SEIU developments. Luís also thanks his family—Alice, Gabriella, Juliano, and Emilio—for enduring his edginess, which only sharpened with this book's sometimes taxing progress. Finally, Luís acknowledges the support of the Social Sciences and Humanities Research Council of Canada (SSHRC) with a research grant (#410–2010–1530) into studying the globalizing of the Justice for Janitors and the publication of this book. Joe in turn is grateful to Luís for inviting him to help shape this project as it moved toward publication, his coauthor and former student Alyssa May Russell Kuchinski for letting him work with her to craft a narrative based on her exhaustive research, his colleague and collaborator Stephen Lerner for generously sharing his wisdom about both SEIU and the dynamics of the twenty-first century labor struggle, and the three women who bring joy to his life every day: Diane, Mara, and Elisa. Both coeditors would like to thank the UBC Scholarly Publication Fund for financially supporting the publication of this book. And, lastly, both coeditors thank the University of Illinois Press and its editors past and present who encouraged this volume along—especially James Engelhardt and Alison K. Syring Bassford, and her team of Ellie Hinton, Nancy Albright, Tad Ringo, and Roberta Sparenberg—for their continued commitment to labor studies like this one.

1

Seeing Purple

An Introduction to the History and Global Significance of SEIU

JOSEPH A. MCCARTIN AND LUÍS LM AGUIAR

That the Service Employees International Union (SEIU) is deserving of study by anyone who cares about the past and future of organized labor is indisputable. With some two million members in occupations that range from janitors to doctors, school employees to social workers, nurses to engineers, and taxi drivers to government workers, and with a membership spanning the geography of Canada and the continental United States and stretching from Hawaii to Puerto Rico, it is a giant among unions.

Chartered in 1921 as a building service union with roots in Chicago, by the early twenty-first century SEIU was managing campaigns and partnerships in multiple countries around the world, from Australia and New Zealand to Mexico, Western Europe, and South Africa. Among the languages spoken by its polyglot membership are Spanish, French, Chinese, Korean, Polish, Italian, Portuguese, Tagalog, Vietnamese, Arabic, Japanese, Creole, and Greek. In short, SEIU is one of the most diverse and expansive unions anywhere in the world.[1]

With over 12,000 employers under contract, SEIU sits at the nexus between the service sector and the public sector, between professionals and the working poor. It serves as the largest union for both healthcare workers and building service workers; it is among the largest unions of public employees, with over a million members working for government. The union comprises four major divisions: hospital systems, public employees, property services and security, and long-term care. Across these divisions, its membership is composed of a higher percentage of women and of minorities than the overall workforce of Canada or the United States: more than half of its members are women, 40 percent are minorities. More than three-quarters come from two-wage-earner families, making it the union with more members among struggling working families than any other.[2]

In part owing to its unique size, structure, and membership, SEIU became by many measures the most influential union in the North American labor movement during the past half-century. Writing in 1989, scholar Michael Piore believed that SEIU's organizational innovations were pointing the way toward labor's future. Citing his own surveys of trade unionists, Piore reported that respondents repeatedly singled out SEIU as "especially innovative and dynamic."[3] While other unions struggled to manage far-flung bureaucracies made larger by a wave of union mergers that began in the 1970s, SEIU was refining a national industry conference structure that it inaugurated in 1974 and hiring consultants from the American Management Association to do staff trainings. Under John Sweeney, SEIU, like many unions in this period, aggressively pursued the absorption of smaller unions as affiliates, a tactic that attracted two-thirds of the union's new members during the years 1980–1985, as historian Timothy J. Minchin has shown. The union also grew due to the expansion of employers it had successfully organized.[4] But what made SEIU so significant is that it prioritized organizing more than any big union of its time.

The union's president in the years from 1980 to 1995, John Sweeney, brought a dynamic organizing director, Andy Stern, to the union's Washington headquarters in 1984. Stern, in turn, recruited some of the best young organizers of their generation to SEIU's campaigns, including Stephen Lerner. During the 1980s and 1990s the union developed a missionary esprit de corps, its leaders and organizers believing their approach could revitalize the entire labor movement. The union's vision was expansive. It debated issues beyond bread-and-butter unionism, and its internal debates were informed by what Piore called an unusual "openness of internal discussion and debate" animated by a passionate "moral vision."[5] This passion animated the young organizers recruited to assist or lead organizing drives. Many came from outside the labor movement and therefore lacked preexisting notions concerning the business climate or business cycles that might have constricted their vision of the possible. These young people often gained their organizing experience mobilizing community members and activists to address emerging issues of citizenship status, immigration, housing, gentrification, public transit, and corporate greed that needed immediate action, often through unorthodox (to the labor movement) and creative ways that pressed for resolution to issues affecting the community.

Their experience with grassroots organizing and inclusive politics fed SEIU's campaigns irrespective of business climate. Their approach invoked people's social characteristics and place-making to tackle such issues as citizenship status (or lack thereof) and neighborhood integrity by drawing on an ethic of solidarity and social justice.[6]

Central to SEIU's moral vision was the movement energy it derived from the most innovative organizing campaign of the 1980s and 1990s—Justice for Janitors—the campaign Sweeney and Stern recruited Lerner to conceptualize and lead. Launched in Denver in 1985, J4J, as it became known, used creative and militant tactics to organize janitors in major cities whose wages and working conditions had deteriorated as commercial buildings increasingly outsourced their service workers to hypercompetitive cleaning contractors. By ignoring the janitors' direct employers—the contractors—and instead targeting building owners with public shaming, repeated "street heat" demonstrations, and political and financial pressure, the union was able to force building owners to ensure their contractors respected workers' rights to bargain collectively.[7] In 1990, the union won its biggest breakthrough in a hard-fought campaign in Los Angeles. Video of the campaign demonstration became the turning point for the Justice for Janitors campaign in Century City, Los Angeles. It contained footage of police brutality, including the beating of a pregnant woman who later miscarried. The video's content elicited public sympathy, and support for the campaign grew within and beyond Los Angeles.[8] By 2000, the campaign resulted in tens of thousands of new members for SEIU, most of them immigrants, women, and/or people of color.[9]

The success of Justice for Janitors helped propel John Sweeney into the AFL-CIO presidency in 1995 while also laying the groundwork for the union's growing international involvements. Under Sweeney the union broke with the cold war foreign policy in Central America advocated by the AFL-CIO in the 1980s, established a progressive International Affairs department, and joined the National Labor Committee in Support of Democracy and Human Rights in El Salvador.[10] SEIU's internationalism both shifted and deepened under the presidency of Andy Stern (1996–2010). While Stern dismantled the union's International Affairs department as a distraction, he promoted a range of new international campaigns.[11] SEIU sent Christy Hoffman to Geneva as the union's European director in 2004, where she coordinated global campaigns against employers like Sodexho and Wackenhut. SEIU also partnered with unions in Australia, New Zealand, the United Kingdom, Ireland, The Netherlands, and elsewhere to launch campaigns inspired by Justice for Janitors.[12] Soon thereafter it applied the same model to international campaigns to organize private security workers at companies such as Securitas and G4S/Wackenhut. By the time it won a global framework agreement from G4S in 2008, SEIU had arguably become the world's most influential union. Its "organizing model" deeply influenced union strategies in Africa, Europe, and Latin America.[13] Furthermore, SEIU influence spread not only through Hoffman and others at Union Network International (UNI) in Geneva but also via a Change to Win (CtW) satellite office in Utrecht, The Netherlands, staffed by former SEIU organizers who assisted and collaborated in organizing campaigns throughout Europe.[14]

As SEIU's vision, strategies, and leading personalities have influenced the course of the global union movement over the past forty years, its impact in the United States has been even more profound. SEIU put its stamp on the U.S. labor movement's leadership when John Sweeney defeated Tom Donahue in 1995 in the first contested election for the presidency of the AFL-CIO. As president, Sweeney installed a range of SEIU veterans in top positions and sought to revamp the structure and direction of the AFL-CIO. Under Sweeney, the labor movement joined with environmentalists and allies on the left to oppose the World Trade Organization and engage in historic protests in Seattle in 1999. When the ambitious vision of the Sweeney administration was undermined by the contested election of George W. Bush to the U.S. presidency in 2000 and the terrorist attacks of September 11, 2001, it was SEIU that again provided impetus for change. As the Sweeney agenda stalled, Andy Stern, who rose to the union's presidency in 1996, broke with his former mentor when Sweeney resisted making sweeping changes in the AFL-CIO's structure that Stern and his allies demanded. Stern then led SEIU and four of the AFL-CIO largest unions out of the federation to form Change to Win (CtW), a rival center, in 2005.[15]

SEIU also influenced the direction of the national labor movement by affecting how unions pursued growth and power, both through its campaigns and its political action. SEIU continuously innovated campaigns, from Justice for Janitors, to the global fight to organize private security workers, to the Fight for $15. More than other unions, its organizers and strategists saw themselves as "campaigners." Its political influence was equally impressive as it became both a lobbying and electoral force. Through the Fight for $15, SEIU successfully lobbied for minimum wage increases lifting wages for tens of millions of workers. Its electoral work also produced breakthroughs. SEIU's endorsement played a crucial role in catapulting Barack Obama to the Democratic presidential nomination in 2008 and then to the U.S. presidency itself.

Not since the United Mine Workers (UMW) instigated the birth of the Congress of Industrial Organizations (CIO) in the 1930s, had any single union so influenced the direction of the broader labor movement in its time. The comparison with the UMW is in many ways apt, for like the UMW before it, SEIU's outsized influence stirred constant controversy. Just as the AFL had once heaped scorn on the renegade UMW for breaking away to found the CIO, so too did prominent labor leaders attack SEIU as a divisive force. In their 1995 contest for the AFL-CIO presidency, interim president Tom Donahue (who had begun his union career at SEIU) slammed John Sweeney for "blocking bridges"—an allusion to the civil disobedience practiced by its Justice for Janitors campaign—instead of "building bridges."[16] Ironically, Sweeney in turn would later denounce his former protégé, Andy Stern, for leading SEIU into CtW in 2005. Just as John L. Lewis's iron-fisted rule of the UMW was attacked as authoritarian in his time, so too would Stern's leadership of SEIU elicit similar critiques. Nothing fed these critiques more than the union's effort to trustee and consolidate locals in order to align them with national union priorities.[17] Stern's effort to consolidate control of healthcare bargaining at the expense of local autonomy would trigger a "civil war" in 2009 as the union's most influential leader in California, Sal Rosselli, broke from SEIU to form the National Union of Healthcare Workers (NUHW).[18] Meanwhile, Stern's controversial involvement in the internal union politics of UNITE HERE, a union that had followed SEIU into Change to Win, drove that union back into the AFL-CIO in 2009, accelerating the unraveling of CtW and no doubt helping to precipitate Stern's sudden decision to step down from SEIU's leadership and leave the labor movement in 2010.[19]

As its influence grew, SEIU drew critics from both the left and the right, from within the union movement as well as from the movement's enemies. Advocates of union democracy called it a staff-dominated union and assailed its practice of trusteeing recalcitrant locals. Union militants claimed that it signed soft contracts with employers in the interest of increasing its membership and building density in strategically important sectors like healthcare. Partisans from other unions regarded it as arrogant and believed that it showed little solidarity with the rest of organized labor. Union opponents accused of it buying political influence through seamy political deals with politicians, such as the disgraced Illinois governor Rod Blagojevich. They pointed out that after receiving an endorsement and $800,000 from SEIU in his successful gubernatorial race in 2002, Blagojevich signed a law that allowed SEIU to successfully organize Illinois' homecare workers. When Blagojevich was later sent to prison for selling political influence and lying about it, SEIU was tarnished even though it was not complicit in the crimes that Blagojevich committed. The range of complaints against SEIU was so broad as to make the union a favored target of both the antiunion *Wall Street Journal* editorial page and left-wing publications like *Counterpunch*.[20] Despite its centrality to the labor history of the past half-century and, notwithstanding the influence of its major campaigns—from Justice for Janitors,[21] to homecare organizing,[22] to the Fight for Fifteen[23]—the only book-length histories of SEIU that we have to date were commissioned by the union itself.[24] Scholarship on the union lags far behind its influence. This book aims to help remedy that problem.

There are no academic books critically examining this giant of the American labor movement. There are, of course, investigations of specific SEIU-mounted union drives, or campaigns where the union plays a significant role.[25] These are important case studies and analyses with significant contributions to understanding aspects of SEIU's strategies, personalities, and motivations in pursuing specific campaigns in the manner the union does. Campaigns mark out the distinctiveness of SEIU approaches to union work by reaching out to marginalized workers or those previously outside of the labor movement and largely considered unorganizable.[26] In studying these campaigns, we learn not only who gets organized but also in which specific places and industries organizing is pursued, in the process revealing important information on regional political economies and the latter's implication for labor in general. Furthermore, relationships with local organizations and social movement activists are especially highlighted in cooperating, participating, and strategizing in the unfolding of campaigns. Needless to say, more of this type of research on SEIU (and other unions, we might add) remains important for tracing the localizing of organizing drives and the initiatives, strategies, and allies developed in place in support of such initiatives.

The need for a broad study of SEIU is indisputable and long overdue. It is also timely.

While this book focuses on SEIU, it contextualizes its relationship to the broader labor movement alongside the neoliberalism of the past 40 years. For some writers much of the innovation, centrality, and even militancy of the American labor movement under neoliberalism was driven by provocative initiatives and campaigns emerging from SEIU. From its articulation and successes with Justice for Janitors (J4J) campaigns in the 1980s and 1990s, spilling onto the organizing of security guards in G4S, including framework agreements, to breaking away from the AFL-CIO to mount the alternative and rival Change to Win federation, to the more recent Fight for a Fair Economy platform focusing on the growing problem of inequality, SEIU has been at the forefront of creatively identifying issues and mobilizing workers, sometimes by partnering with other unions and social allies, and sometimes alone. It is no exaggeration to say that no American union has outdone SEIU in stirring into action large segments of the union movement since the 1980s. And, it has largely done this by defying traditional labor conventions that said that recent immigrants—documented or not—and women were unorganizable. SEIU proved the unorganizable are indeed organizable. And once organized, they are some of the most dedicated and militant members in the house of labor. SEIU has done this through internal organizational reorganizing and restructuring.[27]

But does Piore's 1989 assessment of the union as "especially innovative and dynamic" hold true today? We live in unprecedented times of rising economic inequality, right-wing populism menacing working people and their organizations, as well as the disappearance and reclassification of work as we know it. In addition, a rising wave of precariat status workers is afoot, as are increasing incidents of muted and overt racism, with increasing vulnerabilities and uncertainties for women and immigrant workers in low-wage workplaces with few prospects for occupational mobility or even economic survival. And yet neoliberalism's crisis unfolds and its historic bloc restructures to reassert its legitimacy and dominance over our lives in a more aggressive and authoritarian form. What should labor do? What should SEIU do?

Can the methods SEIU developed in response to the rise of neoliberalism work in pushing back against the forces labor now faces?[28] In 1989 Piore concluded that the union's organizational innovations pointed the way toward the labor's future. Does that assessment still ring true today? [29] The essays in this book suggest a range of answers to that question. Yet, taken together they underscore that we have much to learn from both SEIU's successes and its failures if we hope to develop a powerful 21st century workers' movement.

Our intention in gathering these essays is not to provide a comprehensive picture of SEIU's recent past. Its story is too large, its influence too broad for any single volume of essays to do it full justice. Rather, our aim is to delve into key episodes, themes, and features of SEIU's recent history and to begin to situate and evaluate SEIU as a union with global aspirations and impact. By doing so, this volume seeks to lay the groundwork for more intensive investigations to come. The book's essays are organized as follows.

The volume opens with three chapters that tell the story of SEIU's growth over the course of the twentieth century and early twenty-first centuries. Benjamin Peterson's "From Flats to the White House: A Brief History of SEIU" traces SEIU's rise from its origins among Chicago building service workers in the early twentieth century to the Obama White House. Peterson shows how SEIU's emphasis on innovation emerged from the unique challenges of representing the workers it sought to organize, and he explains how the union's unique characteristics have been a source of both its successes and failures. Kyoung-Hee Yu's essay, "Reconciling Progressive Idealism with Centralized Control," complements and enhances Peterson's historical trajectory of the union while also exploring a central theme in SEIU's recent history. Using Justice for Janitors campaigns as a case study, she explains how the union has struggled to balance its movement culture and aspirations for worker empowerment with its strategic effort to push locals into consolidation and participation in its major campaigns. Adrienne E. Eaton, Janice Fine, and Allison Porter's chapter "Becoming Purple: Organizational Change at SEIU during the Andy Stern Years," picks up the story from Peterson and Yu, closely examining SEIU's history during the tumultuous Stern years (1996–2010).

The next three contributions offer case studies of key SEIU campaigns in the United States. Alyssa May Kuchinski and Joseph A. McCartin's chapter, "Persistence, Militancy, and Power: The Evolution of Justice for Janitors from Atlanta to Washington, D.C., 1987–1998," uses two under-examined battles in the larger Justice for Janitors campaign to trace the evolution of SEIU's campaign strategy over time. They begin with an account of the union's abject failure to achieve a breakthrough in Atlanta during the run-up to the Democratic National Convention held there in 1988, and they conclude with an account of the long fight that led to an ultimate victory in Washington, D.C., a fight that pushed the union to develop an increasingly sophisticated understanding of how to combine street pressure with the targeting of corporate malefactors, illumination of their financial manipulations, and the development of public pressure against them. Veronica Terriquez's chapter, "Rank-and-File Leadership Development and Its Implications for Education Justice," looks at the impact of their union involvement on the civil participation of Latinx immigrants who are members of SEIU's United Service Workers West (USWW), a vibrant local of immigrants that, when it was known as Local 1877, achieved Justice for Janitors' breakthrough in Los Angeles. She finds that the USWW both responded to its members concerns about the problems in LA's public schools and empowered its members to get more involved in the fight for the future of public education in their city, a potential she suggests the union has only begun to tap. Maite Tapia and Tashlin Lakhani's contribution, "Organizing Fast Food: Opportunities, Challenges, and SEIU," examines the origins and development of the Fight for $15 campaign. They emphasize the extent to which the campaign retained local ownership and nurtured local leaders, while also departing from its caricature as a top-down, staff-driven movement. They conclude by assessing the lessons of the campaign for SEIU and the labor movement.

The next three chapters offer case studies of SEIU's efforts in Canada, Australia, Western Europe, and Brazil. Laurence Hamel-Roy and Yanick Noiseux's chapter, "Renewing Union Practices and Strategies: A Case Study of SEIU's Sweet $16 Campaign in Ontario, Canada" considers an ambitious and largely successful homecare workers' campaign launched in 2014. The campaign not only demanded a minimum wage of $16/hour, but also sought secure pensions, a declaration that homecare is an essential service, and ongoing continuing education and specialized training opportunities. Their analysis suggests the campaign's success owed much to SEIU's recognition of challenges created by the gendered division of labor associated with homecare work, the home settings where this work takes place, and the nature of the work itself. Luís LM Aguiar's "The Global Career of Justice for Janitors and the Limits of Institutional Permeability," offers a broad-ranging look at the impact of Justice for Janitors in Australia and Western Europe. His investigation suggests that while the Justice for Janitors model has excited unionists in many countries, it has scarcely offered a silver bullet to efforts to organize low-wage workers. Rather, some of the most significant criticisms that have been leveled at SEIU in the United States—including the charge that it sacrifices member empowerment to centralized control of campaigns—have reappeared in European settings to the detriment of those campaigns. Euan Gibb and Luís LM Aguiar's, "Organizing Strategies without Borders: The Case of Brazil," discusses SEIU's partnership with Siemaco-SP, the union that represents urban cleaners and maintenance workers in the city of São Paulo. Their chapter suggests some of the challenges of transplanting SEIU's methods into different cultural, legal, and political context.

The volume concludes with an interview with Stephen Lerner, the former SEIU official, and architect of Justice for Janitors. Along with SEIU's then president, John Sweeney, and the union's then organizing director, Andy Stern, Lerner was the third person in the triumvirate that led SEIU's most successful campaign. While Stern left the labor movement after stepping down as president of SEIU in 2010, Sweeney retired after three terms as AFL-CIO president in 2009 and passed away on February 1, 2021. This has left Lerner as the only one of the three still active, applying lessons he learned through Justice for Janitors to new campaigns. After departing from SEIU at the end of 2010, Lerner went on to work on a range of exciting new organizing projects, culminating most recently in Bargaining for the Common Good, an effort to reframe collective bargaining to deal with the realities of twenty-first-century capitalism. In this interview, he reflects on the lessons he has drawn from his SEIU experience, on the legacy of Justice for Janitors thirty years after its breakthrough in Los Angeles, and on the challenges that labor faces today.

Notes

1. On SEIU's early history, see John B. Jentz, "Citizenship, Self-Respect, and Political Power: Chicago's Flat Janitors Trailblaze the Service Employees International Union, 1912–1921," *Labor's Heritage* 9, no. 1 (1997): 4–23; John B. Jentz, "Unions, Cartels, and the Political Economy of American Cities: The Chicago Flat Janitors' Union in the Progressive Era and 1920s," *Studies in American Political Development* 14, no. 1 (2000): 51–71; Grace Palladino, "When Militancy Isn't Enough," *Labor History* 28, no. 2 (1987): 196–220. Work on the more recent history of SEIU includes: Leon Fink and Brian Greenberg, *Upheaval in the Quiet Zone: 1199/SEIU and the Politics of Healthcare Unionism,* second edition (Urbana: University of Illinois Press, 2009); Steven Henry Lopez, *Reorganizing the Rust Belt: An Inside Study of the American Labor Movement* (Berkeley: University of California Press, 2004); and Ariel Avgar, Boris, Monica Bielski, Robert Bruno, Wonjoon Chung, "Worker Voice and Union Revitalization: The Role of Contract Enforcement at SEIU," *Labor Studies Journal* 43, no. 3 (2018): 209–233.

2. On SEIU's vital statistics, see https://www.seiu.org/cards/the-complete-stewards-manual/seiu-snapshots/p7.

3. Michael J. Piore's 1989 paper on SEIU was published as "Unions: A Reorientation to Survive," in *Labor Economics and Industrial Relations: Markets and Institutions*, ed. Clark Kerr and Paul D. Staudohar (Cambridge: Harvard University Press, 1994), 512–541 (quotation, 534).

4. Timothy J. Minchin, "A Successful Union in an Era of Decline: Interrogating the Growth of the Service Employees International Union, 1980–1995," *Labor History* 61 nos. 3–4 (2020): 304.

5. Piore, "Unions: A Reorientation to Survive," 529.

6. For a critique of the business climate approach, see Ruth Milkman and Stephanie Luce, "Labor Unions and the Great Recession," *RSF: The Russell Sage Foundation Journal of the Social Sciences* 3, no. 3 (2017): 145–165. On the recruitment of college graduates as organizers, see Lisa Belkin, "Showdown at Yazoo Industries," *The New York Times Magazine*, 21 January 1996. See also Ruth Milkman and Kim Voss, ed., *Rebuilding Labor: Organizing and Organizers in the New Union Movement* (Ithaca, NJ: ILR Press, 2004). Jane McAlevey writes of her time as an environmental activist before joining labor in Jane McAlevey, *Raising Expectations (and Raising Hell): My Decade Fighting for the Labor Movement* (New York: Verso, 2012), 23. For a sample of writing on organizing outside the business climate, see Laura Pulido, *Black, Brown, Yellow & Left: Radical Activism in Los Angeles* (Berkeley: University of California Press, 2006); Jennifer Gordon, *Suburban Sweatshops: The Fight for Immigrant Rights* (Cambridge: The Belknap Press, 2005); Manuel Castells, *Networks of Outrage and Hope: Social Movements in the Internet Age* (Malden: Polity Press, 2015); *Organizing the Transnational: Labour, Politics, and Social Change*, ed. Luin Goldring and Sailaja Krishnamurti (Vancouver: UBC Press, 2007); and Don Mitchell, *The Right to the City: Social Justice and the Fight for Public* Space (New York: Guilford Press, 2003).

7. On public shaming, see Jennifer Jihye Chun, "Public Dramas and the Politics of Justice: Comparisons of Janitors' Union Struggles in South Korea and the United States," *Work & Occupations* 32, no. 4 (2005): 486–503.

8. Tom Balanoff interviewed by Luís LM Aguiar, August 2010. See also Andy Merrifield, *Dialectical Urbanism: Social Struggles in the Capitalist City* (New York: Monthly Press, 2002), 83–89, Edward Soja, *Seeking Spatial Justice* (Minnesota: University of Minnesota Press, 2010), and Ruth Milkman, *L.A. Story: Immigrant Workers and the Future of the U.S. Labor Movement* (New York: Russell Sage Foundation, 2006).

9. Jennifer Luff, "Justice for Janitors," in *Encyclopedia of U.S. Labor and Working-Class* History, ed. Eric Arnesen (New York: Routledge, 2007), 729–731.

10. Andrew Battista, "Unions and Cold War Foreign Policy in the 1980s: The National Labor Committee, the AFL-CIO, and Central America," *Diplomatic History* 26, no. 3 (2002), 423–424.

11. Andy Stern, *A Country that Works: Getting America Back on Track* (New York: The Free Press, 2008).

12. See Luís LM Aguiar in this collection and Kieran Allen, "The Trade Unions: From Partnership to Crisis," *Irish Journal of Sociology* 18, no. 2 (2010), 22–37.

13. Jamie K. McCallum, *Global Unions, Local Power: The Spirit of Transnational Organizing* (Ithaca: ILR Press, 2013), Chaps. 2–3.

14. Heather Connolly, Stefania Marino, and Miguel Martinez Lucio, "Justice for Janitors Goes Dutch: The Limits and Possibilities of Unions' Adoption of Organizing in a Context of Regulated Social Partnership," *Work, Employment and Society* 31, no. 2 (2017): 319–335; Martin Krzywdzinski, "Organizing Employees in Central Eastern Europe: The Approach of Solidarnosc," *European Journal of Industrial Relations* 16, no. 3 (2010): 277–292; and Luís LM Aguiar interview with Ethel Buckley, from the Irish Services Industrial Professional and Technical Union (SIPTU), 1 June 2012.

15. See Ruth Milkman and Kim Voss, "New Unity for Labor?" *Labor: Studies in Working-Class Histories of the Americas* 2, no. 1 (2005): 15–25.

16. Peter T. Kilborne, "Militant Is Elected President of the AFL-CIO, Signaling Sharp Turn for the Labor Movement," *New York Times*, October 26, 1995, D25.

17. On this, see McAlevey, *Raising Expectations (and Raising Hell)*.

18. See Bill Fletcher Jr. and Nelson Lichtenstein, "SEIU Civil War," *In These Times*, December 16, 2009, http://inthesetimes.com/article/5309/seius_civil_war.

19. On the conflict between SEIU and NUHW, see Cal Winslow, *Labor's Civil War in California: The NUHW Healthcare Workers' Rebellion* (Oakland, Cal.: PM Press, 2010); and Steve Early, *The Civil Wars in U.S. Labor: The Birth of a New Workers' Movement or the Death Throes of the Old?* (Chicago: Haymarket Books, 2011). For Stern's evaluation of his tenure, see Leon Fink and Jennifer Luff, "An Interview with SEIU President Emeritus Andy Stern," *Labor: Studies in Working Class History of the Americas* 8, no. 2 (Summer 2011): 7–36.

20. For an antiunion attack on SEIU, see Mallory Factor and Elizabeth Factor, *Shadowbosses: Government Unions Control America and Rob Taxpayers Blind* (New York: Center Street, 2012), 180–185; for critiques of SEIU from the left, see Steve Early, "The

Poison Pill In 'ObamaCare' that Helped Kill Labor Law Reform," *Working USA* 13, no. 3 (September 2010): 405–423; Early, "Purple Bullying, Ten Years Later," *Counterpunch*, April 3, 2018, https://www.counterpunch.org/2018/04/03/purple-bullying-ten-years-later-seiu-trustees-trample-member-rights-on-eve-of-janus-decision/; and Jane McAlevey, "The Crisis of New Labor and Alinsky's Legacy: Revisiting the Role of the Organic Grassroots Leaders in Building Powerful Organizations and Movement," *Politics & Society* 43, no. 3 (2015): 415–441; and also McAlevey, *Raising Expectations (and Raising Hell)*. Finally, see Kim Moody, *US Labor in Trouble and Transition: The Failure of Reform from Above, the Promise of Revival from Below* (New York: Verso, 2007).

21. Work on Justice for Janitors includes: Richard W. Hurd and William Rouse, "Progressive Union Organizing: The SEIU Justice for Janitors Campaign," *Review of Radical Political Economics* 21, no. 3 (1989): 70–75; Liz McNichol, "Fighting on Many Fronts: SEIU in Los Angeles," *Labor Research Review* 9, no. 1 (1990): 37–43; John Howley, "Justice for Janitors: The Challenge of Organizing in Contract Services," *Labor Research Review* 9, no. 1 (1990): 61–72; Roger Waldinger, Chris Erickson, Ruth Milkman, Daniel J.B. Mitchell, Abel Valenzuela, Kent Wong, and Maurice Zeitlin, "Helots No More: A Case Study of the Justice for Janitors Campaign in Los Angeles," in *Organizing to Win: New Research on Union Strategies*, ed. Kate Bronfenbrenner (Ithaca, NY: Cornell University Press, 1998), 102–120; Luís LM Aguiar, "Janitors and Sweatshop Citizenship in Canada," in *The Dirty Work of Neoliberalism*, ed. Luís LM Aguiar and Andrew Herod (Malden, MA: Blackwell, 2006), 16–36; Jason Albright, "Contending Rationality, Leadership, and Collective Struggle," *Labor Studies Journal* 33, no. 1 (2008): 63–80; Luís LM Aguiar, "Sweatshop Citizenship, Precariousness and Organizing Building Cleaners," in *Neoliberal Capitalism and Precarious Work*, ed. Rob Lambert and Andrew Herod (Northampton, MA: Edward Elgar Publishing, 2016), 255–276; Lydia Savage, "Justice for Janitors: Scales of Organizing and Representing Workers," in *The Dirty Work of Neoliberalism*, 214–234; Lydia Savage, "Geographies of Organizing: Justice for Janitors in Los Angeles," in *Organizing the Landscape*, ed. Andrew Herod (Minneapolis: University of Minnesota Press, 1998); Andrew Gomez, "Organizing the 'Sweatshop in the Sky': Jono Shaffer and the Los Angeles Justice for Janitors Campaign," *Labor: Studies in Working Class History of the Americas* 15, no. 2 (May 2018): 9–20; Cynthia Cranford, "Gender and Citizenship in the Restructuring of Janitorial Work in Los Angeles," *Gender Issues* 16 (1998), 25–51; Urvashi Soni-Sinha and Charlotte A.B. Yates, "'Dirty Work?' Gender, Race and the Union in Industrial Cleaning," *Gender, Work and Organization* 20(6) (2013), 737–751; Christian Zlolniski, "Labor Control and Resistance of Mexican Immigrant Janitors in Silicon Valley," *Human Organization* 62, no. 1 (2003), 39–49; Preston Rudy, "'Justice for Janitors', Not 'Compensation for Custodians': The Political Context and Organizing in San Jose and Sacramento," in *Rebuilding Labor*, ed. Ruth Milkman and Kim Voss, 133–149; Minchin, "A Successful Union," 309–313; Stephanie Fairchild, "Urban Farm Workers: A History of the Justice for Janitors Campaign as an Adaptive Response to Neoliberal Restructuring and Union Decline," Ph.D. Dissertation, University of California at San Diego, 2018; and Javier Gonzales, "J4J:

Inside an Epic Victory for American Labor," *Scheerpost*, December 11, 2020, https://scheerpost.com/2020/12/11/j4j-inside-an-epic-victory-for-american-labor/.

22. Work on SEIU's homecare organizing includes: Linda Delp and Katie Quan, "Homecare Worker Organizing in California: An Analysis of a Successful Strategy," *Labor Studies Journal* 27, no. 1 (2002): 1–23; Jacqueline Leavitt and Teresa Lingafelter, "Low Wage Workers and High Housing Costs," *Labor Studies Journal* 30, no. 2 (2005): 41–60; Patrice M. Mareschal, "Innovation and Adaptation: Contrasting Efforts to Organize Home Care Workers in Four States," *Labor Studies Journal* 31, no. 1 (2006): 25–49; Ken Margolies, "Invisible No More," *Labor Studies Journal* 33, no.1 (2008): 81–92; and Eileen Boris and Jennifer Klein, *Home Health Workers in the Shadow of the Welfare State* (New York: Oxford University Press, 2012). Scholarship on nursing home workers includes Dorothee E. Benz, "It Takes a Village to Win a Union: A Case Study of Organizing among Florida's Nursing Home Workers," *Politics & Society* 33, no.1 (2005), 123–152. Writing on child care worker organizing includes Fred P. Brooks, "New Turf for Organizing: Family Child Care Providers," *Labor Studies Journal* 29, no. 4 (2005): 45–64.

23. On the Fight for $15, see: Steven Ashby, "Assessing the Fight for Fifteen Movement from Chicago," *Labor Studies Journal* 42, no. 4 (2017): 366–386; Jonathan Rosenblum, "The Fight for $15: Good Wins, but Where Did the Focus on Organizing Go? *Labor Studies Journal* 42, no. 4 (2017): 387–393.

24. The union-commissioned histories are: Tom Beadling, Pat Cooper, and Grace Palladino, *A Need for Valor: The Roots of the Service Employees International Union 1902–1980* (Washington, D.C.: SEIU, 1984); and Don Stillman, *Stronger Together: The Story of SEIU* (Washington, D.C.: Service Employees International Union, 2010).

25. For example, see Roger Waldinger et al., "Helots no More," 102–119.

26. Hector Delgado, *New Immigrants, Old Unions: Organizing Undocumented Workers in Los Angeles* (Philadelphia: Temple University Press, 1993).

27. Milkman and Luce, "Labor Unions and the Great Recession," 145–165.

28. Jamie Peck and Adam Tickell, "Neoliberalizing Space," *Antipode* 34 (3) (2002): 380–404; William Davies, "The New Neoliberalism," *New Left Review* 101 (Sept/Oct) (2016): 121–134; Chantal Mouffe, *For a Left Populism* (New York: Verso, 2018), and Sefika Kumral and Sahran Savas Karatasli, "Capitalism, Labour and the Global Populist Radical Right," *Global Labour Journal* 11, no. 2 (2020): 152–155.

29. Some are disappointed in SEIU for soliciting an "innovation specialist" in the style of a "Silicon Valley-style innovation guru" to reenergize itself in 2018. See Chris Brooks, "To Hell with 'Innovation Specialists,'" https://jacobinmag.com/2018/11/seiu-labor-movement-innovation-specialist-power.

PART I

Dynamics of Growth and Transformation

2

From Flats to the White House

A Brief History of SEIU, 1910–2010

BENJAMIN L. PETERSON

As one of the few labor organizations that prospered in the resolutely hostile soil of the late 20th and early 21st centuries, activists and scholars commonly point to the Service Employees International Union (SEIU) as the standard bearer of union resilience and adaptation. Scholars including Kim Voss, Rachel Sherman, and Steve Lopez all argue that the union's distinctive use of social movement tactics provides a potent counter to employer resistance.[1] However, the union does not receive universal praise. In an influential review of several works on SEIU entitled "Reutherism Redux," labor journalist Steve Early accuses the union of "craven political maneuvering—such as SEIU's embrace of industry-backed 'tort reform' that would restrict lawsuits against elder-abuse in California nursing homes."[2] Instead of giving workers more control of their lives, Early continues, SEIU made them the pawns of corrupt labor bureaucrats who "have never been a janitor, security guard, nursing home worker, home health care aide or public employee in their own local or anyone else's."[3] Despite years of dueling books and articles, scholars and commentators have achieved little consensus on SEIU. The debate between these two sides remains unsolvable because, in a way, both are correct in their evaluation of SEIU.

From its foundation as a union of flat janitors, SEIU leveraged political power to achieve its ends. In doing so, the union often committed itself to defending the needs of political elites while simultaneously encouraging its leaders to act more as politicians than labor organizers. As SEIU evolved from its roots in Chicago, it became a center of innovative, political unionism, but it also became distracted from the immediate interests of its members. Seen in this light, SEIU appears as neither a hero nor a villain but as an organization that walks a delicate path between exemplifying and casting aside the ideals of the labor movement.

His Majesty, the Janitor

Writing in 1920, a critic of the Flat Janitors' Union (FJU) complained that its president, William Quesse, held "more power and influence with the mayor and state's attorney than anyone here no matter how much property he owns."[4] The FJU—which became the basis of the modern SEIU—faced tremendous challenges in its rise. Widely distributed across the city, flat or apartment janitors were employed by hundreds of building owners. Individually organizing so many workplaces presented a huge logistical challenge to the union.[5] Furthermore, flat janitors lacked a sense of community solidarity. While most flat janitors emigrated from Europe, they came from varied origins and generally worked alone. Divided by space and ethnicity, the janitorial trade also had relatively low bars to entry, allowing workers to be easily replaced. Furthermore, janitors often lived in the buildings they served. To these janitors, angering an employer meant not only unemployment but also homelessness. Yet despite these challenges, the flat janitors became such a force in Chicago that the *Tribune* described their leader as "His Majesty, a Janitor."[6] The union achieved such a stunning success through a combination of traditional labor solidarity, alliances with employer associations, and political influence.

In Chicago of the 1910s, craft unions formed a dense, interwoven fabric of organizations powerful enough that they could effectively govern the labor market in many areas. These unions relied on each other to enforce work rules through sympathy strikes, boycotts, and violence.[7] Quesse recognized that integration into this system could provide the FJU with leverage. Present in nearly every residential complex across the city, janitors naturally watched other craft workers as they went about their daily business. Effectively, Quesse offered janitors as an intelligence network to enforce craft rules.[8] As the head of Chicago's Painter's Union noted in 1935, "[The union] has [its members] trained so that whenever a non-union painter, plumber, steamfitter or electrician comes to an apartment building, we are notified [and usually] the matter is quickly adjusted and the 'scab' painter . . . is replaced by a union mechanic."[9] In return, these unions helped to fund the nascent organization and respected its picket lines. Suddenly, employers faced not only the potential loss of a striking janitor, but also an embargo against coal deliveries from teamsters and maintenance services from carpenters.[10]

Initially, large real-estate associations resisted the efforts of the union. However, to avert a strike and picket lines the Chicago Real Estate Board (CREB) agreed to negotiations in 1916. During these negotiations, the parties found a shared interest in regulating the real-estate market in Chicago. Just as building trades turned to flat janitors to enforce their rules, the leaders in the CREB soon viewed the union as a useful political ally and tool to pressure independent owners into their association.[11]

At the heart of the CREB agreement was a clause that tied janitorial wages to the amount of rent paid to a building owner. This unique agreement between the FJU and the CREB shaped the relationship between the flat janitors and their employers. With their wages tied directly to rent collected by their employers, flat janitors spoke of themselves as participants in the real-estate market.[12] The shared interest in a booming real-estate market provided incentives for union members, and, perhaps more importantly, union leaders to cooperate with employers on a variety of political issues such as rent control.[13]

The alliance between workers and employers proved temporary and contract negotiations broke down in 1919.[14] However, the union averted disaster through an alliance with the city's political elites, particularly Mayor William Hale Thompson. Although many other unions played these games of politics in Chicago, the relationship between Thompson and the janitors proved uniquely lucrative to both sides. As John B. Jentz observes, the ubiquity of the flat janitors throughout the city provided Thompson with "a ready-made, city-wide precinct organization with a staff of over 6,000."[15] Using their relationship with Thompson as leverage, the union expanded their political influence throughout Chicago's city government. The union flexed its political muscle for the first time in 1920 when they won a favorable decision in an arbitration overseen by Thompson's chief of police, William Fitzmorris. The resulting agreement was finally gained and the union closed shop conditions and secured their position in Chicago. For the union's leaders, the lesson could not have been clearer: alliances with the powerful could result in meaningful gains for their members.

Representing a diverse group of African Americans, Belgians, Swedes, Germans, and others, the flat janitors pursued a notable agenda of racial and ethnic inclusiveness throughout their rise. The union insisted on integrating their locals and even introduced a racial quota that guaranteed a minimum number of leadership spots for African Americans.[16] Emphasizing the importance of political participation, they sponsored programs to help their immigrant members become citizens. The union's efforts bore significant fruit. The 1920

Chicago Commission on Race Relations, for example, noted that the union seemed to have few of the ethnic and racial animosities that defined many of the city's other unions.[17] The union's integration helped them garner support throughout both the white and black political establishments of the city.

Success in Chicago helped the union make a case for the foundation of an international union devoted to the building services. Initially, officials in the AFL resisted the union's request because they felt that the failure of a previous organization indicated that uniting the widely dispersed, often weak, building service locals across the country would be a waste of resources. However, impressed with the effectiveness of their partnership in Chicago, Quesse's application gained the support of other tradesmen who, ultimately, managed to secure support for a charter. In 1921, the Flat Janitors' Union formally became Local 1 of the newly chartered Building Service Employees International Union (BSEIU).

The granting of an international charter allowed the BSEIU to expand beyond flat janitors. Building on their political strength, the organization turned its sights to the city's public sector. After the union's support played a key role in ensuring Thompson's reelection as mayor in 1927, the union used the mayor's power over the Chicago Board of Education (CBE) to reform the employment of school janitors. Prior to unionization, school janitors lacked basic job security and commonly worked alongside child laborers. Along with ending child labor in the schools, unionization provided school janitors basic wages, conditions, and due process guarantees. From this base the union expanded broadly throughout the city's public services. By the 1930s, the union included strong locals among the maintenance staff of city hall and the parks department, and even had successfully organized hospital workers in the city's mental health institutions. With a strong base in Chicago, and a jurisdiction that covered a wide swath of the service industry, the future looked bright for "His Majesty, the Janitor."[18]

Victory, Corruption, and New York

Over the course of a few months in the winter of 1934, the BSEIU added 45,000 janitors and elevator operators in New York City. Under the skilled hands of a former printer's union official named James Bambrick, the New York locals, most prominently Local 32B, secured favorable contracts that reshaped the jobs of some 75,000 elevator operators and janitors. Relying on growing popular support for labor activism, the union's picket lines received respect from the general public—particularly tenants—other labor unions, and even some businesses.

The ability of the union to both disrupt the city's elevators and interrupt the supply of coal and other materials to buildings proved key to their capacity to bring employers to the bargaining table. Once forced into bargaining, building owners faced significant political pressure to settle from Mayor Fiorello H. LaGuardia, who developed a quiet political alliance with Bambrick. In March 1937, the union signed an agreement that provided all of its members with pay raises, vacation time, and a forty-five-hour week.[19]

The sudden success of the BSEIU in New York enriched the mobsters who had successfully wormed their way into positions of power inside the union. Prior to the rise of Bambrick and the successful expansion of Local 32B and its various offshoots, mobsters ran the few active BSEIU locals in New York as fronts for protection schemes. At the same time, the union's connections to Mayor Thompson—who notoriously forged an alliance with Al Capone—and its constant search for allies led many of the union's Chicago leaders to become acquainted with and beholden to mob figures. These connections, combined with intimidation and violence, eventually led to the capture of several locals by the Chicago Outfit and the creation of a mob-backed faction in the union's leadership.[20] Comparatively clean leaders in the union—such as Quesse's nephew and leader of the school janitors William McFetridge—refused to expose this corruption because they feared bad press would undermine the organization. Ultimately these failures led to the appointment of a known mafia associate, George Scalise, as head of the union's activities on the East Coast.

The BSEIU's failure to keep the mob out was far from unique. Funded by prohibition-era profits, the criminal syndicates of the late 1920s grew into highly organized, extremely violent organizations that pursued numerous enterprises.[21] These organizations seized power over labor unions through violence and intimidation. Once in control, these gangsters diverted funds, used the union in protection rackets, and accepted payoffs from employers for labor peace. Although unions always struggled with leaders who took more than their fair share, these gangsters, in the words of Andrew Wender Cohen, "viewed the craftsmen as little more than blobs of cash" and happily undermined the union's activities in the name of profitability.[22]

For some scholars of labor corruption like David Witwer, Scalise represents the prototypical model of this new generation of gangsters—what would sometimes be called a racketeer.[23] A close associate of Anthony Carfano, a gangster whom the press connected to both New York's powerful Luciano crime family and Tammany Hall, the Democratic party's political machine, Scalise proved adept at building bridges between mobsters and politicians. By the late 1920s, rumors suggested that Scalise sat at the center of a corrupt network of criminals, labor organizers, and government officials throughout New York. Scalise used this network to gain influence over labor unions, eventually securing his position overseeing the BSEIU in the East. He used the locals under his influence both as a source of embezzled money and as a tool with which to extort money from employers in return for labor peace.[24]

On April 27, 1937, BSEIU President Jerry Horan died, setting off a succession crisis in the union. Eager to profit from the chaos, the Chicago Outfit sought to take direct control over the union, but found their way blocked by the well-known leader William McFetridge. In this tense situation, Scalise emerged as a compromise candidate. To avert a crisis, and potential violence, McFetridge ultimately agreed to accept Scalise, whom he believed would not challenge him in Chicago. After consolidating his power, Scalise began to transform the BSEIU into little more than a vehicle for his own graft. Expanding on an earlier arrangement in which he skimmed money from the union's eastern locals, he soon began to take a cut of all of the union's income. Although he faced little opposition in New York, his efforts to expand his take to include San Francisco met with aggressive resistance from Charles Hardy, the union's most prominent leader on the west coast. Due to some combination of distance and stubborness, Hardy refused to bend to Scalise's threats and enmeshed the gangster in a lawsuit intended to expose his corruption. Hardy's lawsuit—along with the delivery of a mysterious, anonymous dossier on Scalise—attracted the attention of the infamous antiunion journalist Westbrook Pegler, who painted the president as a goon who funded a luxurious lifestyle at the expense of his members. Through his syndicated column, Pegler turned the Scalise story into a national scandal. Despite the accusations, either out of loyalty or fear for their lives, the union's executive board stood by Scalise.[25]

In 1940, future presidential candidate and New York States Attorney Thomas E. Dewey sought to make political use of the scandal revolving around Scalise. After indicting several of Scalise's associates on charges of intimidation, he arrested the union leader on a variety of charges including embezzlement and forgery. Although Scalise, rightly, accused Dewey of using the arrest as part of his campaign to be the Republican candidate for president, his arrest allowed less corrupt—though certainly not clean—leaders to rise, most notably McFetridge, who became president of the BSEIU in 1940. Although he publicly decried Scalise's arrest as a mere pretext for antilabor rhetoric and activity, he privately consolidated his power over the organization and actively worked with Mayor LaGuardia to remove the former president's loyalists. McFetridge proved to be a self-interested reformer and his anticorruption campaign targeted only those leaders whom he viewed as a threat. Concerned primarily with ensuring stability and his authority, McFetridge even used the anticorruption campaign to remove comparatively clean leaders. Whatever his personal ideals, political realities always trumped morality for McFetridge.[26]

The corruption of Scalise and false reforms of McFetridge reveal the downsides of the union's community and political alliance–focused strategy. Heavily reliant on local organizers and on alliances with corrupt politicians and business leaders, the union struggled to maintain an appearance of moral authority. Born out of the vicious, realist politics of Chicago and New York, the union allowed petty grafters and authoritarian leaders to become intrinsic to the organization and, ultimately, its legacy.

Daley's Machiavelli

The entrance of the U.S. into World War II changed the union in unexpected ways. Struggling to recover their public image after months of disastrous press coverage of the Scalise debacle, McFetridge self-consciously threw the union into wartime work and preparations. In Chicago, the union's flat janitors became the official enforcers of the city's salvage and civil preparedness programs. Operating with an eye toward public relations, McFetridge arranged to have many of the union's members sworn in as deputies in civil defense and publicly began to discuss the union as an organization of patriotic defenders of the home front. The union's allies, such as Chicago's mayor Edward Kelly, facilitated this by loudly proclaiming the importance of the union to the war. Kelly even described the union as being "in the business of preventing people from forgetting what this American way of life is, all that it offers for the family . . . and the labor union—and [ask] where are the labor unions in the land that Hitler's Hell has struck?"[27] The union's performance of patriotism—combined with a loud, if largely ineffective anticorruption campaign—helped to restore their place in the labor community and regained a degree of public support for their cause.

After World War II, the BSEIU embarked on an aggressive, nationwide campaign of organizing. Of these efforts, Los Angeles proved particularly notable. Known as a resolutely antiunion city, the BSEIU initially struggled to organize the janitors of LA.[28] In 1946, however, George Hardy—son of Scalise's enemy Charles Hardy—used the solidarity of the Culinary and Hospital Service Workers' Union to form a beachhead in the city's hotels. Within a decade Hardy expanded on this position to organize nearly three quarters of the city's office cleaners, among others. As in Chicago these unions committed themselves to ethnic and racial inclusion with significant numbers of African and Mexican

Americans. Focused more on rapid expansion, Hardy employed a professional staff of organizers supported by a large staff of researchers. In some cases these professionals took over significant leadership posts in the union. Using this organizer-driven approach, Hardy successfully expanded the BSEIU of LA into health care and the public sector. By 1960, LA's largest local, 399, grew into a behemoth of 11,000 workers. While Hardy's approach certainly bore significant fruit, this professionalization ensured a disconnect between the union's members and their leaders.[29]

Similarly, in Chicago union leaders increasingly gained their positions through political connections, not by rising from the ranks. A series of interviews of flat janitors from 1949 vividly displays this with one noting that "union [leadership and administrative] positions [are] lifetime jobs. And it's getting like the way the kings in Europe were. They had their positions and their sons got their positions when they grew up."[30] While janitors complained about the remoteness of their union leaders, few doubted that the union improved their lives. Another interviewed janitor admits that it "wouldn't do any good to talk about the union. Whether you like them or not, you need them. You'd get peanuts without them."[31] As the leaders of the Chicago BSEIU shifted their focus from the union hall to city hall, they prioritized the pursuit of political power over worker agency.

By 1950, William McFetridge stood as the unchallenged leader of this thriving organization. Although he held power throughout the country, the center of his authority—and of the BSEIU's leadership—remained in Chicago. Adept at the patronage politics of the Second City, McFetridge became perhaps the city's most successful and legendary political fixer. While he personally held many positions, including a seat on the Parks Board where he negotiated favorable contracts for many BSEIU members, McFetridge's influence went far beyond this. Through various surrogates, he reputedly controlled the Chicago Housing Authority outright, was consulted on most public employment decisions, and held significant influence over the police.[32]

Through these networks of influence, the union effectively controlled both sides of the bargaining table during many negotiations. Unsurprisingly, this resulted in superb, sometimes scandalous, conditions for public janitors. In 1953, reporter Bryce Engle found that in city hall, the board of health building, and the police garage, night janitors were allowed to count 6-hour nights as 8-hour days. Working 29 to 34 hours per week, these janitors continued, with the apparent knowledge of city officials, to draw full-time salaries. That same year, all public janitors achieved a 40-hour work week and successfully defeated measures to reduce the number of janitors employed by the city.[33] The intimidating political power of McFetridge also translated into gains throughout the private sector. As these gains were made through behind-the-scenes deals between major figures in business, politics, and the labor movement, overt labor struggle among the Chicago BSEIU became rare. In April 1946, for example, the *Chicago Sun-Times* praised Local 1 as "the union which hasn't had a strike in 43 years."[34] Though in theory such a placid relationship suggests the weakness of the union in negotiations, in practice Local 1 successfully achieved both labor peace and strength.

The political prominence of the BSEIU hit its peak with Richard J. Daley's defeat of Mayor Kennelly. McFetridge played a major role in Daley's campaign and, in return, the mayor granted him an exalted place in his administration. McFetridge became known for serving, or being represented by a proxy, on numerous committees including the Police Commission, the Chicago Housing Authority, and the Chicago Board of Education. These positions granted him the ability to direct money, jobs, and influence to his allies. Summarizing McFetridge's relationship with Daley, journalist Len O'Connor writes, "Every prince, in short, needs his Machiavelli—and McFetridge was Daley's."[35] Though McFetridge's influence over a committee or wing of city government was not always apparent, O'Connor continues, "The ubiquitous McFetridge was always in control, navigating these groups into the channels that Daley wanted them to travel."[36] It was difficult to turn around quickly in the hallways of power in Chicago without stepping on the toes of William McFetridge.

Power came with significant costs, however. As a beneficiary of the Daley administration, McFetridge often put the needs of the mayor and his network of supporters over the needs of workers and the cause of social justice. Nowhere did this become more apparent than in race relations. While McFetridge professed racially egalitarian views, his stated opinions never prevented him from allying with racist aldermen or protecting city officials who enforced Chicago's notoriously racist housing policies.[37]

In 1960, William McFetridge stepped down from the presidency of the BSEIU in favor of David Sullivan, president of Local 32B. McFetridge remained in control of Local 1 and in de facto control of the BSEIU in Chicago. While relations between the two leaders were initially amicable, their different visions of the union slowly led to conflict. Born into Chicago's craft community, McFetridge favored building a local, collaborative community of employers, employees, and politicians. Under this system union leaders became effectively public officials who sought to advance the interests of their city's workers, employers, and political elites. Focused on the city, not the nation, McFetridge always favored the needs of the Chicago labor movement over that of the BSEIU and the national labor movement. Indeed, to McFetridge, the success of Chicago as an organic whole went hand-in-hand with the security and growth of his union. In such a vision, the interests of individual workers could be readily sacrificed if they served to increase his power or secure the position of his allies.

Sullivan, on the other hand, viewed himself as an actor inside the national system of labor relations established during the New Deal. Eschewing the intensely local, influence-based, and personal strategies of McFetridge, Sullivan emphasized the need for national campaigns carried out openly through courts, certification elections, and state-assisted bargaining. Further, Sullivan believed that the future of the BSEIU lay not in building service workers but in the growing service sector. To Sullivan, the true face of the BSEIU would be bureaucrats, health-care workers, and similar service providers, not the janitors and attendants who had initially built the union. These strategies required Sullivan to step on the toes of other unions and employers, breaking the collaborative labor peace that McFetridge held in high esteem.

The conflict between McFetridge and Sullivan escalated into open war over nursing home workers organized by Chicago's Local 4. Pressured by National Labor Relation's Board decisions to amalgamate units whenever possible, the leader of Local 4, George Fairchild, organized janitors along with the health-care workers. In doing so, Fairchild poached upon the traditional, craft-based jurisdiction of Local 1. Because Local 4's amalgamated contract fell short of the standard Local 1 contract on several measures, McFetridge viewed Fairchild's efforts as undermining the worth and dignity of janitors in Chicago. When Sullivan ultimately took Fairchild's side, McFetridge declared open war on Sullivan and the International Union. McFetridge even went so far as to set up a picket line around the picket line of another SEIU local! From 1964 through 1969, the two leaders engaged in a byzantine series of public conflicts that undermined the union's reputation and ability to organize workers. Ultimately inconclusive, the conflict ended only with McFetridge's death in 1969.[38]

The McFetridge-Sullivan feud reveals an early example of a disturbing, recurrent theme in SEIU history: the tensions between local leaders and the national bureaucracy exploding into damaging, public feuds. McFetridge viewed himself as defending the superb, pseudo-professional conditions for janitors that the BSEIU achieved in Chicago. To McFetridge, Sullivan and Fairchild's efforts represented a disruption of a harmonious, yet often pro-worker, world of labor relations he had devoted his life to building. Sullivan, on the other hand, viewed McFetridge as a challenge to his authority who refused to adapt to the changing nature of labor relations. Notably, neither leader embodied an idealistic vision of workers' power, but instead represented two different images of how the union's model of politically connected unionism would operate.

A New Generation

Symbolically, a new era began for the BSEIU when, during the 1964 convention, it formally dropped the B and became the Service Employees International Union (SEIU). More than a re-branding, the name change represented Sullivan's efforts to disassociate the union from the legacy of McFetridge and focus the organization on expansion among public and health-care workers. Although the union only held tenuous jurisdiction over many of these workers, they quickly became a significant portion of the organization.

The union needed expansion to offset the decline of its core membership. In New York, the elevator operators—the base of Sullivan's power—lost their jobs due to increasing automation. Between 1950 and 1972, the number of elevator operators in the local collapsed from 10,880 to a mere 1,184.[39] Although few jobs in the union declined as markedly as elevator operators, improvements in heating systems and other changes to residential and commercial buildings impacted the union throughout the country. Despite initial efforts to resist these changes, ultimately Sullivan and his successors began to consciously move SEIU increasingly away from its roots in the building services.

A new generation of leaders, most notably its new president George Hardy, sought to resist this trend by promoting an enthusiastic, progressive agenda for the union. Politically, he aligned the union with the liberal wing of the Democratic Party, even running presidential candidate George McGovern's 1972 labor outreach.[40] Internally, Hardy actively fought latent corruption inside the union, finally purging the last stalwart of the Scalise-era—a notorious mobster named Tom Burke who had long been seen as the Chicago Outfit's representative to the union—in 1971.[41] Believing strongly that the labor movement benefited from connections to larger social movements, Hardy hired staff members and organizers partially for their roots in the civil rights, antiwar, and women's movements. Commonly well-educated but without deep connections to the labor movement, these new hires professionalized and diversified the union's staff.[42]

The new generation of leadership consolidated its power in 1980 when John Sweeney replaced Hardy as president of SEIU. Eager to arrest the decline of the labor movement, Sweeney and his followers combined community organizing, political deal-making, and savvy negotiation to achieve a series of successes between 1980–2005. Most notably, the union achieved an iconic success in organizing Latino janitors in the Los Angeles area.[43] Sweeney emphasized the importance of building meaningful, long-term community and political alliances. These alliances provided the union with critical leverage to force employers to meaningfully bargain.

As Kim Moody summarizes it, the Sweeney's ideology was a "contradictory cocktail—progressive experiments, business methods, and toleration of the old and dubious."[44] This "cocktail" became the basis of the New Voice platform, which eventually elevated him to the presidency of the AFL-CIO. While Sweeney sold this approach to unionism as new, a similar cocktail of business, social movement, and political unionism had long been served by SEIU. Throughout the union's history, leaders like Quesse, Hardy, and McFetridge combined progressive tactics—political and community organizing—with a willingness to compromise with political and business elites. Sweeney thus exemplified the trends that had defined the union since its birth in Chicago.

Judged solely on growth, Sweeney's approach proved successful, resulting in sustained growth for the union during the difficult 1980s. The ability of SEIU to continue growing while many other unions fell into decline made Sweeney into one of the most prominent labor leaders in the country. As Sweeney gained influence, he became disenchanted with the conservatism of AFL-CIO president Lane Kirkland. Supported by a coalition of dissident union leaders, Sweeney challenged Kirkland's chosen successor for the presidency of the AFL-CIO and won.[45]

The absence of Sweeney in SEIU created a power vacuum that the pugnacious Andy Stern quickly filled. A former welfare caseworker, Stern became the first president of SEIU who neither worked in the building services nor served as an organizer among them. Believing that the labor movement needed to radically change to face the needs of a new age, Stern aggressively promoted various forms of "value-added employer relationships."[46] Like Quesse and McFetridge, Stern sought to trade the union's political influence for employer concessions. In his book *A Country that Works*, for example, Stern lauds a joint labor-management lobbying program "in California [where] the [nursing home] industry and union worked with the legislature [to secure] a $660 million state legislative appropriation" that made employers more prosperous and helped the union to achieve better pay.[47] While these tactics paid dividends in new organization, they committed the union to alliances and tactics that had little tolerance for spontaneous worker activism.

After the union's failure to elect John Kerry in the 2004 election, Stern began to publicly organize a coalition against Sweeney, whom he viewed as being unwilling to adapt and insufficiently committed to organization. When Stern's allies failed to gather enough support to unseat Sweeney, he withdrew SEIU from the AFL-CIO. Followed shortly by several other unions, the seceding unions founded a new federation called Change to Win (CtW). In many ways a platform for Stern, the CtW focused on a combination of aggressive organization while forming alliances with liberal political groups and causes.[48]

As the driving force between the CtW and SEIU, Stern placed a high emphasis on cultivating progressive allies. Complaining that the labor movement was run by "whiter people, older people, maler people," Stern began an internal campaign of diversification that partially redressed the longstanding inequalities in the union's leadership.[49] Similarly, Stern sought to link the labor movement to the growing immigrant rights movement and other progressive causes.[50] Recognizing the need to associate the labor movement with the growing progressive wing of the Democratic Party, Stern's efforts sought to cement the role of labor as a key coalition member. While such moves could easily be mistaken as a true disjunction in SEIU, they largely continued the opportunistic political strategy developed by McFetridge and Hardy.

Stern's political maneuvers culminated in SEIU endorsing Barack Obama over Hillary Clinton in the 2008 primary. The early endorsement of Obama helped to cement a perception of the union as among the most important members of the young Senator's electoral coalition. When Obama became president in November 2008, it appeared that Stern had restored labor unions to power in Washington, D.C. Seeking to capitalize on this moment, SEIU began a $50-million-dollar lobbying campaign for universal healthcare and comprehensive labor law reform. However, these efforts helped win the Affordable Care Act, but not universal healthcare or labor law reform. Despite having the president's ear, the union failed to make labor reform a central priority for the new administration and ultimately accepted a severely compromised health-care bill. Part of this failure of influence came from the new president's distancing from SEIU due to scandals involving its close ally Illinois Governor Rod Blagojevich (see Introduction to this collection).

Growing unrest inside SEIU also undermined Stern's influence over the political process. Throughout Stern's presidency, a significant number of union leaders and members objected to his focus on new organization over improving conditions for the union's existing members. Stern justified this tactic as providing "justice for all" and accused his opponents of selfishly guarding their narrow interests. To implement this while quelling internal dissent, Stern's supporters at SEIU's June 2008 convention approved a significant expansion of presidential powers. The critical voices grew into a chorus in early 2009 when Stern placed United Healthcare Workers West—the local over which his harshest internal critic/ Sal Rosselli/ presided—under trusteeship. When Rosselli resisted, an open state of conflict ensued between the 150,000 health-care workers in the local and their parent union. Echoing the struggle between McFetridge and Sullivan, the dispute dragged on until a San Francisco court found that Rosselli had illegally used union funds in his fight against Stern. Despite his notional victory, Stern resigned from the union shortly thereafter.[51]

Although the specific expressions of labor activism embodied in Sweeney and Stern did form a contrast to many other AFL-CIO unions, they remained clearly in line with the union's historical development. Continuing to use political, community, and business alliances to gain leverage for service workers, the new leaders of SEIU sounded and acted remarkably like the old. While this approach led to significant successes, it continued to generate tensions between workers and the politically savvy labor leaders who claimed to represent them.

Conclusion: The Contested History of SEIU

SEIU consistently provokes controversy among scholars, journalists, and activists. On the one hand, many argue that the SEIU of Sweeney and Stern, while certainly imperfect, embraced innovative strategies that helped modernize the labor movement. Ruth Milkman and Kim Voss, for example, praise SEIU for its "pioneering organizing initiative" and view the Sweeney era as having resulted in "some important breakthroughs." Furthermore, they note that "if all sixty-five affiliates of the AFL-CIO were as active and strategically sophisticated in organizing the unorganized as SEIU [there would be] a leap forward."[52] From this perspective, whatever the faults of the SEIU model of labor unionism, it generally represents the future of the labor movement.

Others disagree. Steve Early, for example, argues that the "Stern/SEIU model . . . abhors rank-and-file initiative, shop floor militancy and democratic decision making." In doing so the union becomes distracted from "the workplace issues [of] existing members—because those just get in the way of more important big-picture goals."[53] To Early, the approach of SEIU fundamentally alienates its members by handing the labor movement over to a class of bureaucrats, lawyers, and political sycophants. Early does not stand alone in this assessment. Kim Moody similarly argues that SEIU's efforts to reach nation-wide accommodations with business and political elites required a structural quashing of local militancy, which ultimately damaged the labor movement.[54] While praising certain locals and initiatives, former SEIU official and scholar Jane McAlevey echoes many of these complaints, noting that Stern's strategies "significantly diminished the role of workers in their own emancipation and have contributed to labor's ongoing decline."[55]

All of these different perspectives on the modern SEIU hold elements of truth. SEIU can fairly be seen as both hero and villain depending on one's priorities, perspective, and definition of the labor movement's purpose. From its earliest days in Chicago, SEIU approached unionization through the use of questionable alliances with employers, politicians, and mobsters. Although many other unions pursued similar tactics, the unique nature of building service workers made them unusually effective allies to diverse groups of elites. Through these tactics, the union achieved historic victories among difficult-to-organize workers who otherwise lacked bargaining leverage. Over time, however, these alliances alienated the union's leadership from its membership and aligned their interests with those of political and economic elites. In defense of larger political and economic goals, union leaders increasingly used authoritarian means to restrict uncoordinated, grass-roots activism and militancy. Such actions led to worker resentment, bruising internal conflicts between factional leaders, and embarrassing associations with corrupt politicians. At key moments leaders might have chosen better, more democratic or member-led paths, but the significance of external political, community, and business alliances made these approaches dangerous. Constantly struggling to balance the needs of boardroom allies, political patrons, bureaucratic leaders, and workers, SEIU continues to follow a successful yet morally challenging path.

Notes

1. Kim Voss and Rachel Sherman, "Breaking the Iron Law of Oligarchy: Tactical Innovations and the Revitalization of the American Labor Movement," *American Journal of Sociology* 106 (September 2000): 303–349; Steven Henry Lopez, *Reorganizing the Rust Belt: An Inside Study of the American Labor Movement* (Berkeley: University of California Press, 2004). Parts of this article are adapted from my dissertation: Benjamin Peterson, *Building the Service Employees International Union,* PhD. Diss, (University of Illinois at Chicago, 2016).

2. Steve Early, "Reutherism Redux," *Against the Current,* Issue 112 (September-October 2004). https://www.solidarity-us.org/node/1122.

3. Ibid.

4. "Flat Owners Join to Fight Rent Curb," *Chicago Tribune,* November 27, 1920, 1.

5. *Proceedings of the Seventh Convention of the Building Service Employees International Union* (Chicago: BSEIU, 1935), 4.

6. "His Majesty, A Janitor and His Union Sued," *Chicago Tribune,* October 3, 1920, 10.

7. Andrew Wender Cohen, *The Racketeers Progress: Chicago and the Struggle for the Modern American Economy, 1900–1940* (Cambridge: Cambridge University Press, 2009).

8. Building Service Employees International Union, *Information and Instructions to the Members of Chicago Flat Janitors Union, Local No. 1* (Chicago: Press of John F. Higgins, 1940), 15. Hereafter *Instructions to the Members of the Chicago Flat Janitors Union.*; Peterson, *Building,* 45.

9. *Proceedings of the Seventh Convention of the Building Service Employees International Union,* 12.

10. Georg Liedenberg, *Chicago's Progressive Alliance* (Dekalb: Northern Illinois University, 2006).

11. John Jentz, "Labor, the Law and Economics: The Organization of the Chicago Flat Janitors Union, 1902–1917," *Labor History* 38 (1998): 413–431.

12. Raymond L. Gold, "In the Basement—The Apartment-Building Janitor," in *The Human Shape of Work: Studies in the Sociology of Occupations,* Peter L. Berger ed. (New York: Macmillan Co, 1964), 46; Herrick, "Up the Labor Ladder with William F. Quesse," *Chicago Tribune*, 86; Jentz, "Labor, the Law and Economics," 422–428.

13. John B. Jentz, "Unions, Cartels, and the Political Economy of American Cities: The Chicago Flat Janitors Union in the Progressive Era and 1920s," *Studies in American Political Development* 14 (Spring 2000), 68.

14. Tom Beadling, Pat Cooper, and Grace Palladino, *A Need for Valor (1983 Unpublished Manuscript)*, Box 4, Folder 3, SEIU Historical Records, Walter Reuther Library, Wayne State University. Hereafter, SEIU Historical Records, *A Need for Valor*. Note that this is not the published version of *A Need for Valor* but the longer original draft, which was cut to create the official, published version.

15. Jentz, "Unions, Cartels, and the Political Economy of American Cities," 59.

16. BSEIU, *1919 Yearbook*, Box 1, Folder 6, SEIU Research Department Historical File, Walter Reuther Library, Wayne State University.

17. John B. Jentz, "Citizenship, Self-Respect, and Political Power: Chicago's Flat Janitors Trailblaze the Service Employees International Union, 1912–1921," *Labor's Heritage*, Vol. 9, No. 1 (Summer, 1997): 10.

18. "Well Done McFetridge," *Public Safety*, January 1931, 16; Peterson, *Building*, 92–93.

19. "Parley to Avert Elevator Strike," *The New York Times,* March 14, 1937, 27; "Move to Arbitrate Eases Service Row," March 16, 1937, 7; "Fail to Pick Arbitrator," *The New York Times*, March 18, 1937, 2; "Service Wage Issue Left to Arbitration," *The New York Times*, March 23, 1937, 11; "50,00 Service Men Win Rise in Wages," *The New York Times*, May 11, 1937, 1; Peterson, 175.

20. James Jacobs, *Mobsters, Unions, and the Feds: The Mafia and the American Labor Movement* (New York: New York University Press, 2007).

21. David Scott Witwer, *Shadow of the Racketeer: Scandal in Organized Labor* (Urbana: University of Illinois Press, 2009), 45.

22. Cohen, *The Racketeer's Progress*, 228.

23. Witwer, *Shadow of the Racketeer,* 80.

24. "Scalise's Ann Discovers She Made an 'Error,' *Chicago Tribune*, August 17, 1940, 11; Witwer, "Scandal of George Scalise," 922–925.

25. Witwer, *Shadow of the Racketeer,* 161–166. On Pegler's life and career, see Finis Farr, *Fair Enough: The Life of Westbrook Pegler* (New Rochelle, NY: Arlington House, 1975).

26. Steve Early, *The Civil Wars in U.S. Labor: Birth of a New Workers Movement or Death Throes of the Old?* (Chicago: Haymarket Books, 2011), 93.

27. *Convention Proceedings of the Ninth Convention of the Building Service Employees International Union*, 147.

28. On Los Angeles, see Mike Davis, *City of Quartz: Excavating the Future in Los Angeles* (New York: Verso, 2006).

29. Ruth Milkman, *L.A. Story: Immigrant Workers and the Future of the U.S. Labor Movement* (New York: Sage Foundation, 2006), 62–68.
30. Raymond L. Gold, "The Chicago Flat Janitor," unpublished M.A. Thesis (University of Chicago, 1950), 135.
31. Ibid., 135.
32. "Moats to Sullivan," circa 1964, Box 64, Folder 13, SEIU Secretary-Treasurer's Office: International Executive Board Records Collection, Walter Reuther Library, Wayne State University. Hereafter "Moats to Sullivan."
33. Bryce Engle, "$72,834 Saving on City Janitor Work Possible," *Chicago Tribune*, January 26, 1953, 13.
34. *Chicago Sun-Times*, April 18, 1946, Quoted in BSEIU, *25th Anniversary of the Presidency* (circa 1960), Box 1, Folder 11, SEIU Historical Records, Walter Reuther Library, Wayne State University.
35. Len O'Connor, *Clout—Mayor Daley and His City* (Chicago: Contemporary Books, 1984), 133.
36. Ibid., 134.
37. William Mullen, "Portrait of a Power Broker," *Chicago Tribune*, April 11, 1982, 17; Vernon Jarrett, "A Look at Charles Swibel's Power," *Chicago Tribune*, April 21, 1982; "Charles R. Swibel, 63, Former CHA Chairman, Dies," *Chicago Tribune*, January 20, 1990, 21; Peterson, 294.
38. W. L. McFetridge, "Labor Leader, 75," *New York Times*, March 17, 1969, 39; "Moats to Sullivan"; Peterson, *Building*. 343.
39. Grace Palladino, "When Militancy Isn't Enough: The Impact of Automation on New York City Building Service Workers, 1934–1970," *Labor History* 28(2) 1987, 220.
40. "Union Leaders Will Stump for McGovern Labor Vote," *New York Times*, October 27, 1972, 24.
41. James Strong, "Burke's Ouster Ends Labor Era," *Chicago Tribune*, July 23, 1973, 2.
42. Milkman, *L.A. Story*, 68–69.
43. Ibid., 155–156.
44. Kim Moody, "Saviors from on High," *Jacobin*, July 2015. https://www.jacobinmag.com/2015/07/sweeney-trumka-chavez-seiu-unions/.
45. Steve Early, *Embedded with Organized Labor* (New York: Monthly Review Press, 2009), 97.
46. Andy Stern, *A Country that Works: Getting America back on Track* (New York: Free Press, 2006), 107.
47. Ibid.
48. Early, *Embedded with Organized Labor*, 208.
49. G. Burkins, "Andy Stern Seems a Shoo-in to Lead Aggressive Service-Employees Union," *Wall Street Journal*, March 15, 1996.
50. "A Progressive and Practical Labor Leader," *Wall Street Journal*, January 03, 2002.
51. The preceding two paragraphs are based on Stephen Greenhouse's reporting in the *New York Times* from 2004 to 2009. See also Steve Early, *The Civil Wars in U.S.*

Labor (Chicago: Haymarket Books, 2011); Cal Winslow, *Labor's Civil War in California* (Oakland: PM Press, 2010); and Bill Fletcher Jr. and Nelson Lichtenstein, "SEIU's Civil War," *In These Times* December 16, 2009, http://inthesetimes.com/article/5309/seius_civil_war.

52. Ruth Milkman & Kim Voss, "Introduction" In *Rebuilding Labor: Organizing and Organizers in the New Union Movement*, eds. Ruth Milkman & Kim Voss (Ithaca: ILR Press, 2004), 4–5.

53. Early, *The Civil War in American Labor*, 16.

54. Kim Moody, "Toward an International Social-Movement Unionism," *New Left Review* (September 1997), 59.

55. Jane McAlevey, *No Shortcuts: Organizing for Power in the New Gilded Age* (New York: Oxford, 2016), 71.

3

Reconciling Progressive Idealism with Centralized Control

An Institutional Analysis of SEIU's Growth

KYOUNG-HEE YU

That large organizations develop centralized structures over time is a well-known axiom. From Michels[1] to Merton,[2] scholars have associated the development of structural rigidity in progressive organizations with a conservatization of their goals, or what Zald and Ash termed a 'becalming' of radical ideology. The SEIU case challenges this association.[3] The union embodies progressive idealism albeit in structures where power is highly concentrated at the top, and therefore presents a paradox to observers of the American labor movement and students of social movements. On the one hand, SEIU has been characterized as a beacon of hope that re-introduced militancy into a dormant labor movement suffering from the "iron law of oligarchy."[4] Yet critics of SEIU have maintained that the union is top-down and that it exemplifies a case of professionalized staff dictating low-wage workers' interests, evoking Piven and Cloward's[5] warning against powerful organizations taking over "poor people's movements."[6] This chapter renders a more nuanced understanding of SEIU's past and sheds light on how the apparent paradox—the embodiment of ideological progressivism in a centralized bureaucratic apparatus—came about. It examines how SEIU evolved from its origins as a decentralized craft union to a powerful "social movement union."[7] The chapter brings to light the organizational change process that transformed SEIU from an under-resourced union representing a haphazard combination of service occupations into a command center for national campaigns.[8]

The discussion herein is divided into three periods: (1) the early years of the Flat Janitors Union, SEIU's predecessor; (2) the decades between the 1950s and the 1980s characterized by diversification into public and health services and the development of a federated bureaucracy; (3) the 1980s and 1990s characterized by rapid centralization of control and radical organizational transformation.[9] I conclude with a discussion of what such a historical trajectory means for understanding the many successes and challenges faced by the union today. I also discuss theoretical implications of SEIU case for understanding the tension between radical ideology and centralized command.

Origins and Early Years: A Decentralized Craft Union (1920s–1950s)

As Ben Peterson's contribution to this volume makes clear, SEIU's roots reside in apartment or "flat" janitors' locals in Chicago and New York, and theatre janitors' locals in San Francisco in the early 1900s. Early locals organized janitors against the predominant public opinion, which tended to regard the janitor as a servant whose right to organize was considered "laughable."[10] In fact, SEIU publications point out that the earliest janitor locals were granted American Federation of Labor (AFL) charters at the urging of carpenters' and plumbers' unions who complained that their work was threatened by unorganized janitors, rather than from any sense that the janitors deserved to be unionized.[11] Efforts to organize janitors, elevator operators, and window cleaners in Chicago and New York began in the late years of the 19th century. While organizing efforts by the Knights of Labor in New York failed in 1891, similar efforts in Chicago resulted in contracts with building owners and an AFL charter in 1904 for the Chicago Flat Janitors' union. However, the union quickly fell into disarray, ending in a dissolution.[12] The remaining fledgling group of janitors locals was again organized into an international union, the Building Service Employees International Union (BSEIU), by William Quesse, a janitor who was responsible for the initial organizing in 1902 and who became the first president of the national union in 1921. BSEIU was granted a federal AFL charter. Three out of the seven founding locals of the BSEIU were based in Chicago, and power remained centered in Chicago with New York a secondary base until the 1940s. The prominence of Chicago and New York in BSEIU's history (with San Francisco a close runner-up) owed to the rapid expansion of residential buildings and the militancy of the immigrant workforce in these cities.[13]

During the first few decades, the federation of janitors' unions was distinguished for its decentralized structure featuring a diversity of members and their work and the existence of power bases in key localities that counter-balanced one another. Janitors at the time were predominantly African American and immigrant (the main immigrant groups were German, Swedish, Irish, and Belgian in the early 1900s).[14] A SEIU publication notes that in 1910 approximately 20 percent of janitors in Chicago were African American when only two percent of Chicago's population was African American.[15] The proportion of African Americans in the occupation increased between 1910 and 1920 as a result of migration from the South. The Chicago Flat Janitors' Union had a vice president and three members of the executive board who were African American at a time when most unions excluded African Americans or forced them to join separate unions.[16] The union's first yearbook in 1916 declared that the union was "composed of all creeds, colors and nationalities, and do not allow anyone to use any prejudice in the organization."[17]

Flat janitors, elevator operators, doormen, and theatre janitors all experienced different social conditions and labor market realities; these differences also accounted for decentralized governance. Flat janitors, constituting the largest group of members, experienced social grievances arising from tenuous relationships with tenants who, the Chicago sociologist Everett Hughes said, gave janitors their "status pain."[18] Most flat janitors lived in the basement of residential apartments, were male, and usually were married. The flat janitor's wife was also involved in the work of the janitor as they were expected to work in exchange for "free" housing.[19] In one of the earliest protests in Chicago, flat janitors demanded regular working hours and freedom of their wives from janitorial work.[20] In contrast, the major concern for elevator operators was the threat of being displaced by technology. By the mid-1960s, SEIU also represented X-ray technicians, cemetery workers, racetrack workers, police units, newspaper distributors, court and probation officers, and even the occasional group of doctors.[21]

Between the 1920s and 1960s, Chicago and New York City alternated in dominating the national union. Early union administration was rudimentary at best. At least one BSEIU president—George Scalise—was found guilty of racketeering and the union was linked with organized crime activities in the 1930s.[22] In a 1960 master's thesis at Princeton University, David Delgado noted that the existence of key urban locals that differed in levels of organization prevented the emergence of centralized power. He wrote:

> The union is organized only in a few key urban areas more or less insulated from one another, having differing degrees of union organization, different employment possibilities and in which the extent of automation and profitability of the industries concerned vary somewhat.[23]

The national union, dependent on powerful regional blocs for resources and talent, had no direct authority over locals, having only what Delgado referred to as recommendatory powers: "The locals set their own policies, negotiate their own contracts, and strike at their discretion."[24]

In 1941, the union achieved a master agreement in hospitals with the San Francisco Hospital Conference, marking its entry into healthcare.[25] In the early 1940s, BSEIU established a presence in Canada, initially with janitorial local unions but rapidly moving into healthcare, establishing a local union in Toronto General Hospital in 1944.[26]

Diversification and Bureaucratization (1950s–Early 1980s)

DEVELOPING A NATIONAL SYSTEM OF UNION ADMINISTRATION

I draw from a sizeable literature on formalization and bureaucracy to examine the development of bureaucracy in SEIU, marked by the development of general and formal rules, a hierarchy of positions and roles, a system of authority based on official position rather than personal influence, and full-time commitment to union activities as well as formal training for officials.[27] According to this classification, bureaucratization in SEIU occurred at a relatively slow pace, and, up to the 1980s, was distinctive in that it was not accompanied by a centralization of control into the national union. These trends can be traced back to the 1940s, when then President McFetridge, a nephew to the first president, William Quesse, took over the union after the fall of George Scalise under charges of embezzlement.[28] Mindful of entrenched corruption under his predecessor, McFetridge launched a modernization effort that included introducing financial record-keeping and establishing legal and research departments.[29]

A system of administration developed in which the respective roles of the national and local unions were demarcated. The national union, whose historic role had been to represent local unions in the AFL, strengthened its administrative function. Formal rules giving the national union the right to trustee a local union first appeared in the 1950 Constitution and By-Laws. In 1972 the national union president was given the constitutional power to negotiate and enter into national and regional collective bargaining agreements.[30] Lastly, a system of appropriations from local unions to fund the functional departments of the national union emerged. A national strike fund, controlled by the national President and the Executive Board, was instituted in 1972. National staff careers were formalized: a pension plan was set up for national organizers and business agents, and the first record of a staff union of national organizers appears

FIGURE 3.1 Timeline of historical change in SEIU

Structural consolidation of local unions	**2005**	SEIU breaks away from AFL CIO, founds Change to Win coalition; 30th JfJ launched in Houston, TX
	1987	JfJ launched in LA, Washington DC, Atlanta, San Francisco, San Diego, Seattle
Centralization of control into national union	**1986**	First JfJ launched: Denver
	1980s	Re-organization into Industry Divisions
National union bureaucratizes	**1950s–70s**	Expansion into healthcare and public service
	1921	SEIU founded

in 1970.[31] Figure 3.1 outlines the chronological development of organizational change in SEIU.

GROWTH AND DIVERSIFICATION

In the 1950s and '60s membership declined in the union's building services occupations due to technological change and outsourcing, and forays from other unions into BSEIU's territory prompted national officers to expand organizing outside of building services.[32] The union thus began a trajectory of growth in semiprofessional occupations in healthcare and public services as mentioned above. In the 1960s, David Sullivan and Thomas Donahue, who later became Assistant Secretary of Labor in the Johnson administration, led the union's lobbying effort for collective bargaining rights in health and public services at national and state levels. This conferred collective bargaining rights on public employees, workers in nonprofit hospitals, and nonprofit colleges and universities. By 1965, more than half of BSEIU's local unions included public workers.[33] Under David Sullivan, who held the presidency from 1960–1971, the union dropped "building" from its name and moved its national offices from Chicago to Washington D.C. Table 3.1 lists key national legislative outcomes that aided the union's expansion.

Since the 1970s, tremendous growth in California made the West Coast the center of activity. In 1971, four locals—in Los Angeles, San Francisco, New York City, and Chicago respectively—made up a quarter of the national union's

TABLE 3.1 Key legislative milestones

Wage security for cleaners in federal government buildings (Service Contract Act)	1965
Bargaining rights for workers in "proprietary" hospitals and nursing homes*	1967
Bargaining rights for workers in non-profit hospitals and nursing homes	1970
Bargaining rights for workers in private non-profit colleges and universities	1970

*Groups newly recognized as bargaining units under the National Labor Relations Act.
Source: SEIU. 1971. SEIU International Executive Board Collection. Archives of Labor and Urban Affairs: Wayne State University.

membership of 435,000.[34] These locals dominated the national Executive Board under proportional representation. A decentralized structure of governance in the form of regional and sectoral "joint councils" was the main mechanism for information sharing and coordination of organizing activities up to the mid-1980s. Local union affiliation with joint councils was voluntary for most of the time that they were effective; however, in the 1970s the national union began to assert jurisdictional control over the joint councils, making affiliations with them mandatory for local unions. Piore described the historical system of governance in SEIU as a "conference system" characterized by decentralized and consultative decision-making.[35] The joint councils structure overlapped for several years with a divisional structure based on industry representation introduced in the 1980s.

Under Hardy's presidency, two key affiliations increased total SEIU membership by nearly 35 percent—the affiliation of the National Association of Government Employees in 1983 and that of the California State Employees Association in 1984.[36] Affiliations were typically entered into between an "independent" union and a union that is a member of the AFL-CIO, under which the former agreed to be exclusively represented by the latter in bargaining while retaining its autonomy in internal affairs. During the 1980s, affiliations of independent unions and employee associations in public services and healthcare became the main source of growth for SEIU. As a case in point, SEIU had 600,000 members in 1980; at the end of 1989, its membership had grown to 925,000. Of the growth in membership, 250,000 came as a result of affiliations, and 75,000 from new organizing.[37] Piore attributed SEIU's immense success in acquiring affiliations to the union's tradition of local autonomy, which he pointed out must have been attractive to affiliating unions.[38] Figure 3.2 charts membership numbers in SEIU for all years that data was available since 1940.

FIGURE 3.2 Membership growth in SEIU (Source: SEIU Executive Board records, various years; www.seiu.org [2008])

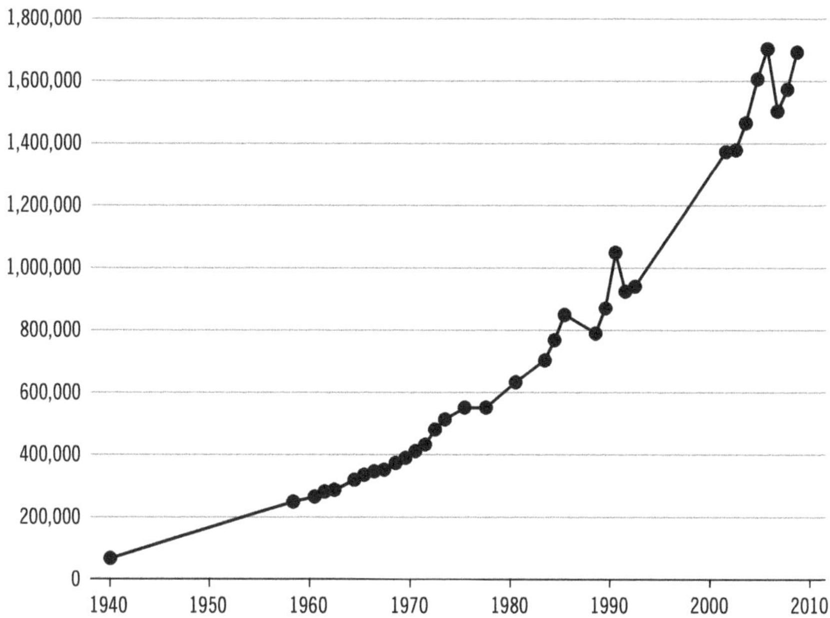

ORGANIZING BECOMES A NATIONAL RESPONSIBILITY

In 1971, George Hardy, who rose to fame as an SEIU field organizer in California, became president of the International Union. Thereupon the international adopted many of the innovative and militant organizing practices Hardy had spearheaded in California and elsewhere. A former janitor at the San Francisco Public Library and the son of a union official, Hardy had organized more than a third of all office buildings in Los Angeles and won 40 percent wage increases over a four-year period.[39] The innovations that Hardy spearheaded foreshadowed SEIU's organizing strategies in later years. Under Hardy, the union influenced policy and legislation to extend bargaining rights to public workers and subsequently convinced the workers and their representatives to authorize SEIU as their bargaining agent. For example, SEIU negotiated bargaining rights for state and local government employees in Pennsylvania, making it possible for relevant local unions to sign up tens of thousands of government workers.[40] In reports, Hardy's mantra was cited as "Organize everything."[41]

Importantly, organizing, which had been the purview of local unions, was made a major responsibility of the International Union under Hardy's presidency. Prior to the 1980s, the international influenced local organizing through subsidies rather than through direct involvement. Under a "cooperative organizing model," the national union subsidized local union officers, usually the President or a business representative, to spend part of their time on organizing efforts.[42] The only full-time national organizers had been regional Vice Presidents, of whom there were merely four to six at any point in time. Typically, regional organizers were joined by staff loaned by other local unions in the area in preparation for a recognition election. An excerpt from President Sullivan's 1968 report to the Executive Board discussing an organizing campaign in the New England region illustrates this:

> Two interesting features of the campaign should be mentioned. One is that this relatively small local asked three of its members to take leave of absence and work for the local at the beginning of the campaign. In the final election week there were about twenty-five people from the local who had taken a week's vacation on their own in order to help in the campaign. We sent in 16 people to man the various polling places and show that we had a good staff. 7 of the 16 were loaned to us by Edward Sullivan's Local 254 [in Boston]. We intend to repeat this cooperative effort when the final election is called.[43]

The near three-fold increase in the organizing budget from $345,000 at the end of the 1960s to $1 million in the early 1970s went mostly to increasing the number of local union staff working on nationally funded projects. It did not increase the size of International Union staff significantly or bring organizing jobs into the national union.[44] Archival records indicate that initial efforts by the international to direct local unions in organizing were often unsuccessful. For example, George Hardy wined and dined local union officers and their wives in an attempt to establish a new joint council in the New England area for organizing public service workers. Yet, powerful locals in the area, such as the Boston local, were reluctant to subsidize less resourceful locals in Rhode Island and Connecticut.[45] Furthermore, organizers sponsored by the international who worked under local unions were routinely fired by local union presidents who had full say over the terms of their contracts.

Rapid Centralization (1984–1996)

The period from 1984 to 1996, when archival data for this chapter ended, was marked by further bureaucratization as well as rapid centralization of control in the International Union under two very strong presidents—John Sweeney (1980–1995) and Andy Stern (1996–2010).[46] First, unprecedented control over local unions was given to the international in this period. In sharp contrast to past constitutions that emphasized the local union and joint council relationship as the basic unit of decision-making, the 1992 Constitution and By-Laws stated that "the International Union has jurisdiction over all local unions and affiliated bodies."[47] Key to strengthening international union control was an organizational restructuring, from a geographic representational structure to an "industry" division structure. This required that local unions hitherto representing diverse occupations exclusively represent workers in one of SEIU's three main industries—building services, healthcare, and public services. Local unions had to "give up" workers who were not in their new industrial jurisdiction, and therefore mounted strong resistance against this directive.[48] Hence, even though the initiative was adopted by the International Executive Board in 1984, implementation took many more years: the plan was successfully rolled out in local unions only after 2000. Under the new structure, the divisions directed policy to the local unions. Distributed decision-making through myriad overlapping conferences was eventually superseded by state-level councils with far less authority than its national or international divisions. Since 2006, the coordinating role of state councils was increasingly assumed by "mega" locals whose boundaries transcended states.[49]

Second, administrative control over locals was strengthened. Between 1980 and 1984, Sweeney increased the number of international staff from about twenty to more than two hundred.[50] In 1994, just before Sweeney left to take the presidency of the AFL-CIO, SEIU had 323 staff on its national payroll.[51] Staff recruited by the international during these years were given unprecedented discretion and entrusted with implementing sweeping reforms and changes in organizational practices. Administrative control was also enhanced through the creation of a Local Union Organizational Development unit directly under the national President that oversaw management systems for record keeping, finances, and human resources.[52]

Third, control was centralized over resources and programs. John Sweeney appointed Andrew Stern, a former member of SEIU's Philadelphia local and later its president, as organizing director in 1984. As organizing director, Stern elevated the status of organizers in the union, increasing their pay and establishing formal training.[53] These developments were significant in a union where historically the bargaining representative had had greater status by virtue of his/her relationship with members holding voting rights and employers. Per capita tax paid by local unions to the international increased from $1.80 per month

TABLE 3.2 Increases in SEIU Organizing Budget

Late 1960s	$345,000
Mid-1970s	$1 million
1980	$2 million
1988	$4 million
1994	$13 million

Source: Report of the International President to the Executive Board, various years

per member in 1980 to $4 in 1984 and doubled to $8 after 1984.[54] Under Stern's presidency beginning in the year 2000, local unions were required to contribute to a Unity Fund that amounted to a further $4–5 per member in addition to per capita tax flowing into the international. Funds from the Unity Fund were earmarked to finance "breakthrough" campaigns, coordinated bargaining, and other activities designed to increase density in SEIU's core industries. In this way SEIU's organizing budget increased from $4 million in 1988 to $13 million in 1994. In 2006, each of the three divisions had an organizing budget that exceeded $13 million. Table 3.2 lists increases in SEIU's organizing budget over various years.

"Cooperative organizing" gave way to a model where the international played a crucial role in identifying strategic targets and directing large-scale campaigns.[55] Under new "strategic organizing," the international took a "new and vigorous role in organizing efforts," as stated in a report from President Sweeney to its convention in 1984:

> In the past, the International's responsibility in organizing has rested primarily in providing technical assistance and funding for local union efforts. Because our membership continues to diversify, however, we must focus more of our efforts on new occupations and new geographical areas—particularly the Sun Belt. And the increasing presence of multinational corporations with their seemingly limitless resources and professional union-busters as our opponents makes it clear that the International must take a new and vigorous role in organizing efforts.[56]

Radical Organizational Transformation

In this section I review the nature of organizational and programmatic transformation that propelled a newly centralized SEIU. Paradoxically, because of the decentralized system, the international president of B/SEIU had always enjoyed a large discretion in identifying new areas of opportunity.[57] Both Sweeney and

Stern designed the union's responses to an external environment that was rapidly and unfavorably changing. A sense of crisis, both within SEIU as well as inside the American labor movement, motivated the architects of reform. Membership in the union's founding building services sector was fast eroding due to outsourcing and demographic changes in the workforce, and at the same time, new members in healthcare and public sectors placed high demands on the union. New immigrants, many of whom were undocumented, now comprised the vast majority of the janitorial workforce, and the union lacked the knowhow to organize them. Externally, labor unions faced antagonism from the Reagan administration.

Amid the crisis in the American labor movement, the international's staff set out to devise a plan for "leading the resurgence of the labor movement," as Sweeney termed it.[58] A breed of radicalism with the goal of social change was introduced by new professional organizers who were recruited into the union in the 1970s and '80s and came to occupy key positions at the helm of functional departments such as organizing, legal, and research.[59] Some, such as Stern, were recruited from within SEIU. Others, such as Stephen Lerner, the architect of the Justice for Janitors, were recruited from outside, mainly from other labor and community organizations. These directors then hired a new generation of managers. This group propelled the innovation, militancy, and unrelenting drive of new campaigns such as the Justice for Janitors.[60] Reformists welcomed extreme uncertainty, favoring a radical break with old ways in order to reinvent the labor movement. In a memo to senior staff in 1992, Stern, then director of organizing, wrote:

> There will be many, many ambiguities. Budgets are mostly inadequate for the task in front of us since this is the area that the labor movement needs the most effort and has the least expertise—creating its own resurgence.[61]

Divisionalization allowed for separate organizational identities in the three sectors even as it helped consolidate the myriad occupational groups represented by the union. In a 1988 Convention report, Sweeney explained the necessity of creating an organizational identity that resonated with the union's diverse membership:

> Just as our strength lies in our diversity, our challenge lies in creating an organizational identity which rings true for our wide range of members. From this challenge, the idea of industry-based divisions within SEIU was born.[62]

For example, the creation of the building services division, comprising office cleaning, security services, and airport workers, was seen as crucial in injecting much-needed resources and morale into janitors' locals previously considered low status in the union.[63]

Inevitably, political battles ensued between proponents and opponents of industry-based restructuring. National union staff cajoled, subverted, and forced local unions into trusteeship in order to win these battles.[64] Ideologically progressive and college-educated—Piore called them members of the New Left who had grown up and gone to college during the 1960s[65]—the worldviews of these newly recruited professionals often clashed with the existing leadership in local unions. Proponents of reform favored putting resources in organizing, rationalizing the operation of local unions, and divisionalizing. Opponents favored local autonomy over directed national policies and were protective of existing practices and relationships with members and at times employers.[66] Among the opponents were presidents of large local unions who had amassed personal status. Staff who had been hired into the change project from outside generally thought of these locals as fiefdoms of labor barons. In addition to being programmatically opposed to old ways, these staff were ideologically repulsed by the nepotism and cronyism that sustained some locals.[67] As the change program unfolded, its breadth was no longer confined to organizing; increasingly, it sought to "transform" local unions, as stated by Andy Stern in a 1989 organizers' training session:

> *SEIU is committed to transforming its locals into organizations that make organizing an integral and essential part of their local union.* Locals who chose to turn the tide, not die of self-inflicted wounds; locals who believe the overall success of the labor movement is directly related to its power to both grow by uniting its existing members with unorganized workers employed by common employers or in similar industries or geography; [. . .] Locals who understand that the only practical way to organize workers on a large scale is by mobilizing currently represented rank and file members, leaders, and staff.[68]

The hallmark of the reform era was national organizing campaigns designed to revitalize the labor movement around the plight of a particular occupation, such as the Justice for Janitors (J4J). The iconic grafted elements of a social movement to a creative reorganizing campaign built around the plight of immigrant workers.[69] The J4J embodied many of SEIU's signature organizing strategies at the time, such as bargaining for employer neutrality, card check ratification, and master agreements that controlled competition across entire urban markets.[70] Strategists in the international sought to capitalize on the imagery of popular campaigns such as the J4J to provide a vision for a renewed labor movement and to differentiate SEIU from other unions it deemed elitist.[71]

Campaigns such as J4J also facilitated reforms by providing an entry point for national intervention in locals and surfacing tensions between old and new management styles. Local union presidents, incentivized by national subsidies, initially invited national organizers to launch a J4J campaign in their locality. Over time, the local union's administration of the campaign made salient any existing problems in management. Conflict often ensued around decisions over resource allocation between national and local staff working on the same campaign.[72] These incidents provided the window for the national union to intervene. Notably, all of the thirty localities in which J4J was waged were trusteed by the national union, automatically displacing the elected leadership in the relevant local. Staff turnover as well as changes effected by the new leadership eventually rid the local union of core members of the old guard. For these reasons, J4J was described by the national Organizing Department as "most valuable in reforming locals."[73]

Conclusion

The preceding discussion provides key insights that help us understand the paradoxical coexistence of centralized command and ideological progressivism in the union. First, SEIU's decentralized past enabled the kind of visioning that inspired a "re-invention" of the labor movement. As Piore argued, the discretion that national leaders enjoyed by virtue of SEIU's decentralized structure freed them from operational concerns to set high goals for the union and respond to changing external and internal circumstances. Second, the diversity of occupations in different sectors as well as racial and ethnic diversity in its membership forced SEIU to be open to outsiders and to novel ideas from within. The union's commitment to respecting diversity and to hiring from outside the labor movement contributed to its ability to adhere to ideological progressivism even while pursuing centralized control.[74] Third, a constant driving force for reforms in the union was the conviction in their moral righteousness.[75] Not only were reforms seen as necessary, they were viewed as the right thing to do to protect workers' livelihoods and rights in an environment where power was stacked against them.[76] Hence, centralized control was seen as a means to building countervailing power against market and corporate structures that rendered workers powerless.

The SEIU case indicates that exceptions to the "iron law of oligarchy" can be found in organizations whose boundaries are porous and hold their leaders accountable to the ideals of the movement. As Leach[77] argued, neither the longevity of a minority leadership nor the relative acquiescence of the membership to leaders' strategies in and of itself is sufficient to determine that an oligarchy has taken hold. Hence, though it may be argued that SEIU leadership has remained firmly in the hands of reformists for decades and that the majority of the union's members are passive participants in union governance, such observations do not amount to allegations that the union's leadership is illegitimate or that the union operates by force or manipulation.[78] Projecting on to recent developments from the vantage point of SEIU's historical development, the union may not have developed the capacity for milestones such as establishing the Change to Win alliance to galvanize organizing in the labor movement,[79] waging the Fight for $15,[80] and helping elect progressive politicians in state and national elections had it not centralized control into the national union. But centralized control also set the union up for internal conflict such as that over the leadership of the former SEIU United Healthcare Workers.[81] Furthermore, as a democratic organization, the difficulty that immigrant workers in particular and members in general have had in impacting policy and practice and the overall intolerance for dissent in the union provide cause for worry.[82]

Notes

1. Robert Michels, *Political Parties; a Sociological Study of the Oligarchical Tendencies of Modern Democracy* (New York: Dover Publications, 1959 [1911]).

2. Robert K. Merton, "Bureaucratic Structure and Personality," *Social Forces* 18, no. 4 (May 1940): 560–568.

3. M. N. Zald and Roberta Ash, "Social Movement Organizations: Growth, Decay and Change," *Social Forces* 44, no. 3 (1966): 327–341.

4. Rick Fantasia and Kim Voss, *Hard Work: Remaking the American Labor Movement* (Berkeley: University of California Press, 2004), and Kim Voss and Rachel Sherman, "Breaking the Iron Law of Oligarchy: Union Revitalization in the American Labor Movement," *American Journal of Sociology* 106, no. 2 (2000): 303–349.

5. Frances Fox Piven and Richard A. Cloward, *Poor People's Movements: Why They Succeed, How They Fail* (New York: Pantheon Books, 1977).

6. Steve Early, *Embedded with Organized Labor: Journalistic Reflections on the Class War at Home* (New York: Monthly Review Press, 2009); Kim Moody, *US Labor in Trouble and Transition: The Failure of Reform from Above, the Promise of Revival from Below* (New York: Verso, 2007); Vanessa Tait, *Poor Workers' Unions: Rebuilding Labor from Below* (Cambridge, MA: South End Press, 2005).

7. Dan Clawson, *The Next Upsurge: Labor and the New Social Movements* (Ithaca, NY: ILR Press, 2003); Fantasia and Voss, *Hard Work*; and Paul Johnston, *Success While Others Fail: Social Movement Unionism and the Public Workplace* (Ithaca, NY: ILR Press, 1994).

8. This chapter is based on a dissertation project examining organizational transformation in the building services sector of SEIU for which data was collected between

the fall of 2005 and spring of 2007. The primary source of data presented in this chapter is the SEIU collections held at Wayne State University's Walter P. Reuther Library's Archives of Labor and Urban Affairs. Collections from the following SEIU organizational units were examined: the Executive Office, the Executive Board, SEIU Conventions, the Research Department, and the Organizing Department. Documents available included meeting minutes, internal memoranda, communication between national and local unions, strategic plans, and internal and external reports. I perused Executive Board minutes for the period starting from the 1950s up to the 1990s in order to get a sense of historical change in SEIU leading up to radical reforms. A more comprehensive reading of all collections mentioned was conducted for the decade of SEIU's "radical" organizational change as it adopted new organizing practices during the 1980s up to 1996, which was the last year archival material was made available to the author.

9. Craig J. Jenkins, "Radical Transformation of Organizational Goals," *Administrative Science Quarterly* 22 (Dec. 1977): 568–586.

10. Tom Beadling, Pat Cooper, and Grace Palladino, *A Need for Valor: The Roots of the Service Employees International Union 1902–1980* (Washington, D.C.: The Union, 1984).

11. Ibid., Don Stillman, *Stronger Together: The Story of SEIU* (White River Junction, VT: Chelsea Green Publishing, 2010), 1.

12. Ibid., 2.

13. Ibid., 6.

14. Beadling, Cooper, and Palladino, *A Need for Valor*.

15. Stillman, *Stronger Together*, 10.

16. Ibid.

17. Beadling, Cooper, and Palladino, *A Need for Valor*, 9.

18. Everett C. Hughes, *Men and Their Work* (Glencoe, Ill.: Free Press, 1958), 50.

19. Stillman, *Stronger Together*, 11.

20. Beadling, Cooper and Palladino, *A Need for Valor*, 10.

21. SEIU (1968) SEIU International Executive Board Collection.

22. David Scott Witwer, "The Scandal of George Scalise: A Case Study in the Rise of Labor Racketeering in the 1930s," *Journal of Social History* 36, no. 4 (2003): 917–940.

23. D. Delgado, "Report on the Building Services International Union, AFL-CIO," Princeton University Thesis, 1960, 2.

24. Ibid., 2–3.

25. Stillman, *Stronger Together*.

26. SEIU Healthcare, https://seiuhealthcare.ca/.

27. Max Weber, *From Max Weber Essays in Sociology*, edited by Gerth Hans Heinrich, C. Wright Mills, with preface by Bryan S. Turner (Milton Park, Abingdon, Oxon: Routledge, 2009); R. H. Hall, "The Concept of Bureaucracy—an Empirical-Assessment," *American Journal of Sociology* 69, no. 1 (1963): 32–40; R. H. Hall and J. E. Haas. "Organizational Size, Complexity, and Formalization." *American Sociological Review* 32, no. 6 (1967): 903–12; and R. Mansfield, "Bureaucracy and

Centralization—Examination of Organizational Structure," *Administrative Science Quarterly* 18, no. 4 (1973): 477–488.

28. Witwer, "The Scandal of George Scalise," and Beadling, Cooper, and Palladino, *A Need for Valor*.

29. SEIU (1940–1960). SEIU Executive Office William McFetridge Collection, Archives of Labor and Urban Affairs, Wayne State University.

30. SEIU International Executive Board, 1972, SEIU Secretary-Treasurer's Office: International Executive Board Records, Archives of Labor and Urban Affairs, Walter Reuther Library, Wayne State University [hereafter cited as SEIU IEB Records].

31. SEIU International Executive Board, 1970, SEIU IEB Records.

32. Grace Palladino, "When Militancy Isn't Enough—the Impact of Automation on New-York-City Building Service Workers, 1934–1970," *Labor History* 28, no. 2 (1987): 196–220, and SEIU, The State of the Union in Building Services. SEIU Research Department Archives of Labor and Urban Affairs, Wayne State University, August 1985.

33. Stillman, *Stronger Together*.

34. SEIU International Executive Board, 1971, SEIU IEB Records.

35. Michael J. Piore, "Unions: A Reorientation to Survive," in *Labor Economics and Industrial Relations: Markets and Institutions*, ed. C. Kerr and P. D. Staudohar (Cambridge: Harvard University Press, 1994), 512–541.

36. President's report to the International Convention, 18th SEIU International Convention Proceedings, 1984, SEIU International Convention Collection, Archives of Labor and Urban Affairs, Walter Reuther Library, Wayne State University [hereafter cited as SEIU International Convention Records].

37. Figures from SEIU Organizing Department reports, 1986–1992. SEIU Organizing Department Collection, Archives of Labor and Urban Affairs, Walter Reuther Library, Wayne State University [hereafter cited as SEIU Organizing Department Records].

38. Piore, "Unions: A Reorientation to Survive," 527.

39. Stillman, *Stronger Together*, 15.

40. Ibid., 15.

41. SEIU (1969–1971), SEIU Executive Office: George Hardy Records, Box 69-5, Executive Board member Sorbie meeting report. Archives of Labor and Urban Affairs, Walter Reuther Library, Wayne State University [hereafter cited as George Hardy Records].

42. SEIU International Executive Board, 1968, SEIU IEB Collection Box 3-21.

43. Ibid.

44. Based on reports, 1969–1971, George Hardy Records.

45. SEIU International Executive Board, 1971), SEIU IEB Records.

46. Richard Cordtz was interim President of SEIU during 1995–1996.

47. SEIU Constitution and By-Laws, 1992, SEIU Publications Collection, Archives of Labor and Urban Affairs, Walter Reuther Library, Wayne State University [hereafter cited as SEIU Publications Collection].

48. For resistance to change in the image of the new SEIU, see Luis LM Aguiar, "Resisting Neoliberalism in Vancouver: An Uphill Struggle for Cleaners," *Social Justice* 31, no. 3 (2004): 105–129.

49. Lydia Savage, "Justice for Janitors: Scales of Organizing and Representing Workers. "In *The Dirty Work of Neoliberalism: Cleaners in the Global Economy*, edited by Luís LM Aguiar and Andrew Herod: Blackwell Publishing, 2006, 214–234.

50. Piore, "Unions: A Reorientation to Survive," 527.

51. SEIU International Executive Board (December 1994), SEIU IEB Records.

52. "Memo from National Organizer to Top Executive: Thoughts on Organizational Development Meeting Discussion," June 23, 1990, Box 3, SEIU Organizing Department Records.

53. Stillman, *Stronger Together*, 20.

54. "18th SEIU International Convention Proceedings," 1984, SEIU Publications Collection.

55. President's Report to the International Convention, 18th SEIU International Convention Proceedings, 1984, SEIU Publications Collection.

56. Ibid.

57. Piore, "Unions: A Reorientation to Survive," 526.

58. SEIU (1986–1992). Andrew Stern memo to senior staff, May 20, 1992. SEIU Organizing Department Records.

59. Kyoung-Hee Yu, "Institutionalization in the Context of Institutional Pluralism: Politics as a Generative Process," *Organization Studies* 34, no. 1 (2013): 105–131.

60. Fantasia and Voss, *Hard Work*. 115–116.

61. SEIU (1986–1992). Andrew Stern memo to senior staff, May 20, 1992. SEIU Organizing Department Records.

62. Report of the President, 1988, SEIU International Convention Collection.

63. Report of the National President, 19th SEIU International Convention Proceedings, August 1985, SEIU Research Department Historical Records, Archives of Labor and Urban Affairs, Walter Reuther Library, Wayne State University.

64. Yu, "Institutionalization in the Context of Institutional Pluralism."

65. Piore, "Unions: A Reorientation to Survive," 530.

66. Yu, "Institutionalization in the Context of Institutional Pluralism."

67. Kyoung-Hee Yu, "Inclusive Unionism: Strategies for Retaining Idealism in the Service Employees International Union," *Journal of Industrial Relations* 61, no. 1 (2019): 33–56.

68. SEIU (1986–1992). Andrew Stern speech at 1989 organizer training, emphasis added. SEIU Organizing Department Records Box 3.

69. C. L. Erickson, C. L. Fisk, R. Milkman, D. J. B. Mitchell, and K. Wong, "Justice for Janitors in Los Angeles: Lessons from Three Rounds of Negotiations." *British Journal of Industrial Relations* 40, no. 3 (Sep 2002): 543–567; R. Waldinger, C. Erickson, R. Milkman, D. J. B. Mitchell, A. Valenzuela, K. Wong, and M. Zeitlin, "Justice for Janitors," *Dissent* 44, no. 1 (Winter 1997): 37–44; and R. Waldinger, C. L. Erickson, Ruth Milkman, D. J. B. Mitchell, A. Valenzuela, K. Wong, and M. Zeitlin, "Helots No

More: A Case Study of the Justice for Janitors Campaign in Los Angeles," in *Organizing to Win: New Research on Union Strategies*, edited by Kate Bronfenbrenner, (Ithaca, NY: ILR Press, 1998), 102–119.

70. Kyoung-Hee Yu, "Organizational Contexts for Union Renewal," *Relations Industrielles* 69, no. 3 (2014): 501–523.

71. SEIU (1986). The State of the Union in Building Services, SEIU Research Department Collection. Archives of Labor and Urban Affairs, Walter Reuther Library, Wayne State University.

72. Yu, "Institutionalization in the Context of Institutional Pluralism."

73. SEIU Organizing Department collection (1990). "Organizing Analysis 1990," Box 3. Wayne State University, Archives of Labor and Urban Affairs.

74. Yu, "Inclusive Unionism."

75. Yu, "Institutionalization in the Context of Institutional Pluralism."

76. Stillman, *Stronger Together*.

77. D. K. Leach, "The Iron Law of What Again? Conceptualizing Oligarchy across Organizational Forms." *Sociological Theory* 23, no. 3 (2005): 312–337.

78. Ibid, 324.

79. Bill Fletcher and Fernando Gapasin, *Solidarity Divided: The Crisis in Organized Labor and a New Path toward Social Justice* (Berkeley: University of California Press, 2008).

80. David Rolf, *The Fight for $15: The Right Wage for a Working America* (New York: The New Press, 2016).

81. Steven Greenhouse, "Infighting Distracts Unions at Crucial Time," *New York Times*, July 9, 2009.

82. Lydia Savage, "Geographies of Organizing: Justice for Janitors in Los Angeles," in *Organizing the Landscape: Geographical Perspectives on Labor Unionism*, edited by Andrew Herod (Minneapolis: University of Minnesota Press, 1998), 225–252.

4

Becoming Purple

Organizational Change at SEIU during the Andy Stern Years

ADRIENNE E. EATON, JANICE FINE, AND ALLISON PORTER

From 1996, when Andy Stern was first elected President, to 2008, SEIU grew from representing 1.1 million workers to 2.1 million during a period when most unions were declining in membership;[1] the union's political fundraising arm went from small by union standards to become one of the largest non-party Political Action Committees in the U.S.; the union brought hundreds of thousands of immigrant workers and workers of color, many of them women, with low-wages and no benefits to union representation with substantial improvements in their standard of living. It went from "SEI-who?" to one of the most recognizable unions in North America. For those who have closely observed the dramatic decline of unions over the past thirty years, SEIU has long been a union to watch.[2]

These changes, and many others, did not happen by accident. Stern and his supporters set out to change the union in very specific and systematic ways and largely succeeded in doing so. In this chapter, we detail the change process, which was rooted in a four-year convention cycle of evaluation, planning, and implementation at all levels of the union. To illustrate this, we look at four highly interrelated dimensions of internal organizational change: resources, structure, leadership, and branding.[3]

A key characteristic of SEIU's change process was careful attention to implementation, not just planning. Thus, it is important to situate our discussion of implementation within theories that have been developed by scholars of organization theory and public administration as well as a path-breaking analysis of union administrative capacity by labor economist Michael Piore.[4] Piore, observing SEIU's unusual "administrative capacity" in the late 1980s, came to what was at the time, a rather surprising conclusion—rather than labor's decline being principally due to a failure to embrace innovative strategies in organizing, bargaining, and worker representation, the major contributing factor was internal—weak "administrative capacity" or poor management.

The process of implementation of policy is most thoroughly studied in the field of public administration. Public policy implementation, particularly that of federal policy by administrative agencies and local governments, bears many similarities to that of a national union implementing policy at the local level. The central starting point of this literature is that the implementation of a law by an administrative agency can be just as complex as the legislative process by which it came into being.[5]

Institutions often fail to accomplish their goals for a variety of reasons: those implementing policies are sometimes acting on incomplete information with limited time and inadequate resources[6] and institutions are not uniform—they are comprised of individuals with different self-interests.[7] Those who are in different roles, physical locations, and levels of the organization will interpret and implement policy differently and their preferences are often ambiguous and shifting, rather than fixed, absolute, or consistent.[8] Additionally, organizations are not guaranteed to draw the right lessons when they do engage in evaluation.[9] At the same time, the external environment in a constant state of flux. Given these challenges, how can national unions—highly political and complex institutions—implement organizational change? How did SEIU?

While some national union bodies, including the AFL-CIO and the National Education Association, began to engage in strategic planning processes during the 1980s and 1990s,[10] the organizational change SEIU accomplished and continues to engage in is, in our view, directly attributable to its creation of a set of organizational norms and practices that ensure diffusion of new organizational strategies throughout the union. The engine driving the establishment of these norms and diffusion of strategy is the deliberative and inclusive leadership forums within the union through which they consider the problem and the range of possible solutions, arrive at a common view of the strategy, and then share that strategy in membership forums culminating in the convention. Post-convention, union leaders engage in extensive implementation planning, including goal-setting and sanctioning mechanisms that become the basis for leadership at all levels to manage staff in pursuit of execution of the plan. Although the precise shape of the planning has varied over the years, there are a set of practices that together have consistently underpinned the organization's exceptional capacity for comprehensive implementation. They also enable a political and practical assessment of how far to push the changes, which contribute to the leadership's willingness to adapt or bend on implementation if they believed it was necessary.

A Foundation for Change

The change undertaken by SEIU from 1996 through 2008 was discontinuous in certain respects, primarily in the move away from a tradition of local autonomy that reflected the historic decentralized employer structure in the building service industry where SEIU began, along with the affiliation agreements[11] with public employee associations that made up almost half the membership, and toward more centralized decision making and control. Nonetheless, that change and many others would likely not have been possible without a strong foundation, a legacy, in large part, of the years that John Sweeney served the union as president. In particular, and as Benjamin Peterson's contribution to this volume describes, John Sweeney led a pro-organizing agenda that moved the union from 650,000 members in 1980 to 1,000,000 by 1992. Sweeney recruited talented national staff, many from the progressive corners of the labor movement or from community organizations (some of whom became major leaders in the union).[12] More people of color and women were encouraged to work for locals and run for office, and the International Union (IU) ran training programs to support rising stars.

Writing in 1989, Michael Piore argued that SEIU's unusual success was a result of a set of internal managerial reforms. These included the establishment of sector-based internal conferences in 1984; an internal planning process in which local unions worked with the national staff to develop performance goals and targets combined with methods of holding local officers and business agents accountable to enforce standards; and a bolstering of the union's internal capacity through expansion of the national staff. Piore[13] also argued that SEIU's organizational coherence was rooted in a moral vision of the union as a means to raise up low-wage workers; a vision that united both the low-wage members of the organization but also the many healthcare and public sector members from the helping professions. Further, he argued that this moral vision was bolstered by a culture of open debate and respect for divergent political views established by John Sweeney when he was elected president in 1980.[14] The success of the changes described above paved the way for further changes. Many of the younger staff had been recruited by Sweeney from activist locals led by '60s and '70s movement activists and community organizers so that they would bring that culture into the national union, including the Organizing Director Andy Stern, and became important advocates of aggressive change in the union.[15]

In 1993, to build support for further changes, Sweeney created a Committee on the Future (CoF) composed of twenty locally elected officers who were either emerging leaders or had a track record in organizing. The CoF spent two years reviewing the economic and political environment, analyzing the union, and preparing recommendations to the convention to be held in Chicago in June of 1996.

Sweeney was elected president of the AFL-CIO in the fall of 1995. Following a brief power struggle in which he challenged and defeated interim president Richard Cordtz, Andy Stern, the union's organizing director, won the presidency having run on a platform to fully adopt the recommendations of the CoF, and having recruited Betty Bednarczyk, from local 113 in Minnesota who chaired the CoF, to run for Secretary-Treasurer on his ticket.[16] The centerpiece recommendation of the committee was that locals would move to committing first 10%, then 15%, and then 20% of their resources for new organizing. The International would also raise its organizing budget from 20% to 50% of total spending. The convention delegates adopted the Committee's "Bold Action" recommendations.

For SEIU's new leaders, the key to reversing the decline in the standard of living of American workers was a reinvigorated, growing labor movement. And to show their commitment to growth, the new leadership directed that headquarters telephones were to be answered with the phrase "SEIU, the organizing union." In their years in power they were to develop and revise, in response to events on the ground, what they sometimes called a "theory of the case"—that is, a set of assumptions about sources of the power "to win" for their members and for working people more broadly, the barriers to developing that power and the ways those barriers could be knocked down. From the beginning they were convinced that unions had to grow in order to make a difference, but they had to grow in a strategic manner that increased union density within specific industries, markets, and political jurisdictions.

The Change Process

In one of his first acts as President, Stern called for a vote to trustee a Chicago building services local long thought to be "untouchable" because of the political power of its top leader, Gene Moats. This move was symbolically important and signified the seriousness of the new leadership's commitment to change. Changing who the leaders were, addressing corruption and organizing to get compliance with national policies were major mechanisms for moving the change process throughout the twelve years. However, a full range of strategies were employed to create alignment including grants, subsidies, staff assistance, leadership involvement, and recognition.

The Stern administration also built upon the success of the Committee of the Future by developing SEIU's four-year convention cycle as the central mechanism for driving organizational change throughout the union. As the highest decision-making body of the union, the membership convention provided an opportunity to consider and adopt ambitious goals. It also gave the new officers a focus for their work as they met to plan for the internal changes needed to implement the platform.

Every four years the convention platform represented real upheaval for local leaders and International Union staff as priorities and structures changed. But by including so many influential leaders and staff in the process of analyzing the issues and drafting the proposals, the national union was able to leave each convention with a mandate to keep changing. This isn't to say that leadership always got just what they wanted, but the inclusive process meant they had early warning on those ideas that faced too much resistance. When that happened, changes were made voluntary or were never fully implemented. One of the most important decisions the national union made was how hard to push.

DIMENSIONS OF CHANGE

Over a twelve-year period, SEIU became a different kind of labor union.[17] Key indicators of that are in its level of available resources, its structure, its leadership, and its shared identity. These four interlocking dimensions developed over time and resulted in a union with dramatically increased influence and results at all levels.

Increased Resources for Growth

Between 1996 and 2006, SEIU's total revenue grew over 150% as a result of both dues increases and membership growth. By 2008, the national union was taking in $247 million in per capita revenue. The funds for organizing increased dramatically, through increased revenues and a larger percentage of funds devoted to organizing.[18] SEIU wasn't the only union during this period that was investing more heavily in organizing, increasing dues and raising per capita payments to the national union. It was, however, doing so at a faster pace and larger scale.[19]

In 1992, of the 370 SEIU locals, only 24 had full-time Organizing Directors and together they spent less than 5% of their budgets on new organizing.

FIGURE 4.1 IU growth-related spending (International Union, Unity Funds in millions), 1996–2006 (Source: SEIU)

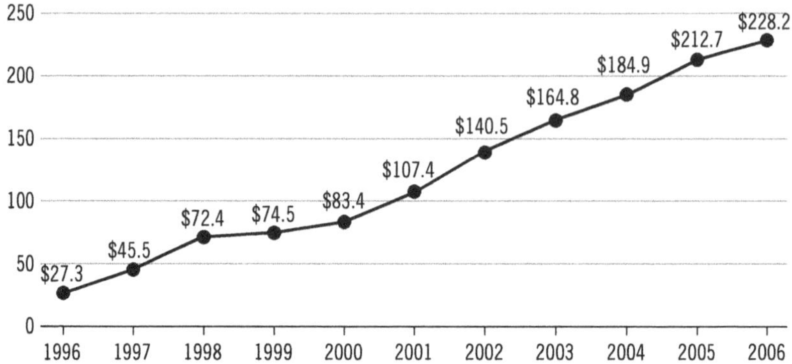

Like most unions, SEIU locals had control of their financial resources. Eighty percent of dues revenues were kept at the local level and the International typically knew little of the details of local budgets. In fact, most locals didn't have detailed budgets or separate their expenditures by program area.[20] Many union locals at that time, rather than breaking out expenditures by program area, followed the template of the federal LM-2 reports they were required to file each year.[21]

By 1999, most local unions were devoting 10% of their resources to organizing, but very few had gotten to 15 or 20%. Compliance was focused on the 50 to 60 largest locals representing 80–90% of the membership. This left 250 to 300 locals who struggled to be financially viable and did not shift dues to organizing on the scale of the larger locals.

The leaders reached two conclusions. One, small locals would have to merge to get sufficient organizing resources to grow. Two, if locals couldn't or wouldn't shift resources away from representation, the whole pie would have to be increased in order to meet the goal of 20%.[22] The 2000 convention approved the proposed dues increase of $1 a week and the restructuring of locals.[23] Delegates also voted to increase dues minimums and to gradually abolish the maximum dues cap. This convention also created the Unity Fund to be administered by the divisions for "breakthrough" industry campaigns and funded by an increase in the per capita tax to the International of $5 per member per month. The national union developed tracking and compliance monitoring for the dues mandate.[24]

At the 2004 convention, for the first time, local unions were constitutionally mandated to spend 20% of their budgets on organizing. They were required to report how they spent the money, and if they didn't spend it, they were required to carry it over to the next year or give it to other locals. In 2008, the convention directed that local unions put their 20% in a separate account. These funds were expected to be used for organizing consistent with the national integrated organizing plan. Both of these mandates were largely aspirational and agitational. Locals were monitored and strongly encouraged to follow the plan (especially those with significant resources) but funds were never actually reallocated without consent. The degree to which SEIU's industry divisions actually developed integrated organizing plans and budgets varied. Nevertheless, the net result was that from 1997 to 2006 the locals and International Union combined spent $1.3 billion on organizing.[25]

The union undertook a similar process for spending on politics. In the 1996–1998 cycle, the union raised less than $5 million for its political action committee and had a few thousand volunteers.[26] In the 2006–2008 election cycle, the union raised over $60 million in COPE funds through voluntary membership contributions and fielded over 55,000 volunteers. The change represents a broader repositioning of SEIU's political influence from one of the least politically active unions to one of the most influential. According to Center for Responsive Politics data, in 2008 the union was the third largest PAC (by total expenditure) in the country, behind only the two political party convention host committees in Denver and Minnesota.[27]

FIGURE 4.2 SEIU growth in political receipts and expenditures 1996–2008 (Source: Center for Responsive Politics)

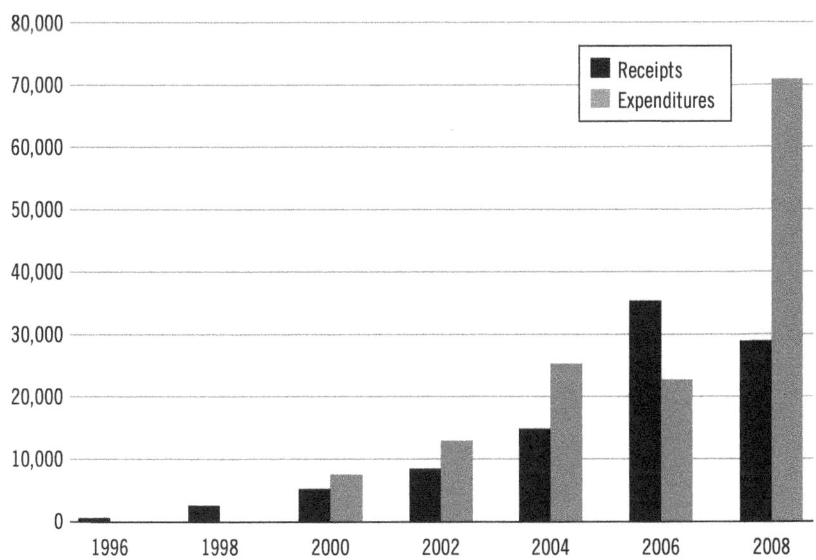

Structure

The union's plan to restructure grew out of the same internal analysis as the decision to increase resources: effective strategies for growth required focusing resources along industry lines. This reflected the reality of the changes in the industries SEIU represented. Property services members, for example, worked for employers that were rapidly consolidating in regional, national, and global corporations. Public sector employers were becoming more adversarial and able to pit locals of the same union against each other in bargaining. As a result, SEIU leaders took the position that they needed to restructure and empower industry divisions. Stern knew that this was taking on a long tradition of local autonomy, but he saw this as a "sacred cow" that had to be challenged for the union to succeed.[28]

The goal of restructuring was to create larger, single-sector locals that each belonged to a division of the union. This meant moving members from one local to another through mergers or swaps. The plan eliminated the regional structure and built up the State Councils to coordinate political activity across locals in a state. At the national level it empowered the Division Leadership Boards [DLBs] and created an Executive Committee of the International Executive Board [IEB].

STRENGTHENING THE DIVISIONS

The national level division structures, begun in 1984, were still fairly barebones operations in 1996, with minimal staff and limited formal responsibility. The Stern administration concluded that for divisions to play a lead role in organizing, they needed focused leadership, dedicated staff, and increased resources.

As divisions became important locations for both organizing plans and bargaining agendas, leadership shifted from Division Directors, who were staff, to national full-time officers, who therefore had more legitimacy to push their peers. DLBs, typically composed of local presidents with significant membership in the industry, became responsible for more and more decisions directly affecting local unions. These boards set policy and standards, developed industry strategies, and approved spending budgets, subject to final approval by the IEB.

RESTRUCTURING LOCALS

Historically, most SEIU locals were amalgamated; they included many bargaining units from different industries in a particular local area. There were also many locals with budgets so small they couldn't afford full-time staff. In California, there were 27 different locals representing workers in the public sector. In Illinois, there were four unions in property services. This mixed and disaggregated membership fragmented the union's power, both vis-à-vis employers and within the political sphere.

As locals were reorganized around single industries, they were also merged to create larger locals that would have, in theory, sufficient resources to fund significant organizing campaigns, engage in more effective bargaining, and wield greater political power. In some instances, SEIU gave bargaining units to other unions, because they "belonged" in another union's industry jurisdiction.[29]

Although there were different paths to reorganization, many were done through a jurisdictional hearing process conducted by an officer designated by the International Executive Board [IEB], which retained final decision-making authority. Hearings were intended to sort out the best and *most politically viable* plan. The vast majority of locals accepted the rationale for the reorganizations and entered into the process willingly; however, in some cases the process was highly contentious. Some mergers went forward in spite of opposition from leaders of some small local unions who felt, understandably, that they would be giving up power, as was the case with some of the California public sector locals who were eventually merged into four new locals. The momentum in the larger locals was strongly in favor of restructuring, and some local officers told us that they felt the outcomes were preordained.

By 2008, with some exceptions, local unions represented members in a single division. The overall number of locals was greatly diminished, from 373 to 140. The average size of a local increased from 2,680 to 14,280. There were 15 locals of over 50,000 members—"megalocals"—representing 57% of the membership of the union. SEIU records listed 136 mergers between 1997 and 2007. These included comprehensive mergers as well as the transfer of bargaining units from one local to another. By 2008, almost all locals were either new to SEIU or had different jurisdiction than they had in 1996.

While there was a lot of attention paid to making mergers happen and completing merger agreements, the post-merger integration process was not always smooth. It took years for some locals to evolve new leadership structures and move past culture clashes. These kinds of problems in some cases undermined the potential synergies of combining organizations. Finally, as locals got larger, more diverse and dispersed, more decisions were made by leaders at the regional and national level, and there were reduced opportunities for members in outlying areas to be heard and develop as leaders. The challenge became how to develop more robust democratic and participatory structures.[30]

In 2008, after much of the restructuring was completed, a significant conflict emerged between the International Union and United Healthcare Workers West (UHW) and its President, Sal Rosselli. UHW was the product of a merger of Bay

Area–based Local 250 and Local 399 in Southern California. In 2008, it had over 140,000 members. The local had worked closely with the Stern administration but had become increasingly critical of the International on a number of issues including centralization of decision-making within the Healthcare Division, the content of particular national agreements with for-profit hospital chains (Columbia HCA and Tenet), and alliance agreements with nursing home providers. Disputes arose specifically around the for-profit hospital chains organizing agreements. The majority of locals participating in the Healthcare Division supported the development by the national union of national agreements because they believed it had enabled major organizing breakthroughs among hospitals that would likely not have been organized otherwise. Likewise, many of the locals viewed the initial basic contracts to which Rosselli objected as baselines to build on, as had been done with nursing home agreements in the past.

In January 2009, as part of the restructuring process, the International Executive Board ordered UHW to transfer its homecare members to a statewide California long-term care local, which it refused to do. The conflict had earlier spilled into the open when Rosselli resigned from the SEIU Executive Committee and launched a website critical of the union. After a prolonged internal conflict, UHW was put in trusteeship, and Rosselli and other former UHW leaders set up a competing organization called the National Union of Healthcare Workers (NUHW).[31]

The dispute was not a simple case of David vs. Goliath, as the NUHW leaders would say, nor "Just Us vs. Justice for All" unionism, as Andy Stern portrayed it, but rather a sad and unfortunate product of the rapid growth and dramatic restructuring of formerly autonomous locals in SEIU. The intention was to build powerful locals capable of running and winning campaigns that would also be aligned and collaborative with a larger national strategy to build power. In this case, the concentration of power in the hands of an independent and effective local leader came back to bite the national union that had made that concentration of power possible.[32]

THE ROLE AND FUNCTIONS OF LOCAL UNIONS

As SEIU worked to strengthen divisions and state councils, its leaders also took a fresh look at the most appropriate role for local unions.[33] The Local Strength Committee was established after the 2004 convention. The committee's ambit was to explore how well local unions were engaging workers in the union and how they could be most effective at their basic functions of organizing, bargaining, representation, and politics. Through conversations with local unions the Local Strength Committee determined that, as the main place where members connect to the union, locals needed to be better at engaging members. To find out how, the committee examined models of member involvement outside of the U.S. labor movement, in megachurches, and in other membership organizations.

A major finding of the committee was that the work of grievances was taking up a disproportionate amount of staff time, with less than 5% of members typically filing over 90% of grievances. After studying the Australian labor movement's use of call centers to handle member calls and grievances, in 2004 homecare and property service locals began to experiment with call centers in the U.S. and Canada. While some of the early models were rejected by some locals, these "member resource centers" took root in many locals across the union.[34]

As with other changes, SEIU moved to put structures in place. At the 2008 Convention, they established goals for member engagement: 1% of the membership of each local union would become leaders, and 9% of each local union would become activists. This was followed up with regional trainings for local union staff on how to recruit and develop member leaders called "Unleashing Our Power." In 2011, they set up a department inside the union—the Member Leadership in Action Department—to promulgate experimentation and track results.

NATIONAL EMPLOYER STRATEGIES

A central goal of the Stern administration strategy was to achieve more coordinated or centralized bargaining relationships in order to match the size and concentration of employers and to wield more bargaining power. Stern referred to this change as moving "from an AFL to a CIO union." While some observers have argued that SEIU's AFL legacy enabled its innovative approaches to organizing, Stern and other leaders viewed CIO-style centralized bargaining and centralized decision-making as necessary for wielding power against large national or even international employers.[35]

As it rolled out, joint bargaining with regional and national employers resulted in significant tensions in the union (see also Yu in this volume). In nursing homes, the division pursued an "alliance strategy" where, in exchange for a very basic contract, a nursing home chain would agree not to oppose its employees' efforts to join a union. In hospitals, some of the early national agreements resulted in groundbreaking union recognition, but they were also made without prior approval and review by leaders of all affected locals.[36]

Despite the tensions, the union had success in creating more centralized bargaining structures, both formal and informal. Reaching agreement with employers covering multiple bargaining units and large geographies was a major accomplishment for a union with the history of autonomous locals that SEIU had. They did this at a time when national and even international trends were going in the other direction.[37]

Leadership

Around the time that Andy Stern became president, Stephen Lerner wrote an analysis of the union's recent past and future strategies in the Building Services industry, pointing the finger at local leaders as a substantial obstacle to change:[38]

> It needs to be clearly stated that we have a leadership problem. . . . We must openly discuss, address and develop strategies to deal with the fact that our major local leaders are sitting on time bombs in their own locals that will set the stage for a replay of our decline of the early 1980s.

From 1996 to 2009, there was a marked leadership turnover among SEIU's full-time elected officials. Of the presidents of the fifty largest locals in 1996 (representing over 70% of the membership at the time), only seven were still with the union twelve years later. Leadership turnover was the result of several factors including the reduction in the overall number of locals, retirements, and the expanded use of trusteeships.[39]

The involvement of the IU in selecting local leaders was controversial. Beyond trusteeships, the creation of new locals through extensive reorganization gave the president the power to appoint officers under temporary bylaws, almost always resulting in the appointed leader's election later on. Stern called the appointments of new leaders "the biggest decisions I make."[40] In June of 2009, eighteen of the presidents of the fifty largest locals were initially appointed to their position by Stern; ten were elected leaders of other locals (including in some cases one of the merging locals) prior to their appointment. Strikingly, the new local presidents were a more diverse group than the years prior to Stern.[41]

Along with turnover of leadership came changes in how leaders functioned, both within their locals and within the International. Elected leaders were running far larger, more complex and powerful organizations than existed a dozen years before. With the creation and strengthening of national decision-making bodies at the division level, local leaders began collaborating more with their peers in making decisions affecting multiple locals. Local leaders also interpreted policy and made decisions as chairs of jurisdictional hearings, trustees, and administrators of other locals, and as participants in state councils and coordinated bargaining councils. More sat on the International Executive Board (IEB) as it expanded from forty members in 1995 to over sixty in 2004 and then again in 2008–9 to seventy-nine.[42] While this leadership participation was central to creating a unified position on union strategies, it required leaders to hold their local and national roles in tension because the interests of a particular local's members might not be the same as the interests of the national union.

To support leadership development and the process of change within the union, SEIU launched the New Strength Unity Institute in 2002. Later renamed the Institute for Change (IFC), and then the BOLD (Building Organizations and Leadership Development) Center, this unit supported leadership teams from selected locals in making both individual and organizational change.[43] The BOLD Center continues to operate a large coaching, leadership and organizational development operation in support of local unions.

Identity: Becoming Purple

Starting in the early years of the Sweeney Administration, there was concern about SEIU's lack of visibility. The union was an organization of 360 locals with 144 different names. Locals had been free to adopt logos that changed regularly or not. The result was that there were nearly as many logos (and color schemes) as there were names. Despite its growing size and influence, when it came to the organization's public image, it was still largely "SEI—Who?", as one staffer joked. In 1996, the new administration decided that in order to move the aggressive agenda they envisioned, they would have to upgrade the union's profile.

The work on an enhanced SEIU identity began at the 1996 convention. A team of communications experts recommended using the abbreviated, bumper sticker length name, SEIU, rather than a catchy new name or the name in full, Service Employees International Union. Planning for the next convention cycle continued the work. The President's Committee 2000 drafted statements of the SEIU mission, vision, and values and tested them with members and the public through polling and focus groups. After review and feedback from the senior staff and executive officers, the team developed a half page mission and a one-sentence mission-statement: "To improve the lives of working people and their families and lead the way to a more just and humane society." This inspired the tagline "leading the way." After receiving criticism for its self-important tone, it was changed to "stronger together." The union also commissioned new designs for the logo, ultimately adopting a stylized path leading to a sun. Next, taking a lesson from AFSCME's use of the color green, the communications team worked on choosing a single color for SEIU materials, ultimately locking onto the color purple, specifically Pantone 268c.

Like many of the change initiatives described here, these changes went from being voluntary for locals to required. At the 2000 convention, members passed a constitutional amendment that required locals to go by the name SEIU, followed by their name or number.[44] By 2008, few remembered a time when there wasn't a unified brand.

The creation of a unified SEIU identity has had a profound impact on the mindset of members, leaders, and observers of SEIU. Many use the word "purple" as synonymous with union power. The *New York Times* reported that "once a movement of rust brown and steel gray, Big Labor is increasingly represented, at rallies and political conventions, by a rising sea of purple."[45] Employers and the general public also began to "see" SEIU where they hadn't before. Members were making connections across locals, such as the California member visiting relatives in Ohio discovering that her cousin was a member when she saw his purple T-shirt.

Implementation

There is much that could be said about SEIU in the Stern years, about its successes and its failures and the controversies it stirred up. Indeed, other chapters in this volume tackle many of those complexities. Few would contest, however, that the union has changed significantly through an intentional process lead from the center. To better understand how they have been successful at this change, we took a close look at the culture of change that developed as well as the rigorous, yet flexible, approach to implementation.

Immediately following each convention came a planning phase that included an officers' retreat to discuss the implications of what was decided. The International Executive Board, Division Leadership Boards, and local union governing boards would also meet to discuss how they would carry out the platform. The IU would align its own departments, programs, and staffing to conform to the new priorities. Deliberative decision-making bodies strongly staffed and committed to specific timelines for implementation are the core of these practices, which appear to have roots in the Sweeney era.[46] At headquarters, both 1996 and 2008 involved painful layoffs, while 2000 and 2004 changes led to major restructuring and reassignment of staff.

SEIU's implementation efforts relied on the setting of clear and measurable goals and their enforcement, long an important aspect of program implementation.[47] Van Meter and Van Horn identify two types of enforcement: technical advice and assistance and sanctions.[48] SEIU took the communication of standards and objectives seriously, often providing staff support and technical advice along with kits with brochures and videos to facilitate implementation. The union also used sanctions. In most program areas, policies were established first as voluntary guidelines with incentives. This stage was often followed by convention or constitutional mandates with both penalties for failure to meet targets and continued incentives to do so. According to Stern, "for us, accountability is a key essence of our success and a key issue that will always create tension in the union."[49]

Van Meter and Van Horn also talk about the importance of the attitudes of the individuals responsible for implementing policy and whether they support, reject, or are neutral to the policy.[50] Probably most interesting in the SEIU case is that the views of implementers were, essentially, not left to chance. The use of committees and task forces in the planning process, plus town halls and other venues for bottom-up communications, worked toward developing and then aligning around a vision and direction, and pulled a broad array of local leaders, staff, and ultimately members into the planning process. Although there was sometimes cynicism that decisions had already been made by the top leadership, the pre-convention planning processes allowed many voices to be heard, compromises to be made and then created widespread buy-in to the final recommendations.

The rapid growth of the union in the early years of the Stern administration, and the infusion of national funds into locals, also created broad legitimacy for the change program. The union leadership used the convention process and the linkage of the change program to the broadly shared goals of increased social and economic justice—what Piore called the union's "moral vision"—to create what Etzioni terms "normative compliance."[51] The bottom line is that most local leaders took action to meet the new standards in part because they believed they were right, but also because they wanted to be part of the engine that was moving the union forward. The national union was also able to leverage its financial subsidies, either to support core expenses or a local organizing program, to gain cooperation from some locals.

Flexibility was a third factor that contributed to the national union's success. This was important given that local unions retained a great deal of power, the national union was a democratic institution that could not rule by edict, and locals differed greatly in size and significance to the overall organization. While SEIU implemented its program with intense focus, it was not rigid. Flexibility was underwritten by political acumen and was demonstrated in the movement from voluntary to mandatory standards in many areas and in the use of carve outs and waivers in many cases. Waivers, for instance, were built into the various financial requirements for locals with particularly difficult circumstances.[52] In this way, the requirements could still be maintained for the locals representing the vast majority of members. As discussed above, flexibility was also demonstrated on local restructuring, though here it was based on political rather than financial considerations.

The union was not always able to implement all aspects of the convention-approved program. For example, the resolution to move to a percentage-based dues system did not achieve the broad sponsorship and alignment that other resolutions garnered. It turned out to be extremely difficult for locals with very low-wage members and they were not in the end required to do it. Similarly, while most of the big local unions over time and with strong support from the national union implemented the resolution regarding a dues increase, some of the low-wage locals did not move to increase dues and were granted waivers by the national union.

Finally, while the Bold Action platform included a commitment to increase member involvement in the union and this theme returned in the 2000 cycle with a plan that called for Member Involvement Programs in each local, participation was once again never mandatory, and some local unions were more successful than others. Across all locals, in the year leading up to the 2016 convention, the organization engaged in a systematic count and determined that it had been able to reach its goal of 10% participation of its members. Union leaders feel that they have made some significant progress in terms of member participation but are far from satisfied and continue to engage in experiments in engaging members outside the workplace. The challenge of membership involvement remains a difficult issue with which SEIU (and virtually every other union) is still struggling today.

A Culture of Continuous Change—Often Effective, Not Always Smooth

The organizational change process we describe earlier is unique in the history of the contemporary U.S. labor movement. Many other unions have created committees to examine the future or have undertaken strategic planning, but very few have developed a lasting culture of change and made such conscious and sustained effort to change. Over time, SEIU developed a culture of planning that helped to ensure, to the degree possible, the union's future would be, in their words "a matter of choice, not chance." Because that planning was (and remains) attached to the convention cycle, it has assured that it is also cyclical, beginning with reviews of earlier plans and the metrics used to track their progress and then moving to envisioning the future and generating ideas.

While the cycle of analysis and goal-setting created an atmosphere where leaders were open to ambitious change and experimentation, the national committee process failed when it came to ideas and practices around union democracy. To be sure, leaders who weren't on the hand-picked committee were engaged through the Division and Executive Boards, but rank-and-file members had few structured avenues to have their voices heard before decisions were made. The planning cycle also failed to evaluate and learn from less successful experiments from the previous period. This was perhaps because the staff moved quickly to adapt, but possibly also because failure was too politically risky to acknowledge and own. There are multiple examples of this, including the Fight for a Fair Economy and the National Member Resource Center. There were clearly some moments when the expectation that people would be "on board" caused groupthink to set in. Some leaders and staff did not feel particularly free to share their feedback for fear of being seen as an obstacle. In the process of identifying barriers to change and knocking them down, numerous controversies were stirred up and damage was done to individuals and organizations. Some would argue the damage was substantial and/or unnecessary.[53]

Perhaps the most egregious and destructive example of leadership overreach was SEIU's decision to actively support UNITE in its nasty breakup with HERE after an unsuccessful 2005 merger. The UNITE faction was likely bolstered by SEIU's willingness to affiliate the new organization they would become: Workers United.

By actively supporting Bruce Raynor, former President of UNITE, and Workers United, SEIU opened itself up to attacks from other unions, many of whom protested publicly and privately. AFSCME President Gerald McEntee accused SEIU of "piracy on the high seas of organized labor."[54] SEIU's involvement in the internal conflict of another union not only touched a nerve with those unions who were already unhappy with what they perceived to be SEIU's aggressive posture but also within the union itself among leaders and staff who strongly objected to the policy.

In 2010, Andy Stern took the union by surprise by suddenly announcing his retirement. Although he endorsed Anna Burger, with whom he came into the union and worked in close partnership for many years, he did not actively campaign and she lost the presidential race to Mary Kay Henry, the Executive Vice President leading the healthcare division and long-time organizer who had also worked closely with Stern for many years. Various reasons have been given for that outcome: that Burger was perceived as focused on electoral politics while Henry was seen as more committed to organizing; that the race was an opportunity for the mega-locals to exercise their power and they viewed Henry as more open to their leadership and more interested in organizing than Burger; and that, as the powerful Secretary-Treasurer, Burger had accumulated some enemies over the years. One of the first actions by Mary Kay Henry, the newly elected president of SEIU in 2010, was to approach John Wilhelm, president of UNITE-HERE at the time, to put an end to the hostilities.

Another early action taken by the administration of Mary Kay Henry was to establish a Member Strength Review Committee which evaluated both the Institute For Change and the Member Action Service Center and recommended sweeping changes intended to recognize a broad desire within the union for local union control over administration and support from the national union for capacity building and strengthening.

While the union made mistakes along the way, its willingness to dismantle customs, structures, and processes that held back change was instrumental to its success. According to Stern, there were "no sacred cows—anything that is not helping win is open for change."[55] Locals changed their names, their boundaries, and their leaders and gave up members in the interest of broader change. Contract language, constitutions and bylaws, job descriptions, and reporting structures—every aspect of the union was open to review. Change wasn't only about what was new: it also involved a commitment to stop doing things that weren't core to the mission.

SEIU in the Stern years succeeded in many areas. It developed a sustained change process that enabled the union to accomplish substantive structural change and to engage in a great deal of experimentation. It succeeded in restructuring the union around its core industries at both the national and local level and in centralizing resources, some decision-making and some collective bargaining at the national level. It succeeded in organizing hundreds of thousands of low-wage workers in homecare and childcare and substantially increased their wages and benefits. And it grew—almost doubling from 1996 to 2008.

In recent years, SEIU has suffered from the setbacks to public sector bargaining along with other public sector unions, and in particular in the home care sector when provisions granting home care workers collective bargaining rights and recognizing unions were reversed by new, Republican governors and ultimately by the Supreme Court's 2014 *Harris v. Quinn* decision, which weakened home care workers' union rights (*Harris v. Quinn*, 573 U.S. 616 [2014]).[56] The Property Services Division launched successful efforts in the 2000s to organize security guards and most recently airport contracted workers. On the public sector side, the union, in partnership with AFSCME, recently achieved a significant victory in California, where the Governor signed legislation that will provide collective bargaining rights to more than 40,000 publicly funded childcare workers and SEIU continued to maintain significant annual organizing numbers. The Fight for $15 changed the national conversation on the wages and working conditions of low-wage workers and, according to a study by the National Employment Law Project, has resulted in 22 million low-wage workers winning $68 billion in annual raises from 2012–2018, through a combination of state and local minimum wage increases and action by employers to raise their companies' minimum pay scales.[57] However, it has not yet resulted in the achievement of traditional bargaining rights for fast food workers.

Change to Win, the breakaway labor federation SEIU spearheaded as part of this same change process, catalyzed important organizing achievements over time but has not led to the exponential organizing gains that was the impetus for its creation.[58] Although the new federation has helped to strengthen the strategic capacity of the Teamsters and the United Food and Commercial Workers, along with several European unions through its European Organizing Centre, it was not the hoped-for second coming of the CIO. UNITE HERE returned to the AFL-CIO in 2009 and the UFCW followed suit in 2013.

Although SEIU has evolved from a weak national union with a high level of local union autonomy to a strong national union with much greater centralization of strategy and resources, with an industry focus, the pendulum has in some ways swung back toward local (albeit, *mega-local*) unions, with a geographic focus. These large local unions have become increasingly independent from the International and politically powerful. These are tensions that the national union must manage, and it does so through its structures and through leadership engagement in the Convention platform planning process. The big locals are important voices in the divisions, which continue to be central deliberative bodies for strategy and policy development, along with IU departments and State Councils. Importantly, the process of national level reflection, shared visioning, planning, and rapid implementation that happens every four years continues to be deeply embedded in the culture of the union. This process along with the substantive changes that resulted from it are the legacy of the Stern years.

Notes

1. Richard Freeman, "Spurts in Union Growth: Defining Moments and Social Processes," in *The Defining Moment: The Great Depression and the American Economy in the Twentieth Century*, ed. Michael D. Bordo, Claudia Goldin, and Eugene N. White (Chicago: University of Chicago Press, 1998), 265–298; Henry S. Farber and Bruce Western, "Accounting for the Decline of Unions in the Private Sector, 1973–1998," *Journal of Labor Research* 22, no. 3 (2001): 459–485; Nelson Lichtenstein, *State of the Union: A Century of American Labor* (Princeton: Princeton University Press, 2013/2002); Barry Hirsch and David McPherson, "U.S. Historical Tables: Union Membership, Coverage, Density, and Employment, 1973–2013," http://unionstats.com.

2. Ruth Milkman, *L.A. Story: Immigrant Workers and the Future of the US Labor Movement* (New York: Russell Sage Foundation, 2006); Rick Fantasia and Kim Voss, *Hard Work: Remaking the American Labor Movement* (Berkeley: University of California Press, 2004).

3. This chapter is based on research conducted by the authors largely between 2005 and 2009 and was commissioned by SEIU to capture the story of the rapid structural changes undertaken during the years that Andy Stern was President and Anna Burger was Secretary-Treasurer. We interviewed 25 national officers, division directors, and headquarters staff. We conducted site visits at seven locals representing different sectors and geographic regions during which we interviewed over 100 local union elected leaders and staff to whom we promised confidentiality. We also examined internal

records, including financial records, and public reports. Although it was a collaborative process and culminated in a report that required the approval of the union and was presented to its executive board, we also negotiated, sometimes fiercely, for our respective points of view in the final document. Under our agreement, the union has the right to review other publications or presentations but cannot approve or veto material. The complete 72-page report to SEIU is cited below as Eaton et al., "Organizational Change at SEIU," Unpublished report (2010) and is available for download at http://www.alvarezporter.com/wp-content/uploads/org-change-at-seiu.pdf.

4. Michael Piore, "Administrative Failure: An Hypothesis about the Decline of the U.S. Union Movement in the 1980s," Unpublished paper (1989), Massachusetts Institute of Technology.

5. Jeffrey L Pressman and Aaron Wildavsky, *Implementation* (Berkeley: University of California Press, 1984).

6. Daniel Mazmanian and Paul Sabatier, *Implementation and Public Policy* (Glenview, III: Scott, Foresman, 1983).

7. Anthony Downs, *Inside Bureaucracy: A RAND Corporation Research Study* (Boston: Little, Brown, 1967). Michael Lipsky, "Toward a Theory of Street-Level Bureaucracy," in *Theoretical Perspectives on Urban Politics*, ed. Willis D. Hawley and Michael Lipsky (Englewood Cliffs: Prentice-Hall, 1976), 196–213.

8. James G. March, "Bounded Rationality, Ambiguity, and the Engineering of Choice," in *Decisions and Organizations*, ed. James G. March (New York: Blackwell, 1988), 266–293.

9. James G. March and Johan P. Olsen, "The Uncertainty of the Past: Organizational Learning under Ambiguity," *European Journal of Political Research* 3 (2017): 147–171, https://doi.org/10.1111/j.1475-6765.1975.tb00521.x.

10. David N. Weil, *Turning the Tide: Strategic Planning for Labor Unions* (New York: Lexington Books, 1994).

11. Existing independent unions or professional associations at the local, state, or national level may decide to affiliate with a national union like SEIU; when they do so, the terms of that affiliation, like dues payments and governance rights, are typically spelled out in a binding legal agreement.

12. Kim Voss and Rachel Sherman, "Breaking the Iron Law of Oligarchy: Union Revitalization in the American Labor Movement," *American Journal of Sociology* 106, no. 2 (2000): 303–349, https://doi.org/10.1086/316963; Fantasia and Voss, *Hard Work*; Piore, "Administrative Failure."

13. Piore, "Administrative Failure," 28.

14. Ibid., 30.

15. Interviews: Anonymous local and national staff and leaders.

16. See *Andy Stern, A Country That Works: Getting America Back on Track* (New York: Free Press, 2006), 61–63.

17. For a thorough examination of this change process, see Eaton et al., "Organizational Change at SEIU."

18. See Figure 4.1.

19. For a comparison of SEIU with AFT, NEA, and AFSCME, see Eaton et al., "Organizational Change at SEIU," 15, Figure 1.

20. Marshall Ganz and Scott Washburn, "Organizing and Unions: A Challenge of the 80s: An Organizer's Perspective," Unpublished paper (1985); Eaton et al., "Organizational Change at SEIU"; Anonymous SEIU staff interviews.

21. Eaton et al., "Organizational Change at SEIU"; Anonymous SEIU staff interviews.

22. For a more detailed description of the process of increasing resources dedicated to organizing, see Eaton et al., "Organizational Change at SEIU," 14–19. Any specific figures were provided to us by SEIU.

23. The significant per capita tax increase to fund the Unity Fund was a key element of the New Strength Unity Plan adopted at the 2000 Convention. See SEIU Constitution, Article XIII, Section 1(d).

24. Compliance was never 100% and some locals were granted waivers for various reasons. For more details, see Eaton et al., "Organizational Change at SEIU," 18.

25. See Eaton et al., "Organizational Change at SEIU," 16–19.

26. For a full discussion of the union's political program, see Eaton et al., "Organizational Change at SEIU," 52–56.

27. Eaton at al., "Organizational Change at SEIU," 52–53.

28. Stern interview, December 14, 2006.

29. For instance, several locals of utility workers (with total membership of over 4700) were transferred to the Utility Workers Union of America in 2002–2003. See Stern, *A Country That Works*, 65–66.

30. See also Lydia Savage, "Justice for Janitors: Scales of Organizing and Representing Workers," *Antipode* 38, no. 3 (2006): 645–666, https://doi.org/10.111/j.0066-4812.2006.00600.x; Kim Moody, *US Labor in Trouble and Transition: The Failure of Reform from Above, the Promise of Revival from Below* (New York: Verso, 2007), 194.

31. For a full discussion, though with an admitted strong NUHW slant, see Cal Winslow, *Labor's Civil War in California: The NUHW Healthcare Workers' Rebellion* (Oakland: PM Press, 2010). See also Bill Fletcher Jr. and Nelson Lichtenstein, "SEIU's Civil War," *In These Times*, December 16, 2009, http://inthesetimes.com/article/5309/seius_civil_war.

32. For a detailed description, see the court decision in *SEIU v NUHW*, 711 F.3d 970 (9th Cir. 2013). According to the 2018 LM-2 reports filed by the unions involved, in 2018 SEIU UHW had 99,673 members; the new California statewide long-term care SEIU local had 188,129 members; the split-off NUHW had 14,158 members.

33. For a longer discussion, see Eaton et al., "Organizational Change at SEIU," 41–46.

34. On the development and performance of the call center at Local 1 in Chicago, see Ariel Avgar et al., "Worker Voice and Union Revitalization: The Role of Contract Enforcement at SEIU," *Labor Studies Journal* 43, no.3 (2018): 209–233.

35. On the union's AFL legacy, see Ruth Milkman, "Divided We Stand," *New Labor Forum*, 15, no. 1, (2006): 38–46.

36. See Jane McAlevey and Bob Ostertag, *Raising Expectations (and Raising Hell): My Decade Fighting for the Labor Movement* (London: Verso, 2012).

37. See Nick Wailes, Greg J. Bamber, and Russell D. Lansbury, "International and Comparative Employment Relations: An Introduction," in *International and Comparative Employment Relations: Globalisation and Change*, ed. Greg. J. Bamber, Russell D. Lansbury, and Nick Wailes (London: SAGE Publications, 2011).

38. Stephen Lerner, Internal SEIU memo, Undated, 12, copy in the authors' possession.

39. From 1996 to 2003 thirty locals were trusteed.

40. Stern Interview, December 14, 2006.

41. Eaton et al., "Organizational Change at SEIU," 32.

42. In 2004, the union created a 20-member Executive Committee appointed by the president, which met more frequently than the IEB. This body later expanded to 35.

43. On the IFC, see Service Employees International Union, *Institute for Change, Service Employees International Union—Working Papers*, Volume 1 (2005).

44. Affiliate agreements prevented the IU from mandating that all locals change logo and color, although almost all the locals did so. On the rebranding of the union, see Stern, *A Country That Works*, 74–75.

45. Matt Bai, "The New Boss," *The New York Times*, January 30, 2005, https://www.nytimes.com/2005/01/30/magazine/the-new-boss.html.

46. Piore, "Administrative Failure."

47. Donald S. Van Meter and Carl E. Van Horn, "The Policy Implementation Process: A Conceptual Framework," *Administration & Society* 6, no. 4 (February, 1975): 445–488.

48. Ibid.

49. Stern Interview, July 2009.

50. Van Meter and Van Horn, "The Policy Implementation Process."

51. Amitai Etzioni, *A Comparative Analysis of Complex Organizations: On Power, Involvement, and Their Correlates (Revised and Enlarged edition)* (New York: The Free Press, 1975).

52. Included were locals with members earning less than $100 per week, members who had not yet achieved a collective bargaining agreement, high dues public locals, and local unions in which a majority were Industrial & Allied service sector workers.

53. See, for example, Fletcher and Lichtenstein, "SEIU's Civil War."

54. UNITE-HERE Convention, June 29, 2009.

55. Stern Interview, June 14, 2009.

56. See Eileen Boris and Jennifer Klein, *Caring for America: Home Health Workers in the Shadow of the Welfare State* (New York: Oxford University Press, 2012).

57. "Impact of the Fight for $15: $68 Billion in Raises, 22 Million Workers," Data Brief, November 2018, National Employment Law Project, https://s27147.pcdn.co/wp-content/uploads/Data-Brief-Impact-Fight-for-15–2018.pdf.

58. For our discussion of the creation of Change to Win see Eaton et al., "Organizational Change at SEIU," 59–60. See also Milkman, "Divided We Stand," 2006.

PART II

Developing the Organizing Model

5

Persistence, Militancy, and Power

The Evolution of Justice for Janitors from Atlanta to Washington, D.C., 1987–1998

ALYSSA MAY KUCHINSKI AND JOSEPH A. MCCARTIN

The Justice for Janitors campaigns of the 1980s and 1990s have not received much attention to date. This chapter will explore how Justice for Janitors campaigns evolved over time with the study of two cities. The first campaign in this analysis occurred in Atlanta in 1987–1988 and proved to be a costly learning experience for the union. The second took place in Washington, D.C. from 1987 to 1998, and it saw the union deploy a range of new tactics to achieve victory. Not only did the D.C. campaign ultimately prove successful and change the lives of the janitors throughout the city, it helped pave the way for the election of SEIU's president, John Sweeney, to the presidency of the AFL-CIO. To understand these campaigns, we must first grasp the dynamics that gave rise to this innovative effort.

Seeds of a New Model

Justice for Janitors emerged from a difficult decade for organized labor. The 1980s witnessed a decisive setback for unions across the United States. Despite increased employer resistance, unions had brought at least half a million workers to union elections supervised by the National Labor Relations Board (NLRB) in each year during the 1970s. Following Ronald Reagan's election to the presidency, his appointment of Donald Dotson to chair the NLRB, and his dramatic breaking of the 1981 Professional Air Traffic Controllers Organization (PATCO) strike, union progress abruptly changed. Beginning in 1982, the number of workers who voted in union elections started to plummet. By 1983, the number had dipped to 165,000. Large unions like the United Auto Workers (UAW) and the United Steel Workers of America (USWA), which had been running aggressive organizing campaigns in the late 1970s, sharply retrenched: by 1982, they were seeking less than half the number of union elections they had sought from 1977 to 1979. The collapse of union organizing was especially apparent in a region historically hostile to union organizing; the number of NLRB elections held in the Southeast dropped nearly 40 percent in 1982, and it never recovered.[1] Not surprisingly, union density suffered its steepest decline in any single decade, falling from 24 percent in 1980 to 16.8 percent in 1989.[2] Even more obvious was the reluctance of unions to go on strike after several prominent private sector employers, such as Phelps-Dodge, followed Reagan's PATCO example and broke strikes by hiring replacement workers. The number of major work stoppages dropped by more than two-thirds, from 289 annually in the 1970s to 83 annually in the 1980s.[3]

As organizing and militancy both stalled, union strategists began to explore new approaches. Three strategies emerged from this ferment. First, recognizing that strikes had become dramatically less winnable, some strategists argued for a creative rethinking of militancy using tactics other than strikes. In 1986, the AFL-CIO published *The Inside Game: Winning with Workplace Strategies*, to further this approach, teaching workers how to mobilize workplace actions, like slowdowns, that could pressure their bosses.[4] A second strategy was the "corporate campaign," inspired by New Left anticorporate activism: the successful boycotts organized by Cesar Chavez and the United Farm Workers (UFW) in the 1960s, the research of organizations like the Corporate Data Exchange (founded in 1975), and the successful publicity campaign led by the Amalgamated Clothing and Textile Workers Union (ACTWU) against J. P. Stevens, which finally won a union at that textile company in 1980.[5] Corporate campaigners "power mapped" their targets and brought pressure to bear on them through boycotts, proxy votes at stockholder meetings, and other new tactics. A third approach was a focus on new organizing. "There must be a renewed emphasis on organizing," argued "The Changing Situation of Workers and Their Unions," the 1985 special report of the AFL-CIO's Committee on the Future of Work.[6] In the 1980s, several unions began to invest in their organizing departments, and the AFL-CIO founded the Organizing Institute in 1989. All three of these influences found traction within SEIU, especially under the leadership of John Sweeney in the 1980s.[7]

As many unions grew lax in their efforts to organize new members in the postwar years, SEIU became more aggressive. By 1968, the union had dropped the word *Building* from its name and was among the first private-sector unions to begin organizing public-sector workers. George Hardy, who led the union in the 1970s, had famously framed his union's expansive vision with the mantra, "If they're breathing, organize them."[8] Not surprisingly, SEIU's largest local, 32B of New York City, incubated two of the most significant labor leaders to rise to power in the second half of the twentieth century: Thomas Donahue and John Sweeney. Donahue served as executive assistant to longtime AFL-CIO president George Meany, and then became the AFL-CIO's Secretary-Treasurer to Lane Kirkland when Kirkland succeeded Meany in 1979. Donahue had led the AFL-CIO's Committee on the Future of Work, which argued for the need to revive organizing in the 1980s. Sweeney, meanwhile, rose to the presidency of Local 32B in 1976, presidency of the merged Local 32BJ in 1977, and then to the general presidency of SEIU, succeeding Hardy in 1980.

No union was more open to new influences in the 1980s than SEIU under Sweeney's leadership. In 1984, he restructured the union to prioritize organizing. He tapped Andy Stern, then president of Local 668, the Pennsylvania Social Services Union, to come to Washington as the union's new organizing director. He also brought in young organizer Stephen Lerner to run the union's property services division, which included its janitorial locals. Stern and Lerner embodied an aggressive approach to labor organizing. Stern was drawn to labor through his flirtation with the New Left while he was a student at the University of Pennsylvania's Wharton School. As a high school student, Lerner started organizing for the United Farm Workers in the early 1970s and had gone on to organize textile workers in the South before joining SEIU.

With these leaders in place, SEIU conducted an internal analysis of its janitorial locals in 1985. What it found was alarming. While it had successfully organized building janitors in many big cities during the post–World War II years, its organizational hold had slipped during the 1970s. The industry was changing rapidly and so was its workforce. In the years when SEIU was building up its janitorial locals, most janitors had been directly employed by the owners of the buildings they cleaned. In the 1970s, however, buildings began contracting out their cleaning to janitorial service companies. These companies were often small, averaging only 18 employees each, and they competed fiercely with each other for contracts. In order to cut costs and bolster the bids they submitted to building owners, the contractors cut employees' wages and benefits. To attract workers willing to take these jobs, contractors increasingly turned to recent immigrants, most from Mexico or Central America, and many of whom had entered the country without documentation and, therefore, found themselves in the most exploited positions in the nation's urban labor markets.[9]

As the union surveyed its janitorial locals, Lerner and his colleagues were inspired by a 1985 strike of Pittsburgh janitors against wage and benefit cuts. Emerging from the Pittsburgh effort, Lerner articulated a strategy that would pressure building owners that contracted with cleaning services, not cleaning contractors themselves. Janitors would demand that building owners employ only contractors that provided decent wages and benefits and allowed their employees to unionize.[10]

This approach was first tried in Denver in 1986–1987. There, the union dramatized the differences in the pay and benefits of the cleaning crews that worked for nonunion contractors in downtown office buildings with those enjoyed by unionized janitors at Denver airport. In the course of the struggle, the union popularized its campaign under the banner "Justice for Janitors." In choosing this language, SEIU framed its efforts as more than a bid to gain union members, but as a vital broader social justice struggle. In the Denver campaign, each of the three new influences that were emerging in labor circles in the 1980s were evident. The campaign sent in young organizers, used militant direct actions more often than strikes, and power-mapped the city to look for ways to pressure powerful building owners rather than their janitorial contractors.[11] The Denver fight received little national attention. But Atlanta, which was schedule to host the 1988 Democratic National Convention, would provide an ideal setting in which to both gain a national audience and pressure a party whose alliance with the labor movement had started to fracture.[12]

A Painful Learning Experience in Atlanta

When Justice for Janitors organizers launched the Atlanta campaign in March of 1987, they believed the locale was ready for success for several reasons. First, they did not need to persuade a local union to take up the effort. Since the city lacked a janitors' local, they established a new one, SEIU Local 679. Second, they believed the city's civil rights movement leaders would support a movement to organize the overwhelmingly African American janitorial workforce. Third, they knew that some of the janitorial contractors in Atlanta owned janitorial operations that were unionized in other cities and, thus, the contractors might be open to their workers organizing or, at the very least, not oppose them in their efforts to unionize. And finally, they reckoned that the impending 1988 Democratic National Convention, which would take place in that city, would provide additional leverage. Organizers believed that neither national nor local political leaders would want to see their gathering marred by controversy, which would help force a settlement to the union's advantage. In the meantime, the campaign would be in a position to garner national press.[13]

Atlanta's roughly 1,300 janitors were mostly African American women, 35 years old or older, who made on average $3.50 an hour, with no health insurance, no sick leave, no holiday pay, no retirement fund, little job security, and who often faced sexual harassment.[14] Organizers hoped to raise wages to a minimum of $5.25 an hour; gain employer-provided health insurance, holiday pay, and respect on the job; and establish seniority rights within the janitorial force.[15]

Organizers believed the key to achieving that goal was convincing the city's largest real estate developer, John Portman Jr., to allow his properties to be unionized. As the multimillionaire owner of eleven square blocks of downtown Atlanta, Portman was the obvious target for the campaign.[16] He was by far the most prominent building owner in the city, where for the previous twenty-five years he had designed and constructed its most iconic structures, including the Peachtree Center complex. Atlanta had a rapid growth spurt in the 1980s, with approximately 225 new office buildings containing 33 million square feet of space created from 1980 until 1988.[17] Much of the quick expansion was attributed to Portman. He was not only "responsible for shaping Atlanta's skyline," he also had helped shape Atlanta's image as the South's most progressive big city: he was a lifetime member of the NAACP and the first person to open an integrated restaurant in the city in 1961.[18]

In order to bring Portman to the table, organizers needed to build a base among the city's janitors. From the outset, they did not fear confrontation. Wearing red jackets with "Justice for Janitors" in white lettering on the back, organizers leafleted downtown buildings to educate nonunion janitors about the pay and benefits enjoyed by unionized janitors. Management often interrupted exchanges between organizers and janitors, even when janitors were on break. On August 6, 1987, two SEIU staffers were arrested because they refused to leave the Peachtree Center where they were organizing.[19] The union responded three days later with a loud demonstration outside of the Center that triggered an injunction prohibiting loud demonstrations and limiting groups of protesters to six. The union in turn protested the injunction. Fifty "J4J" members formed groups of six, tied together by rope, and marched up and down the street with tape over their mouths. One protestor held a megaphone that had the microphone portion taped over, mocking the injunction that prevented them from using it. The protest served as a notice to Portman's Peachtree Center Management Co. that, although the protestors could not vocalize their grievances, they would make sure both management and the general public heard them until organizers were free to meet with janitors in their place of work.[20]

Despite arrests, organizers continued to enter the buildings they were trying to unionize. Their tenacity resulted in their banishment from central downtown buildings. On September 24, 1987, Fulton County Superior Court Judge Clarence Cooper granted Peachtree Center Management Co. a restraining order that prohibited SEIU from soliciting janitors inside workplaces. Although the order inhibited Justice for Janitors organizers from entering Portman's buildings, they continued to leave leaflets and talk with janitors outside, making their presence known to the company.[21]

The Atlanta campaign had its share of supporters despite the strong opposition it encountered. Justice for Janitors won allies among high-profile members of the black community, including Claude "Thunderbolt" Patterson, a professional wrestling champion well-known throughout the South. Thunderbolt had attempted to unionize professional wrestlers in the early 1980s but was blacklisted as a result.[22] He became the most vocal of the four SEIU organizers working for the campaign in Atlanta.[23] Other notable allies were civil rights movement veterans: former SNCC chairman Congressman John Lewis,[24] and Reverend Joseph E. Lowery, president of the Southern Christian Leadership Conference (SCLC). In November of 1987, following the Peachtree Center injunction, Rep. Lewis encouraged the janitors to carry on their efforts and refuse to be "sidetracked."[25] A month later, Rev. Lowery spoke glowingly of the janitors' campaign at Local 679's founding convention.[26]

The courts, however, were decidedly less friendly as the legal battle spilled into 1988. On March 22, 1988, Fulton County Superior Court Judge William H. Alexander, who granted the Peachtree Center injunction, ruled that SEIU was in contempt of court. Although they had been barred from entering the premises for union activities, evidence suggested that the activists continued to distribute union material inside the Center to working janitors. SEIU and three of its activists, including Thunderbolt Patterson, were fined for "unlawful solicitation."[27] Then, on April 26, 1988, Judge Alexander ordered a permanent injunction against SEIU, blocking organizers from soliciting employees at Peachtree Center. Once again, organizers were barred from "blocking entrances, cursing, making obscene gestures, singing loudly, clapping or shouting inside Peachtree Center buildings."[28]

As the Atlanta fight became more bitter, SEIU sought to draw national attention to the struggle. On March 30, 1988, the Atlanta campaign held a rally in solidarity with the national Justice for Janitors movement, and ten other cities, including Los Angeles and San Jose, held vigils.[29] Days later, on April 4, 1988, the

SEIU and allied progressive organizations launched a pilgrimage from Memphis, the site of Dr. Martin Luther King Jr.'s death, to Atlanta on the twentieth anniversary of the assassination of Dr. King. When the pilgrimage entered Atlanta on May 14, 1988, janitors pushing brooms led 10,000 jubilant and chanting marchers through downtown.[30]

The continued protests made some janitorial contractors nervous. On June 14, 1988, Michael Gebhart, the president of janitorial contracting company Gebhart Building Services, Inc., and a target of the Justice for Janitors campaign, pleaded with SEIU to "petition the National Labor Relations Board (NLRB) for an election, and let our people make their own decision by secret ballot in a fair election monitored by the NLRB." SEIU leaders responded they were only interested in a unified contract that included all fifty-six of the largest office buildings, their eighteen janitorial contractors, and the blessing of the forty-three building owners.[31]

As the opening of the Democratic National Convention (DNC) neared, Mayor Andrew Young, a Democrat, former chief aide to Dr. King, and sympathizer with the union cause, grew worried. The DNC would take place July 18–21, and Young did not want it engulfed in tumultuous protest of the kind that had famously disrupted the DNC in Chicago in 1968. He began to encourage Portman and SEIU to sit down and work out a deal. For its part, SEIU sought to pressure Young. On July 7, the union sent out letters to DNC delegates and other politicians, including Democratic presidential candidate Michael Dukakis, asking them not to attend five convention events that were co-sponsored by Portman: a dinner at Portman's home for party leaders, appearances on ABC's *Good Morning America*—which was planning to broadcast from the Portman-owned Marriott Marquis—a benefit fashion show at a Portman-owned building, a *USA Today* brunch to be held at a Portman-owned hotel, and a Delta Air Lines reception cosponsored by Portman.[32] These letters prompted Young to act.

On the very day the letters went public, Young invited two SEIU representatives and two Portman aides to his home for dinner.[33] This gathering was the first face-to-face conversation between the two parties and initiated a four-day period of negotiations, much of which took place in Young's home.[34] Despite Young's encouragement, negotiations stalemated and the two parties headed into the DNC still locked in conflict, much to the mayor's dismay.[35]

As politicians and journalists poured into Atlanta, SEIU prepared to escalate the fight. A small group of janitors set up outside Peachtree Center costumed as giant purple raisins in the 95-degree heat chanting, "We're raisin' hell to get Justice for Janitors."[36] To avoid such demonstrations and the prospect of forcing prominent Democrats to choose between crossing a picket line and canceling interviews, *Good Morning America* moved its broadcasts from the

Portman-owned Marriott Marquis hotel to another location.[37] Yet it was too late to even consider moving most DNC events from Portman-owned locations. A day before the DNC officially opened, more than 100 demonstrators picketed a brunch hosted by *USA Today* at the Apparel Mart, a building partially owned by Portman. Many attendants chose to avoid the picketers by utilizing a sky bridge that linked the neighboring Merchandise Market tower to the Apparel Mart tower. Among those who chose to cross the picket line, was Rep. John Lewis, who had pledged his support to the janitors only eight months earlier. Lewis told reporters that he "didn't have any real problem with crossing the line" because he had spoken to the janitors about it.[38]

SEIU's disruption of the *USA Today* lunch produced its desired effect. That evening, Portman's representatives called SEIU president John Sweeney just as Sweeney was driving to a planned action at Portman's house, where the developer was about to host a dinner for prominent Democrats. Portman's representatives pressed Sweeney to call off the planned protest. Sweeney said he would do so only if Portman "negotiates in good faith." Paul Kirk, the DNC Chairman, assured Sweeney that Portman would negotiate as long as Justice for Janitors refrained from protesting any other DNC planned events. Sweeney agreed to these terms. Arriving at the protest outside Portman's home, he announced to the assembled demonstrators: "we have won a victory." Sweeney assured them that there would be a plan for unionizing janitors at Portman's properties before the end of the convention.[39]

The truce was short-lived. Kirk wrote a letter to Sweeney on July 19 explaining that Portman promised to begin negotiations following the end of the DNC, not during the event.[40] Sweeney believed that this contradicted what he had been promised. He knew that if negotiations began after the convention, he would lose his leverage. So, on July 19, Justice for Janitors resumed their action and picketed a reception for Senators Bob Graham of Florida and Jay Rockefeller of West Virginia at the Portman-owned Marriott Marquis.[41] Protests continued on July 20, the convention's last day. Over two hundred demonstrators picketed outside the Delta Air Lines reception hosted at Portman's Marriot Marquis, singing and shouting anti-Portman slogans. Some Democrats, including DNC Chair Kirk and a few local officials,[42] crossed the picket line, but many Democrats chose not to go to the event or, like Florida delegate Gloria Jackson, joined the picketers.[43]

The confusing turn of events during the convention marked the passing of SEIU's moment of maximum leverage. Thereafter, the Atlanta campaign found itself back in the courts.

On September 2, the National Labor Relations Board (NLRB) ruled that Portman's Peachtree Center Management Co. could not exclude SEIU organizers from its office-retail complex. The NLRB found that the restraining order that had barred organizers from the premises had denied the employees' ability to decide whether to unionize or not.[44] Portman's legal team pushed back. On October 3, 1988, Portman sued SEIU for disrupting his businesses, claiming he lost at least $435,000 alone due to *Good Morning America*'s canceled booking at the Marriott Marquis. Portman also contended that their picketing of his events constituted a secondary boycott that violated Section 8(b)(4) of the National Labor Relations Act as amended by the Taft-Hartley Act.[45]

In response, the Atlanta campaign both widened its demonstrations and intensified its own legal battle. On November 17, it launched an international movement against Portman behind the slogan "Bring John Portman to Justice," with allies in twenty-five U.S. cities and six different countries participating; Portman owned businesses in each of these cities. From Seattle, Washington, to Hartford, Connecticut, to Bonn and Copenhagen, people gathered to demand that Portman pay just wages and provide decent working conditions and benefits to the janitors who cleaned his Atlanta buildings.[46] Then, on January 9, 1989, SEIU filed a lawsuit against Portman's Peachtree Center Management Co., alleging the company violated federal antitrust and civil rights laws during the DNC when it blocked a thirty-minute broadcast SEIU had financed to promote the janitors' cause from airing in the Marriott Marquis, thereby preventing 6,000 downtown hotel rooms from accessing the broadcast. But these legal moves were not enough to turn the tide against Portman. Thus, on January 11, 1989 the union executed a tactical legal retreat shortly thereafter, agreeing to refrain from "illegal picketing, demonstrating, and coercive action" in response to Portman's secondary boycott suit.[47]

The union continued to fight through 1989. Its January 11 agreement did not prevent Justice for Janitors from staging a demonstration at a dinner hosted by the M.L.K. Center for Nonviolent Social Change, Inc. to commemorate what would have been Dr. King's 60th birthday. The large celebration attracted many from Atlanta's elite, including Portman. When Portman rose to speak during the dinner, thirty Justice for Janitors activists began loudly singing "We Shall Overcome" from just outside the ballroom.[48] Yet such efforts could not disguise the fact that the Atlanta campaign was losing steam, a reality that became increasingly undeniable on May 13, 1989, when an administrative law judge[49] dismissed the unfair labor practices charges SEIU filed against the Peachtree Center Management Co.[50]

Organizers attempted one last effort to revive the campaign by taking on a new target. On July 27, fifty Atlanta Justice for Janitors protesters marched outside one of the largest corporations in the United States, Coca-Cola. Like other Atlanta businesses, Coca-Cola's headquarters used nonunion contractors to clean its facility. Many groups supported efforts to organize the Coca-Cola janitors, but the effort made little headway.[51]

By the fall of 1989, the Atlanta campaign was largely confined to courtroom maneuvers. SEIU helped two janitors bring a discrimination suit against Gebhart Building Services, Inc.[52] SEIU claimed two black men were refused applications for positions as janitors with Gebhart Building Services, Inc. at Koger Center in Chamblee, Georgia, a city just northwest of Atlanta, because of their race. One of the men allegedly discriminated against claimed that, when he sought an application as a janitor in August of 1989, he was told "all jobs were reserved for Koreans" at that location. The lawsuit sought $350,000 in back pay and punitive damages for the defendants as well as an affirmative action program to be put in place at Gebhart to prevent further discriminatory practices.[53]

The decision to file a civil rights suit against Gebhart amounted to an admission by the Atlanta organizers that they had exhausted all of the arrows in their quiver. In February 1990, the Atlanta Justice for Janitors campaign quietly ended. Local 679 gave up targeting Portman and their central strategy of targeting building owners, focusing instead on trying to organize a single janitorial contractor, Southern Services Inc. (SSI). SSI was a company owned by John Burks, who proudly touted that he was a successful black business owner. While Rev. Jesse Jackson made a tape imploring workers to vote for the union,[54] Burks pushed back, contending SEIU would not keep its promises to the janitors, and, according to some janitors, threatening to fire them if they voted for the union.[55] The union vote failed and the Atlanta Justice for Janitors campaign sputtered to a close without winning over even one small janitorial contractor.[56]

The spectacular failure of the Atlanta campaign seemingly called the entire Justice for Janitors model into question. Unless organizers could learn from the Atlanta defeat and apply its lessons in other cities, they knew that the future of their innovative organizing model was in doubt. Fortunately, the campaign was already beginning to gain traction in Washington, D.C. There, organizers would choose their targets more carefully, take advantage of a less hostile court system, and, when the time was right, escalate militancy in ways they had not attempted in Atlanta.

Bridge Blocking and Breakthrough in Washington, D.C.

The Justice for Janitors Washington, D.C. campaign officially launched in October 1987, five months after the beginning of the Atlanta campaign, with the establishment of SEIU Local 525, which was created to unionize and represent

Washington's janitors.[57] Prior to the launch of this campaign, D.C. janitors had simply been hoping for increases in the minimum wage[58] with most janitors earning the federal minimum wage of $3.35 an hour with few or no benefits.[59] The minimum wage had remained stagnant throughout the Reagan presidency and janitors and other low-wage Washington workers had repeatedly urged both the D.C. City Council and Congress to pass legislation that would increase their wage. Yet once the Justice for Janitors' campaign began, the janitors lifted their sights well above a meager increase. The campaign not only demanded $6.50 an hour, paid sick leave, an affordable health insurance option, overtime pay, and paid holidays and vacations, but also "justice and fair treatment on the job" and "dignity and respect."[60] With a collective bargaining agreement and union grievance system, the janitors felt they would finally be recognized as the hard-working employees they were.

From the beginning, the D.C. campaign required a more inclusive strategy. Approximately 60 percent of D. C. janitors were women, a large majority of whom were women of color—African American and Latina. Organizers planned actions that were in support of women specifically, such as a "Stop Sexual Harassment Now" press conference and rally on March 23, 1988, five months into the campaign.[61] In addition to suffering the same low pay and degrading working conditions as men, women faced sexual harassment or even sexual assault by supervisors. By emphasizing that issue, organizers sought to make clear their intention to address the needs of female janitors as well as concerns affecting all workers.

The D.C. campaign adopted the same approach regarding the problems faced by immigrants, both documented and undocumented. In 1993, SEIU President John Sweeney released a statement about the abuse immigrant janitorial workers faced on the job from their supervisors. Specifically speaking to the abuses D.C. immigrant workers faced, Sweeney cited a case in which a company hired immigrants living in Texas and drove them to Washington, D.C. in order to employ them. According to Sweeney, these workers were forced to pay exploitative rents to live in housing owned by their employer while earning less than the minimum wage. Sweeney also noted that employers systematically denied immigrant janitors overtime wages and paid them in cash in order to avoid making contributions to the federally mandated benefit of Social Security.[62] By acknowledging the specific injustices that immigrants faced, the campaign made clear it would champion the cause of those underrepresented in the labor movement.

The D.C. campaign also diverged from the Atlanta effort by framing its demands in ways that would appeal to a broad cross-section of Washingtonians.

It did this first by drawing attention to the tax breaks the city gave to downtown developers, who in turn used exploited labor to clean their buildings. Like most cities, Washington gave large breaks, usually on property taxes, to developers in order to encourage them to locate in the city. These tax abatements were often worth millions of dollars, robbing Washington of a great sum of potential tax revenue, an especially important issue in a city in which the largest single property owner—the federal government—was not subject to property taxes. Washington also financed many projects through tax-exempt bonds, in which the city fronted the money for a private company to develop land with an interest-free loan.[63] The campaign framed the tax breaks that large real estate developers received as a drain on municipal taxpayers and working people.

Organizers sought to highlight the costs of this tax drain by pointing to its impact on specific programs, such as the city's Tenant Assistance Program (TAP), which gave rent subsidies to families that earned 80 percent or less of the median income in D.C. TAP was a popular program with an extremely long waitlist and precarious and inadequate funding. Because big developers hired janitors at unsustainably low wages yet still received huge tax breaks, organizers argued, programs like TAP were unable to serve the city's needs.[64] By tying their campaign to a broader issue, organizers mobilized not only those who supported wage increases and better working conditions for janitors but also citizens who cared deeply about these government programs and tax equity.

The D.C. campaign followed the Justice for Janitors' previous strategy in making sure to lift up one developer as the symbol of their campaign. That developer was Oliver Carr. Organizers decided to focus on him because he was the largest antiunion property owner in the city.[65] As Justice for Janitors national organizing director, Bill Ragen, later explained: "We try to pick our targets so they'll have the most resonance."[66] To highlight Carr's role, SEIU paid for a full-page ad in the *New York Times* on July 21, 1994, assailing him for not paying his fair share in taxes and the city for giving him the tax break that shrank its budget.[67] Often using the slogan, "D.C. Is Having Carr Trouble," Justice for Janitors launched a full-scale attack against Oliver Carr. As they had done in their campaign against John Portman, the campaign regularly planned marches and pickets outside of Carr's buildings.[68] They also picketed outside Carr's home, making clear they would keep coming back until he agreed to their campaign's conditions and started to pay his fair share of taxes.[69]

Luckily for campaign organizers, D.C. courts proved more congenial to unions. As happened in Atlanta, building managers throughout the city refused to allow organizers to enter their buildings where they might interact with janitors. The courts, however, blocked their efforts. On December 9, 1989, Superior Court Judge Henry H. Kennedy ruled that the Apartment and Office Building

Association (AOBA)—the association of building managers who were refusing to give organizers access to buildings—had violated D.C.'s Human Rights Act, which banned anyone from discriminating against another person based on their "source of income or place of business."[70] Because the building owners were refusing entrance solely to Justice for Janitors organizers, they were discriminating against the organizers because of their source of income, SEIU. Justice for Janitors viewed this ruling as a big win: "certainly an arrow in our quiver in our efforts to make the real estate industry more accountable to the working poor in the District," as SEIU attorney Reuben A. Guttman remarked.[71] With this ruling in place, organizers began entering buildings, distributing literature, and building their movement. AOBA harassment did not end, however. Four years later, the campaign again sought legal action against the building owners, alleging that they continued to violate the city's Human Rights Act by blocking organizers' entry into their buildings. Again, the court sided with the union and the AOBA was forced to agree to a settlement paying Local 525 $105,000. Jay Hessey, the local's executive director, celebrated the decision as "a classic example of the little people against the big people."[72]

The courts by no means always favored the campaign. When organizers attempted to place a measure on the D.C. ballot called Initiative 35, which would have made the city's tax appeals public while deals were being brokered between the recipient company and the city government, the AOBA raised a successful legal challenge, and the initiative was removed from the ballot on procedural grounds.[73] In December 1994, developer Oliver Carr was also able to secure a court order that limited the size and proximity of the protests outside his offices.[74]

Although D.C. courts were generally less hostile to the union than those in Atlanta had been, organizers knew that courts would not win a janitors' union. Janitors would have to win that in the streets, using militant tactics when necessary, just as the union had done in its successful effort in Los Angeles in 1990. During the first years in Washington, the campaign's primary tactic was holding noisy demonstrations outside of buildings whose janitors it was seeking to organize. But, on October 21, 1993, the union attempted its first act of mass civil disobedience as hundreds of janitors blocked traffic along K Street; four were arrested for unlawfully entering the offices of a cleaning contractor.[75] By December 8, 1994, the campaign attempted its first bridge-blocking protest as thirty-eight people were arrested for blocking traffic on one of Washington's main arteries, the 14th Street Bridge, during a morning rush hour.[76]

By the spring of 1995, the campaign was ready to push its militancy to new levels. Organizers planned a week of action for March 18–24, calling it *Save Our City*. Each day that week Justice for Janitors undertook a major action.[77] On

Monday, March 20, seventy-nine people were arrested for once again blocking traffic on the 14th Street bridge during a morning rush hour. The next day, 150 more protestors were arrested for blocking a busy intersection near the White House during evening rush hour.[78] On Wednesday the 22nd, activists from other cities joined 500 marchers in Freedom Plaza.[79] Even as it blocked streets, the campaign continued to apply political pressure. SEIU research analyst, Manny Pastreich, spoke before the D.C. City Council on March 21 about "Saving Our City by Cutting Corporate Welfare." He explained the campaign's stance against tax abatements and low-to-no interest bonds and substantiated his claims with concrete data.[80] The mix of militant street tactics and public testimony gained the campaign unprecedented attention.

With these protests, the campaign "burst into high visibility" in the words of the *Washington Post*. In ensuing months, organizers kept their campaign in the public eye through militant actions. In mid-September, they launched a series of actions they called "The Days of Rage." Once again, Oliver Carr was their primary target and their most visible action was another bridge-blocking during a morning rush hour.[81] Protestors blocked the Roosevelt Bridge, another key artery crossing the Potomac on September 20. They did so by parking a school bus across the eastbound lanes from Virginia going into the city. Then they set desks, chairs, and blackboards in front of the bus to stage a mock classroom.[82] Their action sought to highlight the revenue lost to public schools because of the tax breaks the city granted to Carr and other developers.

Such tactics were controversial.[83] In a letter to the editor, one woman worried about the "physicians, nurses, expectant mothers, and sick children" who might have been held up on their way to the hospital. The spokesperson for American Automobile Association (AAA) went so far as to label the bridge-blocking "transportation terrorism."[84] At a congressional hearing on October 6, 1995, politicians also condemned the closure of the bridge[85] and urged D.C. officials to increase the penalties associated with blocking major roadways.[86] Even some in the labor movement disowned the protests. Acting AFL-CIO president Thomas R. Donahue criticized his opponent in the October 1995 election for AFL-CIO presidency, John Sweeney, for "blocking bridges" instead of "building" them.[87] Undeterred, Sweeney defeated Donahue for the presidency on October 25, 1995 leading some to speculate that the AFL-CIO had taken "a sharp turn toward militancy."[88]

The struggle continued in Washington for more than two more years before the union finally prevailed. During this period, organizers utilized direct action, political pressure, and an increasingly sophisticated effort to pressure developers' finances. In the fall of 1996, the campaign launched a strike against more than a dozen contractors and threatened to disrupt traffic at National Airport,[89] even as it successfully advanced a ballot initiative that would allow taxpayers to challenge property tax assessments on the public's behalf.[90] After persuading fifteen janitorial service companies to end the strike by bringing over 1,000 workers under union contract on March 7, 1997,[91] the union unveiled a new tool to pressure recalcitrants in the fall of that year: it brought its fight to Wall Street, endeavoring to persuade pension funds to divest from holdings in D.C. that continued to resist the union.[92]

The cumulative effect of this multipronged strategy was decisive. More than a decade after it began, the Justice for Janitors campaign finally won what it had worked so diligently for, a master contract for Washington, D.C. On June 22, 1998, SEIU Local 82, which had emerged in place of the original Local 525, signed a contract with a group of cleaning companies that together accounted for 70 percent of the cleaners of downtown commercial office buildings. By 1999, this agreement encompassed approximately 4,000 janitors, gaining them wage increases, healthcare and retirement benefits, and a fund to help mostly immigrant workers learn other skills that would allow them to move to higher paying jobs.[93]

The Evolution of Justice for Janitors

Between the launch of the Justice for Janitors campaign in Atlanta in March 1987 and the conclusion of the master contract in Washington, D.C. in 1998, the campaign had evolved in important ways. Comparing the Atlanta and Washington campaigns highlights three crucial elements that emerged over the course of that evolution: patient commitment to a program that would take years to unfold, escalating militancy, and a power analysis that allowed the campaign to bring public pressure against powerful financial interests in ways that framed the janitors' fight as a battle against corporate exploitation of the larger community.

Patient commitment was crucial to the success of these campaigns. Organizers launched the Atlanta campaign only sixteen months before the opening of the Democratic convention in that city. They had hoped to use that convention as the leverage point that would bring John Portman to the table and win a union agreement. But they were unable to build enough power before the convention to accomplish their goal. By contrast, the Washington campaign took nearly a decade. Its leaders stuck with the campaign believing that their analysis would eventually lead to a breakthrough—and in the end it did.

The escalation of militancy over time was equally crucial. In Atlanta the campaign did not engage in a series of escalating direct actions. And, just when activists were prepared to picket the house of their key target, Portman, at the moment of his maximum vulnerability, the union pulled back on the vague promise that Portman would negotiate. Portman then delayed negotiations until after the convention when the union's leverage was reduced, and then failed to negotiate in good faith. In Washington, by contrast, the campaign relentlessly ramped up militancy over time and used its militant tactics to build a powerful feeling of solidarity among janitors. If Sweeney had proven reluctant to anger powerful Democrats by disrupting a dinner at Portman's home, he showed no such reluctance when it came to bridge blocking in Washington seven years later. Indeed, he pointed to his union's willingness to block bridges as symbolic of the militancy he would bring to bear if elected as president of the AFL-CIO.

The Washington campaign would not have been successful through persistence and militancy alone. During the course of the D.C. campaign, SEIU honed its power analysis and its ability to portray big developers as rich malefactors who exploited both taxpayers and the working poor who maintained their buildings. In Atlanta, the union had unsuccessfully sought to shame John Portman into an agreement, but it did little to show how Portman, who was widely seen as a paragon in his community, had grown wealthy in large part through public subsidies. In Washington, by contrast, the union carefully worked to portray developers like Oliver Carr as feeding off the public trough in the form of tax abatements and repaying the community with jobs that failed to pay even living wages. Carr's wealth came at the expense not only of the poor janitors that swept his floors, but of the city's schools, which were underfunded because he and his cronies did not pay their fair share of taxes. To the extent that the union could frame the issue this way, it had more political license to employ disruptive tactics, for such tactics were being deployed not only for the benefit of janitors and their union, but for the common good. Thus, not only had Justice for Janitors provided "tremendous identification for SEIU as a low-wage worker union," as one internal union analysis put it, it had provided a model for how to effectively confront concentrated wealth and power.[94]

Those who hope to revive the labor movement in the twenty-first century would do well to ponder the evolution of Justice for Janitors. It is difficult to imagine a union revival that will not draw on the same elements that characterized the evolution of that innovative campaign: patience to pursue a well-founded program that might take years to mature, an ability to escalate militancy and build solidarity over time, and a framing of labor's fight as a fight against corporate elites and on behalf of the common good. To the extent that future movements draw upon these insights, the final fruits of Justice for Janitors have yet to be harvested.

Notes

1. Lane Windham, *Knocking on Labor's Door: Union Organizing in the 1970s and the Roots of a New Economic Divide* (Chapel Hill: The University of North Carolina Press, 2017), 195–196.

2. Timothy Minchin, *Labor Under Fire: A History of the AFL-CIO since 1979* (Chapel Hill: The University of North Carolina Press, 2017), 9–10.

3. Joseph A. McCartin, *Collision Course: Ronald Reagan, the Air Traffic Controllers, and the Strike that Changed America* (New York: Oxford University Press, 2011), 10, 350–351; U.S. Bureau of *Labor* Statistics, "Work Stoppages Involving 1,000 or More Workers, 1947–2016," https://www.bls.gov/news.release/wkstp.t01.htm.

4. Joe Uehlein and Ray Abernathy, *The Inside Game: Winning with Workplace Strategies* (Washington: AFL-CIO Industrial Union Department, 1986).

5. Matt Garcia, *From the Jaws of Victory: The Triumph and Tragedy of Cesar Chavez and the Farm Worker Movement* (Berkeley: University of California Press, 2014); Jarol B. Manheim, *The Death of a Thousand Cuts: Corporate Campaigns and the Attack on the Corporation* (Lawrence Erlbaum Associates, 2001); Charles Perry, *Union Corporate Campaigns* (Philadelphia: Industrial Research Unit, Wharton School, University of Pennsylvania, 1987); Timothy J. Minchin, *Don't Sleep with Stevens!: The J.P. Stevens Campaign and the Struggle to Organize the South, 1963–1980* (Tallahassee: University of Florida Press, 2005).

6. *New York Times*, September 22, 1985.

7. On these tendencies in Canada, see Luis L.M. Aguiar, "Neoliberalism in Vancouver: An Uphill Struggle for Cleaners," *Social Justice* 31:3 (2004): 105–129.

8. Don Stillman, *Stronger Together: The Story of SEIU* (White River Junction: Chelsea Green Publishing, 2010), 17–18.

9. John B. Jentz, "Janitorial/ Custodial," in *Encyclopedia of U.S. Labor and Working Class History*, vol. 2, ed. Eric Arnesen (New York: Taylor & Francis Group, LLC, 2007), 711.

10. Jennifer Luff, "Justice for Janitors," in *Encyclopedia of U.S. Labor and Working Class History*, vol. 2, ed. Eric Arnesen (New York: Taylor & Francis Group, LLC, 2007), 729.

11. Ibid.

12. On the drift of Democrats away from labor in the 1970s, see Judith Stein, *Pivotal Decade: How the United States Traded Factories for Finance in the 1970s* (New Haven: Yale University Press, 2011).

13. Stephen Lerner interview with Alyssa May Kuchinski, May 5, 2017, in author's possession.

14. "Local Janitors Organize for Better Pay, Benefits," *Atlanta Daily World*, November 19, 1987.

15. "Janitors Push for Wages and Benefits," *Atlanta Daily World*, December 20, 1987.

16. "Atlanta Janitors' Fight Spawns Nat'l Boycott," *Los Angeles Sentinel*, October 6, 1988.

17. Mark Calvey, "Window Cleaners Awash with Demand—Demand Is Growing; so Is Insurance Cost," *Atlanta Journal-Constitution*, August 17, 1987.

18. Jim Galloway, "In Streets and On Screens, Labor Seeks Democrats' Attention," *Atlanta Journal-Constitution,* July 15, 1988.

19. Lisa Ricks Crowe, "Union Works to Organize Peachtree Center Janitors," *Atlanta Journal-Constitution,* September 25, 1987.

20. W. Morgan Mallard, "Justice for Janitors Group Marches," *Atlanta Journal-Constitution,* November 25, 1987.

21. Crowe, "Union Works to Organize Peachtree Center Janitors."

22. "The Wrestling Gospel According to Mike Mooneyham," April 20, 2008, https://web.archive.org/web/20080420085351/http://www.mikemooneyham.com/pages/viewfull.cfm?ObjectID=C633DB6F-48A3-4E7B-B98CDB148DC310D4.

23. Kenneth B. Noble, "Ex-Wrestler Fights in a New Arena," *New York Times,* March 21, 1988.

24. "Cong. Lewis Calls Meeting on Janitors," *Atlanta Daily World,* November 17, 1987.

25. W. Morgan Mallard, "Janitors Plan Downtown Demonstration—Group Asking Pay Raises Is under Court Injunction."

26. Wanda Yancey, "Downtown Janitors Rally for Union, Higher Pay," *Atlanta Journal-Constitution,* December 13, 1987.

27. "Business Report," *Atlanta Journal-Constitution,* March 23, 1988.

28. Duane Riner, "Court Enjoins Janitors Union from Soliciting Peachtree Center Employees," *Atlanta Journal-Constitution,* April 27, 1988.

29. Henry Weinstein, "Janitors Stage Vigil as Part of National Protest," *Los Angeles Times,* March 31, 1988.

30. "March That Began in Memphis Draws Thousands in Atlanta," *Tri-State Defender [Memphis, Tenn.],* May 18, 1988.

31. W. Morgan Mallard, "Janitors Union Challenged to Call for Worker Election," *Atlanta Journal-Constitution,* June 15, 1988.

32. Henry Weinstein, "Union Seeking Boycott of 5 Atlanta Convention Events," *Los Angeles Times,* July 9, 1988, sec. Part I.

33. Jim Galloway, "Young Opens House, Office to Union, Builder—Mayor Trying to Avert Picketing of Convention," *Atlanta Journal-Constitution,* July 9, 1988.

34. Galloway, "Young Opens House, Office to Union."

35. "Portman Seeks to Head Off Protest by Janitors," *Atlanta Daily World,* July 14, 1988.

36. Manuela Hoelterhoff, "Gone with the Windbags," *Wall Street Journal,* July 20, 1988.

37. David Treadwell and Henry Weinstein, "Demonstrators Gathering for Usual Sideshow: Officials Hope to Avoid Disruptions as Varied Groups Advocate Views," *Los Angeles Times,* July 17, 1988.

38. Bert Roughton Jr., "DECISION '88—Janitors Shelve Plans for Demonstrations," *Atlanta Journal-Constitution,* July 18, 1988.

39. Ibid.

40. Bert Roughton Jr., "DECISION '88—Kirk: Portman Didn't Renege on Union Pledge," *Atlanta Journal-Constitution*, July 21, 1988.

41. Bert Roughton Jr., "DECISION '88—Janitors Union, Saying Portman Reneged on Talks, Pickets Event for 2—Senators," *Atlanta Journal-Constitution*, July 20, 1988.

42. Roughton, "DECISION '88—Kirk."

43. Monte Trocheck Plott, "DECISION '88—Delegates Get Big Taste of State's Many Products," *Atlanta Journal-Constitution*, July 21, 1988.

44. Ronald Roach, "Labor Board Files Suit to Allow Janitor Union at Peachtree Center," *Atlanta Journal-Constitution*, September 2, 1988.

45. Tom Hallman, "Portman Firm Sues Janitors Over Picketing," *Atlanta Journal-Constitution*, October 14, 1988.

46. "Atlanta Janitors' Fight Spawns Nat'l Boycott," *Los Angeles Sentinel* (1934–2005), Los Angeles, Calif., October 6, 1988.

47. "Metro Report—DeKalb Board Elects Lanier Presiding Officer," *Atlanta Journal-Constitution*, January 11, 1989.

48. "Mrs. King Announces Son to Take Over Presidency of M. L. King Center Here," *Atlanta Daily World*, January 17, 1989.

49. Judge Phillip McLeod presided over this ruling and had not ruled in any of the J4J cases prior to this instance.

50. "Metro Report—Richard Starrett Charged in Fourth Assault on Teen," *Atlanta Journal-Constitution*, May 13, 1989.

51. "Janitors March for 'Justice' at Coca-Cola," *Atlanta Journal-Constitution*, July 28, 1989.

52. Although Portman did not own the building where the alleged discrimination took place at Koger Center, he was harmed by the publicity against Gebhart Building Services, Inc. because it was a major subcontractor he hired to clean his properties.

53. Michelle Hiskey, "Janitors' Suit Claims Portman Contractor Won't Hire Black Workers," *Atlanta Journal-Constitution*, October 26, 1989.

54. SEIU Justice for Janitors Cassette Tape, "A Message of Love, Hope, and Justice for SSI Janitors from Rev. Jesse Jackson and Linda Riggins," February 10, 1990, SEIU Public Relations Record File 90, Box 3, Walter Reuther Library of Wayne State University, Detroit, MI.

55. SEIU Justice for Janitors Flyer, "Justice for Janitors, Atlanta, 1990," 1990, SEIU Public Relations Record File 34, Box 1; and SEIU Justice for Janitors DVD "#10," February 10, 1990, SEIU Public Relations Record Box 4, both in Walter Reuther Library of Wayne State University, Detroit, MI.

56. Lerner interview with Alyssa Russell Kuchinski, May 5, 2017.

57. Rene Sanchez, "Janitors Swept Up in Union Drive: D.C. Janitors Swept Up in Union Drive," *Washington Post*, November 15, 1987. Here we would like to gratefully acknowledge the work of Jennifer Luff who led the project creating a digital history of Justice for Janitors in D.C., http://georgetownlaborhistory.org, which collated many of the raw materials we drew on for this part of our story.

58. Patrice Gaines-Carter, "Janitors Seek Pay Raise: D.C. Panel Weighs 3-Tiered Minimum Wage," *Washington Post*, October 16, 1986.

59. Hamil Harris, "Union Voices Its Support for Minimum Wage Increase," *Washington Afro-American*, March 31, 1987, https://news.google.com/newspapers?id=2JglAAAAIBAJ&sjid=ZfUFAAAAIBAJ&dq=Union+voices+its+support+for+minimum+wage+increase&pg=3302,1165448&hl=en.

60. "Our Contract Demands: This Is Why We Are Fighting for Our Union," Justice for Janitors Organizing Committee, Justice for Janitors D.C.: A Digital History.

61. "Stop Sexual Harassment of D.C. Janitors Now!" Justice for Janitors Organizing Committee, Justice for Janitors D.C.: A Digital History, http://georgetownlaborhistory.org/ephemera/stop-sexual-harrassment-dc-janitors-now.

62. John Sweeney, "Corporate Abuse of Immigrant Workers," *Washington Post*, February 1, 1993.

63. Terrance Lynch, "There's Plenty of Money for TAP without New Taxes," *Washington Post*, December 25, 1988.

64. Ibid.

65. Lerner interview with Alyssa Russell Kuchinski, May 5, 2017.

66. Peter Kaplan, "The Union versus Oliver Carr," *Washington Business Journal*, Justice for Janitors D.C.: A Digital History, August 26, 1994, http://georgetownlaborhistory.org/sites/default/files/collection/news_articles/The%20Union%20versus%20Oliver%20Carr%20%28Washington%20Business%20Journal%2008.26.94%29.pdf.

67. "Display Ad 17—No Title," *New York Times*, June 21, 1994.

68. Kaplan, "The Union versus Oliver Carr."

69. Mary Ann French, "Taking It to the Streets: Justice for Janitors Causes a Dust-Up," *Washington Post*, April 14, 1995.

70. Steve Twomey, "Janitors Win Rights Ruling," *Washington Post*, December 9, 1989.

71. Ibid.

72. Jeanne Cooper, "Building Owners, Janitors Union Settle," *Washington* Post, May 25, 1993.

73. Kaplan, "The Union versus Oliver Carr."

74. Maryann Haggerty, "Judge Restricts Union's Protest Against Carr," *Washington Post*, December 10, 1994.

75. Linda Wheeler and Cindy Loose, "D.C. Janitors Trash Working Conditions," *Washington Post*, October 22, 1993.

76. Maryann Haggerty, "Protest of Carr Companies Blocks Bridge," *Washington Post*, December 9, 1994.

77. Pamela Constable, "Janitors Union Expands Its Campaign," *Washington Post*, March 23, 1995.

78. "Save Our City! Tax Oliver Carr!" Justice for Janitors Organizing Committee, Justice for Janitors D.C.: A Digital History, http://georgetownlaborhistory.org/ephemera/save-our-city-tax-oliver-carr.

79. Constable, "Janitors Union Expands Its Campaign."

80. Manny Pastreich, "Saving Our City by Cutting Corporate Welfare," (testimony before the Committee of the Whole, Washington, D.C., March 21, 1995), Justice for Janitors D.C.: A Digital History, http://georgetownlaborhistory.org/sites/default/files/Saving%20our%20city%20by%20cutting%20corporate%20welfare%20%2803.21.95%29.pdf.

81. "Help Stop the Beast That's Eating D.C.," Justice for Janitors Organizing Committee, Justice for Janitors D.C.: A Digital History, http://georgetownlaborhistory.org/advertisement/help-stop-beast-thats-eating-dc-0.

82. Marianne Kyriakos, "Roosevelt Bridge Blocked in Protest of D.C. Budget," *Washington Post*, September 21, 1995.

83. "Don't Block That Bridge," *Washington Post*, September 29, 1995.

84. Kyriakos, "Roosevelt Bridge Blocked."

85. U. S. Congress, House of Representatives, Committee on Government Reform and Oversight, Traffic Disruption Campaign By "Justice for Janitors," 104th Congress, 1st Session, October 6, 1995.

86. Charles W. Hall, "Rush-Hour Protests Assailed," *Washington Post*, October 7, 1995.

87. Peter Kilborn, "Prospective Labor Leaders Set to Turn to Confrontation," *New York Times*, October 25, 1995.

88. Peter Kilborn, "Militant Is Elected Head of AFL-CIO," October 26, 1995.

89. Frank Swoboda, "D.C. Janitors Say They're Ready to Strike," *Washington Post*, September 30, 1996.

90. Vernon Loeb, "Union Puts Assessment Issue on the Ballot," *Washington Post*, October 31, 1996.

91. Frank Swoboda, "Janitors Approve Contract, End 5-Month Strike," *Washington Post*, March 8, 1997.

92. Frank Swoboda, "Janitors Take Fight to Wall Street," *Washington Post*, November 17, 1997.

93. Frank Swoboda and Maryann Haggerty, "Janitors Approve Contract: Agreement Ends Lengthy Conflict," *Washington Post*, June 21, 1998.

94. Quotation from Timothy J. Minchin, "A Successful Union in an Era of Decline: Interrogating the Growth of the Service Employees International Union, 1980–1995," *Labor History* 61, nos. 3–4 (2020): 313.

6

Rank-and-File Leadership Development and Its Implications for Education Justice

VERONICA TERRIQUEZ

> The schools in this community are overcrowded. . . . That's why I helped with the campaign to open new schools. I talked to other parents so they would get involved. We collected signatures and organized a protest so that the government would pay attention to us and give us new schools.
>
> —Graciela, janitor member of SEIU United Service Workers West (USWW), 2005

Graciela came to the United States from El Salvador in the late 1990s. She found a job as a janitor in a large unionized skyscraper in downtown Los Angeles, and before long, she was recruited by the Justice for Janitors campaign of the Service Employees International Union (SEIU) to participate in building meetings, worksite actions, and other union activities. Although she did not much care for politics at the time, she felt her interactions with the union gave her no choice but to get involved. "When you are with the union, you realize that you need to participate with other people," she later recalled. "Together, you have to stand up for your rights, or you will never get what you need, what you want."

As an undocumented immigrant, Graciela believes the union taught her that she had the right to organize and stand up for herself. It also gave her plenty of experience of how a campaign works. So when a local community organization launched a campaign to address the school overcrowding in the Pico Union neighborhood of Los Angeles where many fellow union members live,

Graciela felt prepared to play a leadership role and help conduct outreach for the campaign. "This is what we do in the union—get other people involved," she explains. As an active member of SEIU United Service Workers West (USWW), a local dominated by Latinx immigrant janitors, Graciela's testimony speaks to SEIU's potential to foster civic engagement in an arena that has long-term implications for the future well-being of working-class families: children's schools.

Drawing on surveys, interviews, and a map of the union's membership, this chapter focuses on how USWW shapes the civic participation of Latinx immigrant members. It begins by highlighting the importance of schools as a site for nonunion civic participation for low-income parents, and then it summarizes prior research that shows how unions, particularly those with a social movement orientation, can bolster members' civic skills and capacities. Next, it describes USWW, and how the union's mobilization efforts in Los Angeles not only successfully engaged immigrant members in union activities, but also created opportunities for members to develop civic skills that bolstered their parental school involvement. This chapter demonstrates the important role of unions in empowering rank-and-file members to become civically engaged and to work toward advancing the interests of their families and communities.

Civic Engagement in Schools

Schools represent unique sites for understanding the ways in which SEIU USWW affects union members' independent civic participation. They offer a variety of opportunities for civic engagement including critical forms of participation that provide parents opportunities to voice their concerns and exercise leadership.[1] Critical forms of school-based civic engagement contrast with more passive or "plug-in forms"[2] of involvement (like volunteering) in which parents act under the direction of school personnel. Critical engagement includes contributing to decision-making processes and collective efforts to improve children's schools.

Labor union members with children enrolled in public schools can become involved in a range of school decision-making groups, particularly at the school site level. For example, federal and state education policies require many public schools, including Title I schools (i.e., schools that serve low-income communities and receive federal funds), to maintain decision-making bodies, such as school-site councils and English Learner Advisory Committees. Additionally, some schools have informal advisory committees, and in some school districts, parents have the opportunity to participate in them. Although parents' power to exercise agency within decision-making or advisory committees varies across schools and districts, these committees potentially offer parents a space in which to contribute to decisions about spending or educational policies.[3] Parents can also participate in grassroots organizations focused on school reform, or in informal collective efforts to improve their children's educational opportunities. These efforts, which parents themselves may instigate, entail working with school stakeholders, including teachers' unions, to advocate for more school resources and policy changes that address safety, health, programmatic, and curricular concerns.

Participation in school decision-making or improvement efforts may entail critiquing school practices and questioning the actions of school authorities.[4] These critical forms of engagement have the potential to promote education justice (i.e., a more equal education system that provides similar opportunities for academic achievement regardless of students' socioeconomic and racial background) and are particularly warranted in schools serving Latinx immigrant and other working-class communities, which disproportionately suffer from classroom overcrowding, poor facilities, a shortage of qualified personnel, and the absence of challenging curricula.[5] This educational inequality is, in part, exacerbated by a general disinvestment in the public school system since the late 1970s.[6]

Union Membership and Civic Engagement

It may not be surprising that SEIU USWW's labor mobilizations provide their members with relevant experiences that enable critical forms of civic participation in schools. After all, labor unions have historically played an important role in fostering the civic and political participation of working-class individuals, including immigrants. With varying levels of success, they have mobilized their members and their families to vote,[7] and some have directed and guided their members through a variety of non-workplace campaigns and civic efforts.[8]

Labor unions vary in the extent to which they provide their members with opportunities to participate in the public sphere.[9] Those that encourage their members to participate in worksite mobilizations, engage in electoral and other campaigns, and assist with outreach for a range of political and community-building activities are likely to have the greatest potential to develop the civic capacity of their members. Such locals, sometimes referred to as *social movement unions*, likely provide members with specific advocacy and organizing skills, or *claims-making repertoires*, that they can later apply to their children's schools or other civic arenas. These claims-making repertoires, like theatrical repertoires, consist of scripts—that is, a set or sequence of actions and strategies—that individuals have performed or at least observed previously.[10] As such, union involvement serves as a catalyst for some rank-and-file workers to take initiative in leading efforts outside the worksite and within their communities. As Nissen's study of SEIU's Florida Health Care Union (FHU) shows, this social movement experience can prompt members to express greater interest in politics and community issues.[11]

UNEQUAL INVOLVEMENT AND CIVIC DEVELOPMENT AMONG MEMBERS

It is important to consider that SEIU membership does not necessarily result in workers' involvement in or endorsement of union's activities. In any union mobilization or action, only a portion of the membership participates, even in the unions that work hardest to involve their rank and file. Unequal participation could in part be attributed to members' exposure to their union's workplace advocacy and organizing efforts. This is especially true in industries that SEIU organizes (janitors, security officers, and homecare workers) where members are scattered throughout many worksites and differ in their direct contact with their union.[12] As prior research demonstrates, interaction with other active peers, contact with union staff, and direct exposure to union activities—that is, individualized socialization practices—tend to generate greater union involvement, independent of members' individual disposition to become involved in union activities.[13] Worksites with greater union exposure and activity can also create social incentives (i.e., expectations of participation in collective action among coworkers)[14] that may be absent in other worksites.

While targeted mobilizations might shape patterns of participation, some members may be more inclined to participate than others. For example, union participation can be related to sociodemographic characteristics of members. As Cynthia Cranford's ethnographic research on USWW (when it was known as Local 1877) suggests, women may be particularly motivated to participate since motherhood can motivate activism.[15] However, having to work a second shift[16] comprised of household responsibilities may also be a hindrance to participating in union-related activities at the worksite and beyond. Those with prior civic and political experience, or certain political views, might be particularly motivated to become involved. This includes immigrants with political experiences prior to migration.[17] Personality traits, including those that lead some people to be particularly social or prone to become involved in group activities, could lead some to gravitate toward participation.[18] Individuals who exhibit a tendency toward activism and group involvement may become involved in the union regardless of recruitment efforts. Such individuals are also likely to become involved in nonunion civic activities, such as children's schools.

Exploring patterns of SEIU USWW members' involvement in their union can provide insights into whether this local's mobilization efforts or other factors are motivating workers to become involved in union activities. Such investigation also provides an understanding of the degree to which members are expanding their civic capacities in order to become involved in community or political affairs.

United Service Workers West and Justice for Janitors

Formerly known as Local 1877, USWW's roots lie in the Justice for Janitors campaigns of the early 1990s, which won union recognition for janitors in Los Angeles.[19] The union's intensive, highly visible campaigns emerged as a response to subcontracting, deunionization, and the decline in wages and working conditions that occurred in the 1980s. The mass mobilization of the largely Latinx immigrant janitorial workforce has figured prominently in the union's success,[20] as the union engaged janitors and other members in numerous contract campaigns over the past twenty years. Typical of SEIU's Justice for Janitors efforts across the country, USWW not only turns out its janitors and other members for workplace actions, it also mobilizes members for political rallies, immigrant rights marches, other protests, and actions organized by other unions.

The local's highly active and well-coordinated committee structure enables leaders to regularly recruit significant numbers of rank-and-file members to a range of union activities. The union's Leadership Committee trains shop stewards on contractual issues, worksite problem solving, running meetings, and communication skills. Stewards learn to run workplace meetings that generate discussion and debate among members; they also receive training in how to involve their peers in collective problem solving around shared grievances or other workplace concerns. USWWs Committee on Political Action (COPA) raises money for political campaign contributions, shapes the union's political plan for the region, lobbies public officials, trains members on political issues, and engages members in voter mobilization and other political activities. The Organizing Committee helps develop campaigns at nonunion worksites and coordinate mobilizations during union contract fights. In addition to these three committees, the union involves members in geographically based action teams that coordinate meetings and mobilizations in areas of Los Angeles County employing high concentrations of members.

Despite its active committee structure, the labor union does not regularly invite all of its membership to participate in its efforts. The union represents workers employed in hundreds of buildings throughout Los Angeles County, the majority of whom clean buildings in the evening or at night. To maximize the efficiency of staff time and union resources, organizers focus their recruitment for union protests, rallies, and campaigns on large buildings with many evening- and night-shift workers. These buildings tend to have a high level of union activity and generate most of the turnout for union protests and other campaigns. The union also targets for mobilization non-janitorial staff working at sites with high concentrations of members and during the most populated shifts. In the following, I draw on 2007 survey data collected from USWW members to account for the extent to which targeted mobilization might contribute to unequal patterns of member involvement.[21]

Union Mobilization and Participation

Table 6.1 shows that 29% of respondents were "active" members of the union, meaning that within the previous year, they attended a union action or rally, conducted phone banking or other outreach, or participated in precinct walking for a union-backed campaign. Active members were more likely to work night or evening shifts (84% compared to 64% of inactive members). This is in part due to the fact that the union concentrated resources in mobilizing nighttime workers. In interviews, many active members spoke about how recruitment efforts by USWW or organizers helped motivate many to become initially involved in the union. Almost all active participants I spoke to worked night shifts in large buildings or had done so in the past. Meanwhile, among inactive union members, about three-fourths were rarely if ever targets of mobilization because they worked day shifts or in small buildings. These findings point to the importance of the union's in-person mobilization efforts in prompting members to become involved in USWW's activities.

At the same time, survey results suggest there may be few, if any, sociodemographic patterns to members' involvement. While the survey shows that approximately three-fourths of USWW members lack a high school degree or equivalent, educational attainment nonetheless does not correlate with patterns of involvement. These results suggest that USWW is successful in involving workers with lower levels of education. This is noteworthy because individuals who did not have the opportunity to complete high school and/or attend college often exhibit low levels of civic and political participation,[22] whether or not they are immigrants.

Survey results also suggest gendered patterns of involvement. Women make up 59% of the sample, and they are more likely than men to participate in the union's activities. This in part has to do with the fact that women

TABLE 6.1 Descriptive Statistics for Active and Inactive SEIU USWW Members

	Active Union Members (n = 111)	Inactive Union Members (n = 267)	Total
Percentage of Sample	29%	71%	100%
Workshift			
Works evening/night shift	84%	64%***	70%
Background Characteristics			
Gender			
Male	34%	45%+	42%
Female	66%	55%+	59%
Educational attainment			
Less than high school	77%	74%	75%
Latino	97%	96%	96%
Born in the U.S.A.	3%	9%***	7%
Naturalized citizen	14%	16%	15%
Speaks English well	15%	23%+	21%
Child is enrolled in high school	29%	34%	33%
Critical Engagement in Children's Schools			
Attended advisory meeting at school	35%	24%*	28%
Attended meeting discussing school improvement	41%	27%**	31%

+p = <.10, p = <.05, **p = <.01, ***p = <.001, two-tailed tests

disproportionately work at night. However, the small survey sample does not preclude the possibility that women might be more involved in the union, even after accounting for their work shift. After all, Cranford's earlier research on this union found that women were particularly motivated to participate because they were concerned about the welfare of their children.[23]

Survey results also suggest that U.S.-born and English-speaking survey participants are less likely to be involved in the union than immigrants and Spanish-speakers. However, this finding is related to the fact that contractors prefer to hire English-speaking janitors—who are disproportionately U.S-born—to work day shifts because they can more easily communicate with tenants.

This statistical analysis, however, cannot account for all the factors that might determine whether or not individuals become involved. In my interviews with twenty inactive USWW members (defined as those who had not participated

TABLE 6.2 USWW Participation and Critical School Engagement: Predicted probabilities from logistic regression where gender, education nativity, citizenship, English-speaking ability, and child grade level are all held constant

	School Decision-Making	School Improvement
Union participant	0.36	0.44
Union nonparticipant	0.24	0.29

in union-sponsored rallies or campaign activities within the previous year), I found that a handful were regularly invited to participate in union activities but declined. Two disagreed with or disliked their union, while a few reported other priorities. Overall, though, survey and interview findings suggest that participation is not simply a result of individual proclivities for attending protests or engaging in campaign activity. Rather, individual socialization practices[24] and social incentives are likely to contribute to USWW members' involvement in social movement union activity.[25] Specifically, USWW members experience encouragement, and sometimes extensive pressure, from peers and organizers to participate in union activities. Members may also be motivated by the camaraderie and solidarity they experience through their involvement.[26]

UNION INVOLVEMENT AND CRITICAL ENGAGEMENT IN CHILDREN'S SCHOOLS

The bottom of Table 6.1 highlights differences in active and inactive union members' critical engagement in their children's schools. Survey results show that 35% of active members with school-aged children reported becoming involved in some type of decision-making body, compared to 24% of inactive members. Meanwhile, 41% of active members became involved in some sort of school improvement meeting, compared to 27% of inactive members. Survey results demonstrate that active union members tend to be more involved in school activities than inactive members. These results hold up after accounting for other key factors that might shape school involvement, including gender, educational attainment, nativity, citizenship, English-speaking ability, and children's high school enrollment. Table 6.1 illustrates differences between active and inactive members' likelihood of participation in school decision-making and school improvement efforts for the average USWW survey participant. These findings, although not conclusive, point to the possibility that USWW members with school-aged children may transfer union claims-making repertoires to critical engagement in school settings.

In-depth interview data, however, provide additional evidence that members borrowed from what they learn through their union experience to actively engage in their children's schools. In-depth interview data cannot be used to draw conclusions about the whole survey sample, but they do suggest that the effects of union participation were not uniform among active USWW members. As I discuss in the following, union experience dramatically changed the way a subset of members interact with the public arena. For other active members, union experience expanded their existing repertoire of civic skills, compelling some to exercise leadership at the school site. In general, active union members were more likely than their inactive counterparts to exercise leadership at the school site, voice their concerns, challenge authority figures, and coordinate other parents in efforts to address shared concerns.

FINDING A VOICE: EMPOWERMENT THROUGH UNION PARTICIPATION

Whether or not they were critically engaged in their children's schools, nearly half of the active Local USWW interview sample reported that they learned how to speak up and voice their concerns because of their union experience. For example, Carlos, a Honduran immigrant, said: "Sometimes you don't want to talk, but they [the leaders] ask you for your opinions—what you think. Little by little you learn to speak up, and then they can't shut you up." Workers found their voice through participating in meetings where they collectively tried to resolve worksite problems, in discussions leading up to an action, and in campaign efforts. Jorge, a union member who previously worked for a nonunion cleaning agency, said: "At my old job, the workers were very submissive; the bosses would yell at us and mistreat us. But not here [at my union job], if the supervisors mistreat you, we all stop working. Here you defend yourself, and this gives you a lot of self-worth."

Lucia's story reflects that of a few other reserved individuals who acquired the confidence to publicly express themselves. Lucia, an immigrant from Mexico City with an eighth-grade education, began working as a janitor in a large building in West Los Angeles soon after her arrival in the United States in the early 1990s. Before long, coworkers recruited her to participate in SEIU's Justice for Janitors campaign efforts. She attended numerous worksite meetings, trainings, and major actions in support of organizing nonunion janitors. She described her labor union experience as transformative:

> I was a very timid person, honestly, a very timid person. If I had to speak in public, I would turn red and would not know what to say. Getting involved in the [union] trainings has helped me become unafraid. . . . It has given me confidence, it has helped me defend myself and speak to other people.

A newfound confidence, coupled with organizing and advocacy experience, propelled some active USWW members with children to become critically engaged in their children's schools. After her involvement in union campaigns, Lucia became more outspoken at her sons' schools and in other public settings. For example, at a town hall meeting, she questioned a local elected school board member about his plans to address parents' safety concerns. "I'm not afraid to speak up, I tell them what I think," she said in reference to her ability to communicate with elected officials, school administrators, and teachers.

Lucia also applied her union experience to mobilize other parents. Like Graciela (who was introduced at the beginning of this chapter), Lucia, a former resident of the Pico Union neighborhood, recruited parents to participate in a local campaign to build new schools. Lucia believed that shared concerns can be resolved by a collective response from affected individuals. Echoing the words of other union members, she claimed, "We [the parents] need to work together to make sure that our children get a better education."

For Lucia, gaining self-confidence went hand-in-hand with developing civic skills that facilitated her critical engagement. But not all parents were reticent before they joined the union; a few parents claimed to be naturally outgoing people. Yet they contended that the union made them "stronger" by allowing them to engage with individuals of higher social status and giving them concrete experience in addressing shared concerns. "You learn how to communicate with all different types of people—your supervisor, the politicians," Carlos said. Members also reported taking greater initiative in addressing challenges. As Haydee declared, "You can't wait for others to solve your problems. You've got to take action."

UNION REPERTOIRES AND SCHOOL-BASED CIVIC ENGAGEMENT

Maria, a Mexican immigrant, said, "The union teaches you how to work with others to resolve problems." She was among a handful of union members who reported active school participation before becoming a union member. These parents attributed their prior school involvement to their personalities, commitment to their children's education, or schools' parent involvement programs (i.e., parent education and workshops). Nonetheless, evidence suggests that union experience enhanced problem-solving, advocacy, and organizing skills among individuals who are already civically engaged. For such parents, union involvement may have been less a determinant of whether they participated in school decision-making or improvement efforts than of how they participated. The union's well-developed committee structure, discussed earlier, provided a range of civic skill-building opportunities, particularly for highly motivated individuals, by engaging them in local politics, leadership training, and a range of campaigns that extended beyond the worksite. This range of experiences expanded members' capacity to take the lead in addressing concerns at the worksite and potentially in other civic settings.

Francisco's story offers an example of how union involvement can enhance the leadership of a parent who regularly participates in school-sponsored activities. A Guatemalan father with a sixth-grade education, Francisco immigrated to the United States in part to obtain better health care for his eldest son, born with spina bifida. In Los Angeles, Francisco and his wife, Marta, enrolled their son in an elementary school with a large special education program. Both parents were active in the school's parent support group, which provided them with an understanding of special education laws as well as strategies for supporting their son's personal and academic growth.

Francisco obtained a job as a janitor soon after his arrival in the United States and, like most people at his worksite, was quickly recruited to participate in the union's organizing efforts. After a few years, his coworkers selected him to serve as their union steward. Required to attend numerous trainings organized by the union's Leadership Committee, he learned to "use the process and go as far as you can to help people," as well as "how to get the other people to fight and stand up for their rights." Through the course of the interview, it became clear that Francisco had mastered the union contract, helped other workers use the process to resolve grievances, and mobilized them for union-sponsored actions.

No longer a shop steward when I spoke with him, he nevertheless performed a similar function at his children's schools, assisting and organizing other parents, including parents with special needs children. "Some parents that I know," he said, "they call me so that things at the school get fixed as quickly as possible." Francisco regularly helped other parents resolve their "grievances"—a union term he used to describe parents' school-related problems. He also mobilized a handful of parents to advocate for installing a new ramp for special education children, and he coordinated a parent and teacher effort to demand that the district clean up the school's drinking water, which was allegedly contaminated with lead.

Francisco credited school programs and his union experience for his school involvement. He claimed that parent involvement workshops offered at his son's special needs program were especially informative, but he had no doubt that his union experience helped him "use the processes to help other parents," "manage the politics of the school administration and bureaucracy," and "involve the other parents in what is going on." In other words, the problem solving, advocacy, and organizing skills Francisco acquired through his union participation subsequently contributed to his leadership at his children's schools. Francisco likely would have been actively engaged in his children's schools regardless of union membership. Yet, as with a few other parents in the sample, his USWW experience enhanced his leadership at the school site.

The in-depth interviews suggest that for many active members, union participation motivated or enhanced their school participation. However, this study does not rule out the possibility that for some union members, personality characteristics and political experience elsewhere (including in immigrants' native countries) might motivate their critical engagement in their children's schools.

SEIU's Potential to Support Education Justice Efforts

Survey and interview findings indicate that USWW's worker mobilizations serve as a catalyst for members to actively address concerns in their children's schools. However, there are limitations to the scope of this activism on their children's behalf. USWW members, like many of SEIU's membership nationally, typically do not possess bachelor's degrees. At the time this research was conducted in 2007–2008, USWW members I interviewed acted on issues that they understood, such as insufficient seats in the classroom, unclean bathrooms, poor quality food in the cafeteria, or the unfair treatment of their own children. Unless they were connected to community-based or other organizations working on issues of education reform, most SEIU USWW members had a limited understanding of education policy and the systemic inequalities (such as inadequate funding and high teacher turnover) affecting their children's schools. Consequently, members are often advocating for solutions to immediate and short-term problems (i.e., teacher with poor classroom management skills) that, to a limited degree, advance educational justice. However, because they lacked access to information and analysis regarding broader structural inequities in the school system, most rank-and-file members (regardless of their English language ability) do not have a sense of broader school policy changes that need to be made to better ensure their children's academic success (i.e., rigorous academic preparatory curriculum and more instructional time).

Overwhelmingly, USWW members view their children's education as the key to securing the future well-being of their families, especially since the economic gains obtained through a janitorial or other low-wage service sector contract can go only so far. In fact, survey results indicate that over 90% of USWW members believed that their union should become involved in efforts to improve their children's education. Interestingly, at the time, survey results showed that education was the top issue members wanted their union to work on, ranking above immigration or health care reform.

USWW took several steps to respond to their members' concerns about their children's education. The USWW leadership has expressed public commitment to addressing unequal learning opportunities, which many of their members' children encounter in low-performing, under-resourced schools. Starting in 2006, USWW sought to provide its members with a better understanding of how to support their children's academic success and advocate for equitable school improvements. The union developed a parent education program known as the Parent University, with the assistance of the UCLA Labor Center, UCLA Institute for Democracy Education, and Access. Saturday, weekday, and worksite trainings offered through the Parent University were geared to meet the learning needs and interests of the members, many of whom have limited formal education. Topics of instruction included parental rights, school governance structures, understanding report cards and standardized tests, English Language Learner classification and testing, resource inequalities in the public school system, the California education budget, and college access. Workshops took place at the union hall, and abbreviated learning sessions also occurred at the worksites during the workers' lunch breaks. Indeed, these workshops aimed to develop members' understanding of educational inequalities and ways to advocate for policy changes that improve opportunities for students from immigrant, high-poverty, and working-class communities. In 2007 the Parent University was implemented through its newly established sister nonprofit, the Building Skills Partnership, which has aimed to provide training and services focused on workforce development, immigrant integration, and community advancement. Notably, in collaboration with the nonprofit, the union was able to support positions for members to serve as parent educators.

USWW has used labor contract negotiations to support union members' parental school involvement. In some contract negotiations, USWW has obtained commitments from employers to pay a few cents per hour worked per employee to fund the Building Skills Partnership's Parent University and other adult education programs. Additionally, some of the union contracts have referenced the California Family-Schools Partnership Act, which affords parents and guardians the right to take time off from work (up to 40 hours per year) to participate in activities at their child's school. As my research revealed, some employers were denying workers their rights to attend their children's school activities. Through the Parent University, the union familiarized members with the Act and distributed a brochure to further educate members about their right to attend children's school functions. By inserting language from the Act into the contract, USWW has been able to create a process to ensure rights that otherwise had no enforcement mechanism.

As the zip code map of Los Angeles County (Fig. 6.1) indicates, USWW members are residentially concentrated in certain neighborhoods in Los Angeles, lending to localized partnership with community groups and members of their own union or other SEIU locals around shared concerns. Large numbers of members live in L.A. neighborhoods, such as Pico Union, East Hollywood, and various communities in South Los Angeles, where the majority of youth failed to graduate from high school in four years at the time this study was conducted. Though they may not know it, many union members send their children to the same under-resourced neighborhood schools. The 2007 survey showed that 14% of respondents knew at least one other USWW member whose child(ren) attended the same school as his/her own child(ren). Meanwhile, additional analysis not shown here indicated that several hundred members (300–700) resided within the attendance boundaries of just a handful of public high schools. Indeed, the residential concentration of union members facilitated union organizing and activism.[27]

FIGURE 6.1 SEIU USWW residential concentration in Los Angeles County

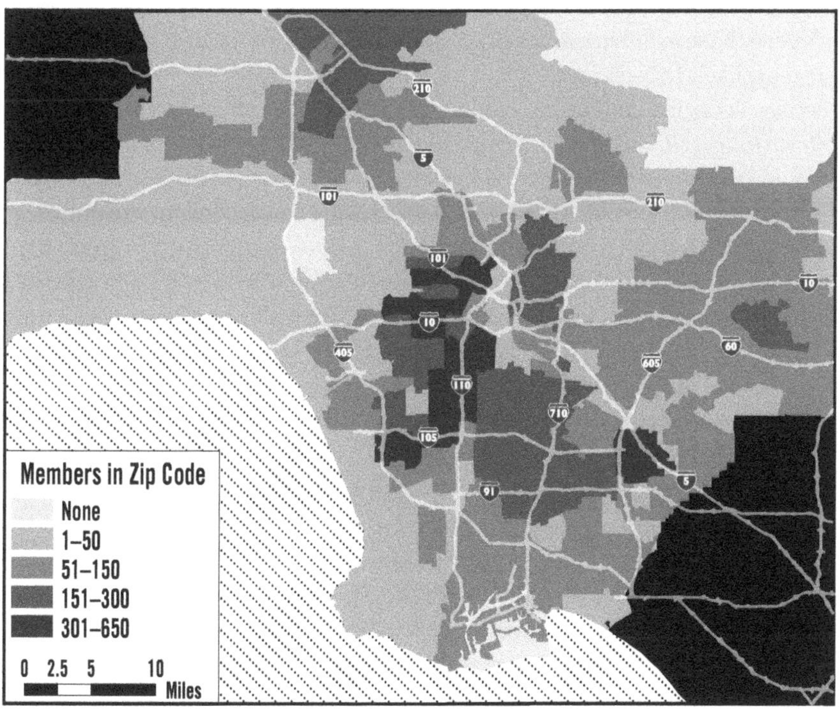

To this end, SEIU USWW formed partnerships with community-based organizations, including the Community Coalition and InnerCity Struggle to address resource and other inequities affecting the education of members' children. Additionally, in 2019, USWW came out in support of the teachers' strike led by United Teachers of Los Angeles (UTLA), which adopted a framework focused on "bargaining for the common good." UTLA's wins included wage increases, but also contract provisions that aimed to enhance learning opportunities for students.[28] Such coalitional work, along with the union's direct efforts to engage members around children's education, evidences USWW's ongoing efforts to remain a social movement union that is responsive to the broader needs of members and their families. The union's attentiveness to workers' concerns beyond the workplace likely deepens members' identification with their union and can thus serve as a model for other unions, especially those operating under a right-to-work context.

Implications for Education Justice

SEIU USWW's mobilization strategies play a role in determining which members become active in the union. The targets of USWW's concentrated outreach efforts—those members who work evening and night shifts in large buildings—are more likely to become involved in union actions, regardless of whether or not they speak English. While they can be characterized as staff-driven or top-down, efforts to recruit and engage night-time workers in large buildings effectively empower workers to find their voice and participate in actions at the worksite and beyond. Indeed, active workers themselves credit the union's outreach efforts for their own participation. At the same time, this research suggests that mothers disproportionately become active in the union's campaign efforts, indicating that union campaign involvement may play a uniquely transformative role in women's leadership development. Women's disproportionate investments in union campaigns may be attributed to the ways in which the union frames worker issues as family issues, which tend to motivate mothers' involvement in particular.[29]

The research presented here also suggests that involvement in USWW's actions, door-to-door campaigns, and other worker outreach efforts enhances the civic capacity of union members. Specifically, labor union involvement corresponds with being critically engaged in schools—that is, in decision-making and school improvement activities that allow parents to activate the civic problem-solving, advocacy, and organizing skills they acquire in the process of participating in social movement union activities. Because this study focuses on members' participation in a setting distinct from their labor union, these findings suggest that union members independently (i.e., without prompting by their union) draw upon their union-acquired skills to effect change in nonunion settings conducive to critical forms of engagement. Moreover, by focusing on differences in civic engagement between active and inactive union members, this study indicates that recruitment into union campaign efforts, rather than the simple fact of membership, is what enhances an individual's civic capacity. When compared with inactive USWW members, respondents who participated in the union's social movement activities appear more confident and better equipped to exercise leadership and voice their interests within the context of the school site.

While prior civic experience and personality characteristics cannot be completely ruled out as factors contributing to the findings, this study illuminates different pathways by which organizational participation affects the civic development of members who vary in their prior disposition toward civic engagement. For some active members, union involvement stimulates critical engagement in their children's schools; these union members experience a vivid transformation in their confidence levels and civic capacity in the course of their union activism. For other members, union experiences enhance their civic participation by expanding the repertoire of organizing, advocacy, and problem-solving skills they can apply to nonunion settings.

USWW has responded to its members' interest in education issues. In addition to winning contracts that helped fund the Parent University and ensured that employers respected the California Family School Partnership Act, the union has encouraged its members to attend district school board meetings to support policies that can benefit children from low-income families. Due to the geographic concentration of its members, this local has the potential to connect members to existing grassroots efforts to improve local schools and neighborhoods.

Findings based on this one particularly active local are likely to apply to other SEIU locals that provide members opportunities to develop their leadership skills, engage in collective action, and participate in non-workplace campaigns. This research suggests that those SEIU members who obtain such experience will be equipped to critically engage in their children's schools or participate in other civic affairs, without direction or guidance from their union. Although, I should note here that schools in Los Angeles may be more welcoming to immigrant parents when compared to those in other parts of the country with fewer Latinx and Spanish-speaking staff.

USWW's response to members' interest in children's education offers some lessons for other locals. First, the union contract can be used to leverage support for members' interest in education. Second, members' interest in their children's future can be used to expand leadership opportunities for the rank-and-file members. According to Aida Cardenas, the director of the Building Skills partnership, the Parent University has attracted members with little prior involvement in the union's workplace or other political campaigns. As a result, the Parent University has served as a mechanism to recruit otherwise disconnected members to other union activities. Finally, the geographic residential concentration of members presents opportunities for coordinated school-based or other localized campaigns. Many USWW members are likely to send their children to the same schools, creating the possibility for them to collectively draw on their union experience to address shared concerns. Maps of other SEIU locals' membership in Los Angeles County, including Local 99 (Classified School Employees Union), Local 721 (County Employees Union), SOULA (Security Officers Union Los Angeles), and ULTCW (Long Term Care Workers), show that members of these unions are also residentially concentrated. This is likely to be true of SEIU locals outside of Los Angeles.

Addressing concerns about public education has largely been the purview of the teachers' unions. Yet for many reasons, SEIU Locals, like USWW, might also focus on promoting education justice, perhaps in partnership with community-based organizations, advocacy groups, and teachers' unions that prioritize equity. Children in working-class families continue to attend college at very low rates,[30] and class inequality in access to higher education is on the rise.[31] Initiatives like the Parent University can help members support their children's learning, strengthening ties that extend beyond the workplace as members identify collectively as parents of children who primarily attend public schools. Such initiatives can ultimately help infuse the often-neglected voices of working-class parents into public debates about educational reform. Given its significant political leverage, SEIU's investment in the education of members' children can help promote education justice for working families.

Notes

1. Veronica Terriquez, "Schools for Democracy: Labor Union Participation and the School-Based Civic Engagement of Latino Immigrant Parents," *American Sociological Review* 76, no. 4 (2011): 581–601.

2. Paul Lichterman, *Elusive Togetherness: Church Groups Trying to Bridge America's Divisions* (Princeton: Princeton University Press, 2005).

3. Melissa Marschall, "Parent Involvement and Educational Outcomes for Latino Students," *Review of Policy Research* 23, no. 5 (2006): 1053–1076.

4. Mark Warren and Karen Mapp, *A Match on Dry Grass: Community Organizing as a Catalyst for School Reform* (Oxford: Oxford University Press, 2011).

5. Jeannie Oakes and John Rogers, *Learning Power: Organizing for Education and Justice* (New York: Teachers College Press, 2006).

6. Dowell Myers, *Immigrants and Boomers: Forging a New Social Contract for the Future of America* (New York: Russell Sage Foundation, 2007).

7. Herbert B. Asher, Eric S. Geberlig, and Karen Snyder, *American Labor Unions in the Electoral Arena* (Lanham, MD: Rowman & Littlefield, 2001).

8. Janice Fine, "Community Unionism in Baltimore and Stamford: Beyond the Politics of Particularism," *Journal of Labor and Society* 4, no. 3 (2004): 59–85; Bruce Nissen, "Political Activism as Part of a Broader Civic Engagement: The Case of SEIU Florida Healthcare Union," *Labor Studies Journal* 35, no. 1 (2010): 51–72; Lowell Turner and Daniel Cornfield, *Labor in the New Urban Battlegrounds: Local Solidarity in a Global Economy* (Ithaca: ILR Press, 2007).

9. Kim Voss and Rachel Sherman, "Breaking the Iron Law of Oligarchy: Union Revitalization in the American Labor Movement," *American Journal of Sociology* 106, no. 2 (2000): 303–349; Dan Clawson and Mary Ann Clawson, "What Has Happened to the U.S. Labor Movement? Union Decline and Renewal," *Annual Review of Sociology* 25, no. 1 (2003): 95–119.

10. Doug McAdam, Sidney Tarrow, and Charles Tilly, *The Dynamics of Contention* (New York: Cambridge University Press, 2001).

11. Nissen, "Political Activism," 51–72.

12. Steven Henry Lopez, *Reorganizing the Rust Belt: An Inside Study of the American Labor Movement* (Berkeley: University of California Press, 2004); Christian Zlolniski, *Janitors, Street Vendors, and Activists: The Lives of Mexican Immigrants in Silicon Valley* (Berkeley: University of California Press, 2006); Roland Zullo, "Shaping Political Preferences through Workplace Mobilization: Unions and the 2000 Election," *Advances in Industrial and Labor Relations* 12 (2003): 173–196.

13. Clive Fullagar, Daniel Gallagher, Michael Gordon, and Paul Clark, "Impact of Early Socialization on Union Commitment and Participation: A Longitudinal Study," *Journal of Applied Psychology* 80, no. 1 (1995): 147–157.

14. Bert Klandermans, "Mobilization and Participation: Social-Psychological Expansions of Resource Mobilization Theory," *American Sociological Review* 49, no. 5 (1984): 583–600; Bert Klandermans and Dirk Oegema, "Potentials, Networks, Motivations, and Barriers: Steps Towards Participation in Social Movements," *American Sociological Review* 52:4 (1987): 519–531.

15. Cynthia Cranford, "'It's Time to Leave Machismo Behind!' Challenging Gender Inequality in an Immigrant Union," *Gender and Society* 21, no. 3 (2007): 409–439.

16. Arlie Russell Hochschild, *The Second Shift: Working Parents and the Revolution at Home* (New York: Viking Press, 1989).

17. Roger Waldinger, Christopher L. Erickson, Ruth Milkman, Daniel J. B. Mitchell, Abel Valenzuela, Kent Wong, and Maurice Zeitlin, "Helots No More: A Case Study of the Justice for Janitors Campaign in Los Angeles," in *Organizing to Win*, ed. Kate Bronfenbrenner, Sheldon Friedman, Richard W. Hurd, Rudolph A. Oswald, and Ronald L. Seeber (Ithaca: ILR Press, 1998), 102–119.

18. Steven Tepper and Yang Gao, "Engaging Art: What Counts?" in *Engaging Art: The Next Great Transformation of America's Cultural Life*, ed. Steven Tepper and Bill Ivey (Abingdon-on-Thames, UK: Routledge, 2008), 17–47.

19. Waldinger, et al., "Helots No More," 102–119.

20. Ruth Milkman, *L.A. Story: Immigrant Workers and the Future of the U.S. Labor Movement* (New York: Russell Sage Foundation, 2006); Waldinger, et al., "Helots No More," 102–119.

21. This research relies on both survey and in-depth interview data. My colleagues at UCLA IDEA (Institute for Democracy Education and Access) and I collected telephone survey data from a simple random sample of the Local 1877 Los Angeles County membership list in 2007. We restricted the sample to parents with coresident school-age children and excluded individuals for whom current telephone information was missing from the union's roster. The survey data contain 378 respondents and include information on union members' demographic backgrounds, work shifts, labor union participation, and involvement in the school of one randomly selected school-age child. To complement survey findings, I conducted in-depth interviews with forty union members. Half of the sample participated in union activities; the other half did not. I asked respondents about their civic participation at different points in time to understand the temporal ordering of their labor union, school, and other forms of civic engagement. In addition to collecting data from members, I obtained additional information on how USWW involves its members in union activities, particularly nighttime workers, through participant observation of union meetings and other activities and through interviews with staff and member leaders. I also used the union's membership database to map out its membership and conducted interviews and participant observations that were focused on USWW efforts to support members' interest in their children's schooling. For more information about the study data and methodology, see Terriquez, "Schools for Democracy."

22. Sidney Verba, Kay Lehman Schlozman, and Henry E. Brady, *Voice and Equality: Civic Voluntarism in American Politics* (Boston: Harvard University Press, 1995).

23. Cranford, "It's Time to Leave Machismo Behind!": 409–439.

24. Fullagar et al., "Impact of Early Socialization on Union Commitment and Participation": 147–157.

25. Klandermans, "Mobilization and Participation": 583–600; Klandermans and Oegema, "Potentials, Networks, Motivations, and Barriers": 519–531.

26. Leslie A. Bunnage, "Social Movement Engagement over the Long Haul: Understanding Activist Retention," *Sociology Compass* 8, no. 4 (2014): 433–45.

27. Lydia Savage, "Geographies of Organizing: Justice for Janitors in Los Angeles," in *Organizing the Landscape: Geographical Perspectives on Labor Unionism*, ed. Andrew Herod (Minneapolis: University of Minnesota Press, 1998).

28. Joseph A. McCartin and Marilyn Sneiderman, "Collective Action and the Common Good: Teachers' Struggles and the Revival of the Strike," in *Strike for the Common*

Good: Fighting for the Future of Public Education, ed. Rebecca Kolins Givan and Amy Schrager Lang (Ann Arbor: University of Michigan Press, 2021), 28–29.

29. Cranford, "It's Time to Leave Machismo Behind!": 409–439.

30. Veronica Terriquez and Sandra Florian, "Socioeconomic Inequalities in the Post-secondary Enrollment, Employment, and Civic Engagement of California's Youth," *Pathways to Postsecondary Success* (UC ACCORD, 2013).

31. Sean F. Reardon, "The Widening Academic Achievement Gap between the Rich and the Poor: New Evidence and Possible Explanations," in *Whither Opportunity? Rising Inequality, Schools, and Children's Life Chances*, ed. Greg J. Duncan and Richard J. Murnane (New York: Russell Sage Foundation, 2011), 91–116.

7

Organizing Fast Food

Opportunities, Challenges, and SEIU

MAITE TAPIA AND TASHLIN LAKHANI

On November 29, 2012, two hundred fast food workers in New York City held a day of protest demanding better pay and the right to form a union. In less than two years, the movement spread rapidly with strikes occurring in over 230 cities, involving thousands of workers in the U.S. and globally, and representing the largest series of job actions in the fast food industry in history. This movement of fast food workers stands out as both a challenge to the traditional model of trade unionism as well as an opportunity toward a new model of organizing and bargaining.

This chapter lays out the overarching challenges faced by SEIU and others in organizing fast food workers in a highly fragmented and franchise-driven industry. We address the following questions: How does a fragmented industry structure affect the traditional model of union organizing? Where do workers get the leverage or power to organize in the low-wage restaurant sector? More broadly, do the strategies and tactics of the fast food movement represent a new, sustainable model of organizing in low-wage, fragmented industries?[1]

Shifting to a Low-Wage Economy: The Fast Food Sector

Decades ago, American companies such as General Electric and U.S. Steel paid their hourly employees more than the median household income. Today, the largest employers are companies that pay the minimum wage. The U.S. fast food industry, a nearly $250 billion industry, is one of the fastest growing sectors in terms of employment as well as one of the lowest paid. So-called "McJobs," or jobs based on "starvation" wages subsidized through public assistance, are becoming increasingly pervasive. A 2013 report showed that due to low earnings, 52% of the fast food workers receive some sort of government benefit, such as health insurance, food stamps, income tax credits, and basic household income assistance, compared to 25% of all workers. Fast food workers rely heavily on public benefit programs to make ends meet, costing nearly $7 billion per year.[2] At the same time, according to a 2014 analysis by the National Employment Law Project (NELP), the greatest employment growth in the U.S. during the 2010–2013 economic recovery occurred in lower-wage industries such as the food services industry.[3]

In 2013 there were 3.8 million fast food workers in the U.S. making up about 3% of the private sector workforce. The large majority of these workers face poor working conditions. The median hourly wage in fast food was then just under $9.00 per hour, with 13% earning the $7.25 federal minimum wage or less, and 70% earning between the federal minimum and $10.10 per hour. The median number of working hours was 30, with nearly half of the fast food workforce working between 20 and 35 hours per week, resulting in median annual earnings of about $11,000.[4] In addition, a 2014 national survey showed that almost 90% of fast food workers were the victim of some sort of wage theft, referring to late or bounced checks, overtime violations, and off-the-clock violations.[5]

Almost 90% of all fast food jobs are front-line occupations with an extremely limited possibility for upward mobility. Managerial, professional, and technical occupations make up only about 2% of jobs in the industry while first-line supervisory positions make up an additional 7%. As a result, workers in low-wage entry-level jobs are unlikely to advance to managerial positions. In addition, fast food workers are even less likely to experience upward mobility through franchise ownership, given the significant capital requirements for opening a restaurant.[6]

Contrary to popular perceptions, the majority of fast food workers are not teenagers or high school dropouts. In fact, fast food jobs represent a primary source of income for many workers with families. For example, a 2013 analysis of Current Population Survey data revealed that 70% of fast food workers are above the age of 20, with more than one-fourth raising at least one child. Among those over the age of 20, almost 85% have attained a high school degree or more and at least one-third has some college education.[7]

Finally, during the 2020–2021 COVID-19 pandemic, food service workers have been amongst some of the most visibly impacted as state stay-at-home orders have forced restaurants to close or adapt to takeout-only service.[8] Even though designated as essential workers, many food service workers lost their job, with an unemployment rate of about 16% in December 2020 and slowly bouncing back to about 12% in March 2021.[9] As a result, some states, such as California, granted two weeks of supplemental paid sick leave to food-sector workers, including fast food workers.[10]

Clearly, there is an unmistakable need to organize fast food workers. Yet many unions have steered away from the fast food sector due to high employee turnover rates (in some cases, over 100%) and its fragmented and franchised industry structure, which poses challenges to traditional modes of organizing and representing workers. As we will discuss, the main union involved in the fast food movement has been the Service Employees International Union (SEIU). Other unions, such as the United Food and Commercial Workers (UFCW), who advocate for grocery, retail, meatpacking, and food processing workers, have so far played a lesser role, mainly showing their support in local campaigns and via social media.[11]

Organizing Low-Wage Fragmented Workplaces

The challenges of organizing low-wage workplaces are not new.[12] However, over the past few decades, unions have faced additional challenges due to the changing nature of industry and ownership structures, which involve an increasing degree of fragmentation or "fissuring" of the employment relationship.[13] The organization of work has shifted from large employers to complex networks of smaller, geographically dispersed business units.[14] Although legally independent, these smaller units operate under the influence, and in some cases direct control, of large lead firms.[15]

The fast food industry is no exception. It is the most highly franchised industry in the United States with over 150,000 establishments and 3 million employees working in franchise businesses.[16] The franchise business model allows individuals to be in business "for themselves, but not by themselves." In exchange for an upfront lump sum and ongoing royalties, companies (franchisors) provide individual entrepreneurs (franchisees) with the right to sell their product or service using their brand name and established business system. The latter includes standardized operating procedures and ongoing guidance regarding menus, décor, advertising, customer interactions, and the like. The franchisee, however, is responsible for day-to-day operations, including the hiring and management of employees. Although franchisors often provide franchisees with assistance in the training of employees, franchisees tend to have much more control over the hiring, firing, pay, and other conditions of employment in their operations.[17] One reason for greater franchisee latitude in the area of employment practices appears to be franchisor fears over direct or indirect ("vicarious") liability for franchisee employees. Active control and/or monitoring of employment relationships in franchised operations could subject franchisors to liabilities for the actions of franchisees toward their employees or of franchisee employees toward customers. As a result, franchisors are often advised by attorneys and trade organizations to "assign responsibility for employment practice issues to the franchisee."[18]

This poses significant challenges to traditional modes of union organizing. Although individuals work for ostensibly identical establishments—for example, there are an estimated 700,000 workers in 14,000 McDonald's restaurants across the U.S.—they often have different employers and working conditions. Fast food corporations directly employ only a small fraction of the individuals working under their brand name in company-owned and operated restaurants, while the remaining workers are employed by individual franchisees. As a result, unions looking to organize in fast food restaurants would, under the National Labor Relations Act (NLRA), have to do so on a unit-by-unit basis. This not only requires substantial resources, but also results in smaller bargaining units due to the small size of fast food restaurants[19] and, in turn, lower bargaining power. Previously successful strategies used by unions in other industries, such as negotiating for employer neutrality, are also out of the question since franchisors do not typically involve themselves in the labor relations matters of their franchisees (the rare exceptions to this are discussed later). As history shows, organizing drives in the fast food sector in the U.S. have been virtually nonexistent, although there have been examples of very small, localized strikes on a restaurant-per-restaurant basis.[20] In other words, pursuing traditional models of organizing has been proven both highly unlikely and undesirable.

The challenges of organizing workers in this industry are reflected in low union density rates—less than 2% of all restaurant and food service employees in the U.S. are currently unionized, most of whom work in establishments within larger organizations such as hotels, airports, and stadiums.[21] Nevertheless, fast food workers have recently engaged in innovative actions, demanding better working conditions from their employers. Where are these workers getting the power or leverage to organize, and what strategies and tactics are they using to overcome the obstacles of a highly fragmented industry structure?

Where Lays the Power of Fast Food Workers?

In the literature, two main types of worker power have been described: structural and associational.[22] Workers can exert structural power depending on their location in the economic system or workers' scarce skills. A classic example is the 1936 Flint sit-down strike where workers were able to push through their demands as they occupied a key node in the supply chain system of General Motors. More recently, subcontracted warehouse workers at distribution centers of big retailers such as Walmart have attempted to use structural power to further their interests by striking and shutting down operations that represent an important link in the company's highly efficient, "just-in-time" global supply chain. Often, however, workers do not find themselves in these positions. In these cases, associational power can compensate for weaker levels of structural power. Participation in collective associations such as trade unions or other worker organizations can give workers effective associational power to demand better working conditions.

Unlike the Flint GM workers or the Walmart warehouse workers, front-line fast food workers lack significant structural power. On the contrary, these workers are easily replaceable, considered low-skilled, and as a result, unlikely to be a threat to the employer. In addition, given their extremely low unionization rate, fast food workers lack the associational power necessary to collectively demand or negotiate better working conditions. Given their extremely weak structural and associational power, where do these workers get the leverage to stand up and fight for their demands? Moreover, given the fragmented industry structure and the many franchisees, who should the workers fight against: the franchisees themselves or the big corporations behind them?

In line with Jennifer Chun's work, we argue that fast food workers are leveraging "symbolic" power in an attempt to rebuild associational power by winning public recognition and legitimacy for their struggles.[23] By engaging in so-called "classification struggles," fast food workers are attempting to redefine the employment relationship in the eyes of the public rather than how it is narrowly defined by law. In other words, it is about convincing or demonstrating to the broader public who the employer is (or should be) and what the working conditions are in order to ultimately put political pressure on lawmakers and the employers themselves to implement changes. They manage to do this by engaging in public demonstrations, shifting the issues from narrow workplace disputes to broad themes regarding dignity and justice for all workers. In the case of franchising, this also entails putting pressure on the direct employers, the franchisees, and the larger, more visible brands they represent. According to Chun, this form of symbolic power, expressed through public dramas, can be considered an important third type of power, resulting in critical organizing strategies for the most vulnerable workers. In line with this, Stephen Lerner, SEIU strategist and organizer, noted: "The key thing is not letting how workers organize be defined by the legal regime which has not only failed to protect workers but also was constructed for a very different kind of workplace."[24] And as one of our interviewees mentioned, "I don't think anyone expects folks being able to wait for those labor boards to allow all these workers to organize . . . we'd be waiting forever if we went by the rules of the labor law right now."[25]

Significant structural changes have occurred in the world of work and employment, making organizing under traditional labor laws difficult at best. As a consequence, in an era of increasingly fragmented employment relations due to the proliferation of multilayer contracting arrangements such as franchising, subcontracting, and offshoring, many worker organizations have come to realize that new models for organizing and representing workers are necessary. As we show in this chapter, leveraging symbolic power through public dramas can be considered one innovative form of organizing.

The Fast Food Campaign: Origins, Tactics, and the Role of SEIU

Before the fast food campaign officially went public with its first strike in November 2012, months of organizing took place on the ground. In New York City, the community-based organization New York Communities for Change (NYCC)—formerly an ACORN chapter[26]—employed organizers across the five boroughs to gather contact information, speak with workers from the fast food industry through house and phone meetings, and identify leaders among the workforce.[27] The organization had forty to fifty organizers on the ground responsible for collecting petitions and gathering vast amounts of data. Workers in about 400 stores were contacted in all five boroughs. Initially, organizers visited Starbucks, Subways, and Dunkin Donuts locations as well, but eventually, these were dropped due to different working conditions (organizers mentioned that Starbucks employees, for example, enjoyed better working conditions relative to the other establishments) as well as the low employee count in family-run franchises such as Subway and Dunkin' Donuts.[28] While the initial conversations were around affordable housing and how that relates to low wages, the organizers soon delved into working conditions and, ultimately, a conversation about unionization. During the months before the first public action, the main goal was thus to identify the key issues, empower and organize workers around those issues, and build momentum.

It is important to mention that during this time, different organizing initiatives and experiments were also taking place across the country led by different unions and community organizations trying to organize bank tellers, pizza parlors, retail workers, and baristas among others. Perhaps the most ambitious of these efforts was SEIU's Fight for a Fair Economy, launched in January 2011. According to some of our interviewees, the fast food campaign originated out of SEIU's Fight for a Fair Economy. The latter was launched recently in which SEIU targets cities across the nation to build a grassroots movement, working closely together with local activists and community groups. The goal is to find out what the big issues are facing low-income families in different locations and to organize, mobilize, and educate workers around those issues. For example, one city would focus on foreclosures while in another city the emphasis would be on raising wages. Although the fast food campaign can be considered within the same mindset of Fight for a Fair Economy's broader framework, there is no direct link between the staff of Fight for a Fair Economy and the fast food campaign.

According to David Rolf, International Vice President of SEIU, the fast food campaign took off due to synergies across organizations working on similar issues: "because of the Fair Economy work, the existing coalition work, etcetera, these were ideas that came together and eventually found some synergy . . . there were a number of experiments and the one that clicked was in New York with a partnership between NYCC and the Fair Economy campaign." The fast food industry was targeted as it is a large industry in NYC and across the country in which the jobs cannot be offshored;[29] the industry consists of a large supply of minimum wage workers, and these workers are among the least organized due to high turnover rates and widespread franchising.[30] In addition, organizing fast food workers presented an opportunity to bring a sea change, reducing incoming inequality and providing vast amounts of people with a living wage.

Accordingly, a number of organizations became involved in the fast food movement. The NYCC hired organizers from the Working Families Party (WFP), a (minor) progressive grassroots political party with active chapters in about 11 states including New York, New Jersey, Ohio, and Wisconsin. Their cooperation was natural because these two organizations share an office in Brooklyn, and there is a strong coordination mechanism at play between them with the WFP helping to leverage political support for the NYCC and the NYCC raising community support for WFP campaigns. Yet to launch an effective fast food workers' movement, they required the assistance of SEIU, which became one of the most important players throughout the different phases of the campaign. According to some of the NYCC organizers, the day-to-day issues were run by the NYCC, but SEIU closely monitored the collected data, oversaw operations, and—together with the executive team at the NYCC—provided the overall direction for the campaign. Although not involved in the day-to-day operations, SEIU has a strong coordination role and also provides critical financial and logistics support.[31] The union, for example, will fly in organizers and workers from all over the country during strike days and train them to coordinate strikes later on in their city of origin.

The campaign, and the role of SEIU in particular, has been criticized from the Right as well as the Left. The Center for Union Facts—a right-wing anti-union organization—and its founder Richard Berman argue SEIU is the driving force behind this "fake" grassroots movement, but the union is hiding behind "a tangled web of front groups" or worker organizing committees. In addition, they argue SEIU has been funneling over $15 million to worker organizing committees to support the fast food campaign and that most people on strike are paid organizers rather than actual employees.[32] From the Left, similar critiques have been made. Some pro-labor media outlets such as *In These Times* and *Labor Notes* have asked whether Fight for $15 is an actual workers' movement or a "march on the media." In addition, the sustainability of the campaign has been questioned. According to these sources, it is not clear what SEIU's endgame is and what would happen to the workers if SEIU's leadership decides to stop funding the campaign.[33] Others, however, such as Steven Greenhouse—a labor journalist up until 2014 working for the *New York Times*—have rebuked these criticisms and have emphasized the potential for workers' mobilization and collective action.[34]

Despite these criticisms, the campaign used a variety of innovative strategic actions, including geographically coordinated short strikes, the use of a broad injustice framework, non-majority organizing on job sites, and the filing of class-action suits. Rather than following a traditional model of organizing, these workers and organizers were inspired by the Occupy movement as well as the taxi, carwash, and retail workers' organizing waves taking place in New York City and other cities across the U.S.[35] The main strategy has been to generate a grassroots movement while simultaneously pushing through the political goal of raising the minimum wage at a city, state, or federal level. This campaign, on the heels of the Occupy movement, the Walmart campaign, and others, has generated crucial public support and might be considered a turning point in placing attention on the plight of low-wage workers.[36] Forming labor-community partnerships and holding conversations not just in workplaces or in union halls, but also in front of the broader public about improving working conditions, raises again the debate around economic inequality and puts low-wage workers back on the map. In line with Chun, the campaign found that winning public recognition and legitimacy for workers' struggles through public demonstrations are critical when the traditional forms of power have been eroded.

The first strike took place on November 29, 2012, in NYC, with approximately two hundred workers at more than twenty restaurants walking out on strike that day. The workers put forward two basic demands: $15/hour and unionization without retaliation.[37] While ministers and city council members accompanied many workers when they returned to work the next day, Shalonda Montgomery, one of the workers who worked at a Wendy's downtown Brooklyn, was fired for striking. Within hours, however, mass pickets emerged outside the restaurant and forced management to rehire her. A second action took place on April 4, 2013, coinciding with Martin Luther King Jr.'s assassination 45 years earlier. The strike was framed as a broader civil rights fight to win dignity and a living wage, signaled by the symbolic importance of this date. Protestors held signs using the slogan "I AM A MAN" or "I AM A WOMAN" echoing the 1968 Memphis sanitation workers' strike that MLK Jr. supported just before he was assassinated. Meanwhile, there were local strikes in St Louis, May 8; Detroit, May 10; Milwaukee, May 15; and Seattle, May 30.[38] A third large action was held on July 29, 2013, with about 500 workers in sixty restaurants in Manhattan, as well as workers in Chicago, Detroit, St. Louis, Milwaukee, Kansas City, and Flint walking off the job. On August 29, 2013—the day after the 50th anniversary of the March on Washington for Jobs and Freedom[39]—another strike was coordinated, spreading and expanding to a national scale, involving at least sixty cities across the U.S. On December 5, 2013, the nationwide protests doubled as they took place in over one hundred cities across the country, from the East to the West coast and from the North to the deep South. This demonstration followed one week after Walmart workers walked out from at least 1,500 stores across the country on the day after Thanksgiving, "Black Friday," one of the busiest shopping days in the U.S.

On May 15th, 2014, a shift in scale occurred as the one-day strike went global, including participation in 150 U.S. cities as well as across the globe from Tokyo to London to Casablanca, and Auckland to Venice. Representatives of the global union federation IUF (International Union of Food, Agricultural, Hotel, Restaurant, Catering, Tobacco and Allied Workers' Associations), representing 12 million workers in 126 countries, and union leaders from more than two dozen countries met in NYC beforehand to prepare for this global day of solidarity for fast food workers. According to Ron Oswald, the then general secretary of the IUF, the fast food workers had inspired employees across the global industry to join them "in a fight for higher pay and better rights on the job."[40] On May 22nd, 2014, nearly 2,000 protesters were brought in by over thirty buses to hold a rally at McDonald's annual shareholder meeting in Oak Brook, Illinois. Among the protesters were hundreds of employees from fast food companies as well as fifty clergy members and community activists, holding these signs: "We Are Worth More" and "My Union My Voice." Notably, the president of SEIU, Mary Kay Henry, and officials from the civil rights organization NAACP joined the picketers as well. They were met by police in riot gear and when the demonstrators tried to cross the barricades, over 100 people, including Henry, were arrested. On September 4, 2014, the next one-day strike took place in over 150 cities across the U.S. Under guidance of SEIU, the fast food workers were joined this time by home care workers, broadening the base of the movement. This time, nearly 500 people were arrested for civil disobedience. On December 4, 2014, fast food workers in approximately 190 cities went on strike, this time joined not only by home care workers but by airport workers, federal contract workers, and retail employees of dollar and convenience stores as well. On April 15, 2015 (a date chosen because it corresponds to the movement's wage demand—for $15 on 4/15—as well as U.S. tax day), the biggest demonstration so far took place across the U.S., involving at least 60,000 workers in over 220 cities. At the time it was considered the largest protest by low-wage workers in U.S. history.[41] Perhaps more importantly, it has raised discussion about the potential for a new social movement wave as the Fight for $15 campaign becomes a broad coalition of community, labor, racial, and environmental justice groups (including groups such as #BlackLivesMatter and 350.org) demanding and fighting for a more just future for all low-wage workers. On May Day 2015, the Fight for $15 joined thousands of people that rallied across the U.S. to fight against racism and police brutality in the wake of the police killing of Freddie Gray in Baltimore. These organized strikes and walkouts for economic and racial justice have continued over the past years with most recently strikes in twenty cities against McDonald's failure to protect its employees during the COVID-19 pandemic.[42]

The main goal of these short-term, geographically coordinated strikes has been to raise awareness among the broader public. Most of these strikes have been based on a strategy of minority-unionism rather than waiting to mobilize or make demands until it has been shown that the majority of workers support these actions. These one-day strikes can become transformative moments for both the workers who participate and their colleagues who were previously skeptical about the campaign, with each strike escalating in the number of workers involved. During these strikes, the organizers and workers often focus on the big corporations behind the franchisees in an effort to "name and shame" the brand. For example, videos and pictures circulate of workers cleaning the shoes of Ronald McDonald, exposing the extreme contradiction between the wealth behind the fast food corporations and the poor working conditions of its own employees. By staging these highly visible demonstrations, workers attempt to place (political) pressure on the franchisor—even though not legally their direct employer—as well as lawmakers to improve working conditions.

Alongside strikes and public demonstrations, workers have simultaneously pursued legal action against large companies and their individual franchisees. For example, McDonald's settled a class-action lawsuit over wages and working conditions with 800 workers at five franchisee establishments in San Francisco in 2016.[43] Likewise, McDonald's faced a class-action lawsuit against corporate-run locations in California over wages and working conditions and agreed to a $29 million settlement in 2019.[44] In 2016, fifteen McDonald's workers filed sexual harassment complaints against the franchise and detailed their experiences in a video released by Fight for $15. In November 2019, this culminated in Michigan McDonald's workers filing a class action lawsuit alleging that the company has a systemic sexual harassment problem.[45] And a final example, in May 2020, McDonald's workers filed a class-action lawsuit over Coronavirus precautions.[46] In all of these cases, McDonald's was targeted both as an employer in its own company-operated units, as well as a "joint" or indirect employer in franchisee-operated units, a strategy that has been derailed during the Trump administration but that could become a viable option again during the Biden administration.[47]

Evidently, the fast food campaign is not about winning an NLRB election, but about building a broad consensus, generating public support, and changing public perceptions regarding low-wage workers and the employment relationship. Furthermore, the workers are building political power and pushing through debates on raising the minimum wage at the city, state, and federal levels. Workers are thus utilizing a variety of levers to put pressure on their fragmented employers: media attention, legal and political pressure, international solidarity, and local fights in the workplace.

Finally, regarding SEIU's role, given the highly publicized and politicized nature of the fast food campaign, information on long-term strategies are understandably not available. While it is clear that big unions such as SEIU are a key player in the fast food strikes, as described earlier, further details about their precise role remain unknown. These strikes have been portrayed in the media to be led by different actors such as "Fight for $15," "Low Pay is not OK," or "Fast Food Forward." From our brief conversations with SEIU representatives, we know SEIU provides substantial funding for the campaign as well as research, legal, and logistics support. This includes, for example, training community organizers on the ground and assisting with the filing of unfair labor practice complaints in response to employer retaliation for worker participation in strike activity and collective action.

Although the campaign began with NYCC in New York City, it has quickly spread across cities and has been described by SEIU representatives as a decentralized workers' movement rather than a top-down operation. Coordination is occurring across organizations and cities, but there is widespread experimentation in both the strategies and tactics of the movement from one location to another. Nevertheless, SEIU has clearly played a strong role in orchestrating the fast food campaign nationally. As one of SEIU officers told us "we are not looking for silver bullets . . . but rather planting a thousand flowers and harvesting the best blooms." This is the beginning of a long, iterative process, based on trial and error. What works in one state or city may not work in another, but in some cases what works in one place can be leveraged in others.

Lessons from the Past?

As other chapters in this book clearly demonstrate, SEIU has been at the forefront of trying to organize low-wage workers such as janitors and home healthcare workers. There seems to be important parallels between these workers and the fast food workers and as a result, these other campaigns may contain some important lessons for the fast food movement. These workers are part of a growing service industry, characterized by shifting employment patterns and an increasing presence of migrant workers. The existing framework of U.S. labor law does not translate well to these new forms of business and therefore makes it difficult to organize using traditional NLRB organizing drives. Employment increasingly takes place in small businesses, with a high incidence of turnover as well as part-time and temporary work. Due to the small size of many workplaces, workers are often isolated from each other, creating another barrier to successful organizing. On the other hand, most of these jobs cannot be offshored but must be done where the customers are. Mobilizing workers and community groups, engaging them in public actions and campaigns, trying to build a communitywide movement, and developing rank-and-file leadership have been critical.[48] In the case of the Justice for Janitors campaign, for example, the union put pressure on both the contractors and owners of buildings to achieve union recognition via card check within metropolitan areas.[49] Justice for Janitors used different tactics at once, such as corporate campaigns targeting building owners that are more vulnerable to public opinion, mobilizing and educating janitors, filing every unfair labor practice complaint ("guerilla-style"), maximizing media coverage, as well as mounting political pressure. In the case of the home healthcare workers, rather than directly targeting the many small employers, the union tried to push through legislation and redefined who the employer was.

Marches were organized on state capitols, the workers and union lobbied representatives and tried to elect legislators and governors that would improve the working conditions of those workers, and broad-based coalitions were formed with senior citizens and other recipients of home health aides—with the customers themselves.[50] In essence, a type of state-by-state policy advocacy was used to raise the labor standards for these workers across the industry. While there are some differences across these cases—for example, the home healthcare workers do not often engage in strikes as it might directly affect the people they care for, and the justice for janitors case strived for card check recognition, not in line with the current tactics of the fast food workers—important parallels come to the forefront in terms of coalition building and redefining the employment relationship that might bring lessons to the current fast food movement. Indeed, in each of these industries, workers are faced with complex industry and ownership arrangements such as subcontracting and franchising as well as questions about the responsibilities of direct and indirect employers.

Arguably, other campaigns or broader movements have also been critical in pushing forward the fast food campaign. The Occupy movement is often cited as a recent pivotal moment in the U.S. that was really able to shape the debate around income inequality on a national level. The fast food movement to a certain extent was built on Occupy by putting forward two very clear and tangible demands: $15 per hour and unionization without retaliation. According to some commentators, having a straightforward agenda is one way in which the fast food workers go beyond the "Occupiers."[51] The "OURWalmart" campaign, which was launched in 2011, and the campaign to organize carwash workers in Los Angeles and other settings helped create the sense of an emerging broad-based movement of low-wage workers fighting for justice.[52] These campaigns did not evolve in their own silos but instead created synergies in which each drew energy from the others.[53]

Finally, there may be important lessons for the fast food movement from previous worker campaigns involving franchisees and franchisors. Although franchisors typically take a hands-off approach to franchisee labor relations and employment practices due to concerns over legal liability, there is some historical and anecdotal evidence to suggest that franchisors can and do get involved when such matters directly affect their brand. For example, Felstead details how the Coca-Cola Company negotiated with the IUF in Guatemala after the global federation of trade unions responded to a franchised bottler's anti-union campaign by orchestrating international work stoppages and consumer boycotts.[54] In a more recent example, in March of 2013, McDonald's removed a franchisee in Pennsylvania for alleged exploitation of foreign student guest workers after workers engaged in public protests publicizing poor working conditions and labor violations.[55] Similarly, recent allegations over foreign worker practices in franchised Canadian operations have prompted McDonald's to investigate restaurants that employ temporary foreign workers.[56] These cases suggest that public demonstrations and corporate campaigns that threaten a franchisor's brand reputation (arguably, its most valuable asset) can be an effective strategy for dealing with a highly fragmented industry structure.

Potential Impact and Future Challenges

Over the past three decades, there has been an increasing degree of fragmentation or "fissuring" of the employment relationship.[57] With the fast food industry dominated by franchisees, workers are trying to redefine the employment relationship by holding the larger parent corporations accountable for their working conditions rather than targeting individual franchisees. They argue that in the same ways the corporate offices dictate standards for food, uniforms, or purchase agreements, they could also dictate working conditions and pay.

Since November 2012, fast food workers have engaged in broad struggles over justice and fairness, involving trade unions and community organizations in over two hundred cities in the U.S. as well as abroad. Arguably, building on the Occupy movement, they have raised awareness regarding the persisting economic inequality in the U.S. (and globally) as well as the need to raise the minimum wage. Some commentators have indeed argued that the fast food movement has been instrumental to raising Seattle's minimum wage to $15/hour, shifting the bargaining efforts from the workplace level to Seattle's Municipal Hall. As a result, over 100,000 workers in Seattle will receive a legally enforceable 65% raise, quite unheard of when compared to traditional firm-level collective bargaining agreements.

While it is fair to say the Fight for $15 movement has not led to any significant increase in unionization—the franchise structure and joint-employer regulations being some of the main reasons—most gains have been made in building a multiracial grassroots labor movement that pushes for minimum wage increases across the country.

At the moment of writing, many cities and states across the U.S. are engaged in minimum wage debates. In 2015 in New York State, for example, then Governor Cuomo authorized a Fast Food Wage Board to investigate the fast food industry and make recommendations to increase the minimum wage. The Wage Board's recommendation to increase the minimum wage to $15/hour for fast food workers went into effect for NYC in December 2018 and for all fast food workers in New York State in July 2021. At the federal level under the Biden administration, raising the minimum wage to $15 per hour by 2025 is back on the table. Groups such as the fast food movement can be credited for helping to put this issue on the agenda.

A 2018 report estimates that since 2012, 22 million low-wage workers have won about $68 billion in annual raises sparked by the Fight for $15 movement. The majority of these raises come from $15 minimum wage laws that Fight for $15 won in California, New York, Massachusetts, Flagstaff, Los Angeles, San Jose, San Francisco, the District of Columbia, Montgomery County, the Twin Cities, Seattle, and SeaTac.[58] Since then, $15 minimum wage laws have been enacted as well in Connecticut, Illinois, Maryland, and New Jersey.[59] In other words, while the fast food strikers are demanding a higher wage and fighting for unionization without retaliation from their employers, their demands extend well beyond the workplace. Many of the discussions currently held in city halls across the country, or at the state or even federal level, revolve around raising the minimum wage.[60] According to Jonathan Westin, Director of NYCC, "we definitely changed the conversation in this country where the President is talking about a $10 an hour minimum wage . . . we went out and our first demand was $15 an hour . . . which was pretty groundbreaking and earth shattering to people . . . but has now become something that people actually believe that people deserve, and I think that's . . . one of the important things about how we choose our tactics and what our demands are because it's not just about trying to win this incremental dollar raise."[61]

Some might argue that the demands of the fast food movement are too narrow and do not allow for a broad enough platform to build alliances. Certain opportunities, such as forming a coalition with the growing U.S. food movement, might be missed. Indeed, for coalitions to be successful there is a need for mutual interest. If the issues of the fast food workers are considered too narrow and only pertain to wages and unionization—as opposed to, for example, sustainable food sources—there could be a missed opportunity for an even broader movement, involving big, national advocacy groups, such as Slow Food USA and Food Democracy Now, the many local chapters and organizations, or the more worker-based organizations, such as the Restaurant Opportunities Center (ROC).[62]

On the other hand, alliances were formed between fast food strikers, Walmart strikers, and carwasheros, for example, under the New York umbrella campaign New York Workers Raising. This movement has also been about more than economic justice and has connected economic justice to racial justice with the Fight for $15 Movement fighting in alliance with the Black Lives Matter movement and the #MeToo movement.[63] Furthermore, in 2017, New York City passed the Fast-Food Worker Empowerment Act, requiring fast food employers to create and administer a payroll deduction scheme under which employees could contribute a portion of their wages to a nonprofit organization that can advocate on their behalf. As a result, with at least 1,200 New York fast food workers contributing, Fast Food Justice was launched. While this nonprofit organization (or worker center) cannot collectively bargain with employers, it provides advocacy and education, aiming to build change not just in the workplace but focusing on affordable housing, immigration reform, better police-community relations and improvements to New York's subway system.[64] Even though it is not a union, Fast Food Justice could help further fund the movement, increase worker participation over the long term, and focus on demands outside the workplace.

In sum, in this climate of union membership decline, the labor movement has often been criticized for using the same strategies and expecting different results. Discovering new models of organizing or experimenting with innovative, groundbreaking strategies does not occur that often or automatically. Unions must balance between short-term, pragmatic strategies, and serving their existing members on the one hand, and long-term, transformative organizing strategies on the other hand. One historical example of a paradigm shift within the labor movement occurred when the unions shifted from craft to industrial unionism in the 1930s. Today, however, the need for a new model (or new models) is not only desirable but also necessary. However, the critical challenge for unions and other worker organizations will be to sustain these models over time. For example, although there appears to be some recent efforts by SEIU locals to organize fast food workers into formal unions in large cities like Manhattan, some have suggested SEIU's support for the Fight for $15 campaign has been decreasing over time, at least financially.[65] This may prove particularly challenging for the movement if SEIU cuts resources where it is needed most—local organizing committees responsible for worker outreach.[66]

SEIU is a union that has been at the forefront of innovative worker organizing. As the union represents the growing sector of low-wage workers, especially in the service industry, they have been challenged to break through traditional ways of organizing workers, build alliances with other organizations—such as community or migrant associations—and engage in experimental strategies and tactics to fight for better living and working conditions. In addition to the groundbreaking work of SEIU, during the 2014 AFL-CIO convention, for example, the umbrella organization proposed a significant shift in its strategy as the federation is opening up its ranks for outside groups—nonmembers—to join, such as environmental groups, migrant associations, or community organizations in an effort to build strong community-coalitions or networks and reestablish itself as a movement for a more diverse working class. Nevertheless, it remains a challenge to find scalable, (self-) sustainable models of organizing and representing traditionally unorganized low-wage workers. The initial fights, strikes, and demonstrations of the fast food workers may be the foundation for a new, groundbreaking paradigm. Workers are involved in collective action and mobilization across the country, building symbolic power to redefine the scope of the employment relationship and to restore justice and dignity for the working and middle class.

Notes

The authors gratefully acknowledge funding support from the Labor Research and Action Network (LRAN) New Scholars Research Grant Fund and the Labor and Employment Relations Association (LERA) Susan C. Eaton Scholar-Practitioner Memorial Fund.

1. This chapter is based on interviews with participants and observers of the fast food movement. We interviewed SEIU representatives, community organizers from New York Communities for Change (NYCC), and people from the Working Families Party. In addition, our analysis draws on news and social media reports.

2. Sylvia Allegretto, Marc Doussard, Dave Graham-Squire, Ken Jacobs, Dan Thompson, and Jeremy Thompson, "Fast Food, Poverty Wages: The Public Cost of Low-Wage Jobs in the Fast-Food Industry," University of California, Berkeley, Center for Labor Research and Education and the University of Illinois at Urbana-Champaign Department of Urban & Regional Planning, October 15, 2013, http://laborcenter.berkeley.edu/pdf/2013/fast_food_poverty_wages.pdf.

3. National Employment Law Project, "The Low-Wage Recovery: Industry Employment and Wages Four Years into the Recovery," Data Brief, https://www.nelp.org/wp-content/uploads/2015/03/PR-NELP-Low-Wage-Recovery-Report-Release-4-28-2014.pdf.

4. National Employment Law Project, "Going Nowhere Fast: Limited Occupational Mobility in the Fast Food Industry," Data Brief, 2013, https://www.nelp.org/publication/going-nowhere-fast-limited-occupational-mobility-in-the-fast-food-industry/; John Schmitt and Janelle Jones, "Slow Progress for Fast Food Workers," Center for Economic and Policy Research, 2013, https://cepr.net/documents/publications/fast-food-workers-2013-08.pdf.

5. Hart Research, Memorandum re: Key Findings for Survey of Fast Food Workers, April 1, 2014, ttps://big.assets.huffingtonpost.com/NationalWageTheftPollMemo.pdf.

6. National Employment Law Project, "Going Nowhere Fast."

7. Schmitt and Jones, "Slow Progress for Fast Food Workers." See also, Ester Reiter, *Making Fast Food: Out of the Frying Pan and into the Fryer* (Montreal: McGill/Queen's University Press, 1993).

8. Pew Research Center. 2020, https://www.pewresearch.org/fact-tank/2020/03/27/young-workers-likely-to-be-hard-hit-as-covid-19-strikes-a-blow-to-restaurants-and-other-service-sector-jobs/.

9. Bureau of Labor Statistics, 2021. https://www.bls.gov/iag/tgs/iag722.htm#workforce. At the same time, before COVID-19, the Bureau of Labor Statistics projected food and beverage service-related work to grow 7 percent or about 1 million jobs between 2019 and 2029, which is much faster than average, https://www.bls.gov/ooh/food-preparation-and-serving/home.htm.

10. Executive Order by Governor Newsome. This order was meant to fill the gap by federal relief that provided similar paid leave benefits for employers with fewer than 500 workers, https://www.gov.ca.gov/2020/04/16/governor-newsom-announces-paid-sick-leave-benefits-for-food-sector-workers-impacted-by-covid-19-additional-protections-for-consumers/.

11. SEIU is the driving force behind the fast food campaign, while the UFCW had been supporting the "OUR Walmart" campaign.

12. See, for example, Kate Bronfenbrenner and Tom Juravich, "It Takes More than House Calls: Organizing to Win with a Comprehensive Union-Building Strategy," in *Organizing to Win: New Research on Union Strategies*, eds. Kate Bronfenbrenner, S. Friedman, Richard Hurd, R. Oswald, and R. Seeber (Ithaca: Cornell University Press, 1988), 18–36; Ruth Milkman and Ed Ott, eds. *New Labor in New York: Precarious Workers and the Future of the Labor Movement* (Ithaca: Cornell University Press, 2014).

13. David Weil, "Enforcing Labor Standards in Fissured Workplaces: The US Experience," *The Economic and Labor Relations Review* 22, no. 2 (2011): 33–54.

14. Lydia Savage, "Geographies of Organizing: Justice for Janitors in Los Angeles," in *Organizing the Landscape: Geographical Perspectives on Labor Unionism*, ed. Andrew Herod (Minneapolis: University of Minnesota Press, 1998), 225–252.

15. Alan Felstead, *The Corporate Paradox: Power and Control in the Business Franchise* (Routledge: London, 1993).

16. International Franchise Association, "Economic Outlook for Franchising," 2013, https://www.franchisetimes.com/February-2013/Economic-Forecast/.

17. Felstead, *The Corporate Paradox*; Tony Royle, *Working for McDonald's in Europe: The Unequal Struggle* (New York: Routledge, 2000); Tashlin Lakhani, *Our Business, Your Employees: The Management of Human Resource Systems in Franchise Businesses*, Working Paper, 2013.

18. See, for example, Dominick Bratti, "Employment Issues: What Franchisees Should Expect from Franchisors," June 2008, http://www.mondaq.com/unitedstates/discrimination-disability-sexual-harassment/62274/employment-issues-what-franchisees-should-expect-from-franchisors.

19. This can range from 10 employees in smaller restaurants like Subway to 50 employees at a McDonald's restaurant.

20. In addition, some small organizing efforts have been taking place since the mid-2000s at coffee chains such as Starbucks and sandwich shops such as Jimmy John's, supported by the Industrial Workers of the World (IWW), http://www.jimmyjohnsworkers.org/. In December 2021, however, Starbucks baristas in Buffalo, New York, have been the first to unionize a company-owned Starbucks. This win in Buffalo has kicked off organizing efforts by Starbucks baristas across the country. At least 130 stores across 24 states have filed to unionize (https://www.labornotes.org/2022/02/buffalo-baristas-touch-starbucks-organizing-wave; https://www.npr.org/2022/03/09/1085583068/three-more-starbucks-locations-in-buffalo-area-vote-to-unionize). See also Royle, *Working for McDonald's in Europe, 85–88.* On early fast food organizing, see Keith Kelleher, "How Decades of Fast Food Worker Organizing Led to 'The Fight for 15'," *Huffington Post*, October 16, 2017, https://www.huffpost.com/entry/how-decades-of-fast-food-worker-organizing-lead-to_b_59dfd015e4b02e99c58354f6. For a history of organizing fast food workers in Canada, with a focus on McDonald's, see Jeremy Milloy, "Learning on the Job: The 1988 Squamish McDonald's Campaign and New Possibilities for Fast Food Workers." *Left History* 16, no. 1 (2012): 55–89.

21. Barry Hirsch and David Macpherson, Union Membership and Coverage Database from the CPS, http://www.unionstats.com/.

22. Erik Olin Wright, "Working-Class Power, Capitalist-Class, Interests, and Class Compromise," *American Journal of Sociology* 105, no. 4 (2000): 957–1002; Beverly Silver, *Forces of Labor: Workers' Movements and Globalization since 1870* (Cambridge: Cambridge University Press, 2003).

23. Jennifer J. Chun, *Organizing at the Margins: The Symbolic Politics of Labor in South Korea and the United States* (Ithaca: Cornell University Press, 2009).

24. Sarah Jaffe, "McJobs Should Pay, Too: Inside Fast-Food Workers' Historic Protest for Living Wages," *The Atlantic*, November 29, 2012, https://www.theatlantic.com/business/archive/2012/11/mcjobs-should-pay-too-inside-fast-food-workers-historic-protest-for-living-wages/265714/.

25. Authors' interview with an SEIU organizer, January 2014.

26. The Association of Community Organizations for Reform Now (ACORN) was a well-known national network of community organizations that disbanded and closed many of its chapters due to a nationwide controversy in which right-wing activists used hidden cameras to disclose fraudulent activities. On its history, see John Atlas, *Seeds of Change: The Story of Acorn, America's Most Controversial Antipoverty Community Organizing Group* (Nashville: Vanderbilt University Press, 2010).

27. Similar actions were taken in Chicago by the independent union "Fight for 15."

28. Although Starbucks appears to have relatively better working conditions than some fast food outlets, they have recently faced backlash for some of their work practices such as pay and scheduling. Importantly, in December 2021, Starbocks

baristas in Buffalo, New York, won a union election at a company-owned shop. Up until then, Starbucks remained vehemently union-free. This historic victory has ignited unionization efforts across the country. At the moment of this writing, Starbucks workers have won union elections at 135 stores since December 2021. Moreover, they are joining Workers United, an affiliate of SEIU (see https://thehill.com/blogs/congress-blog/labor/590090-will-the-starbucks-union-victories-light-a-fuse-of-organizing; https://www.nytimes.com/2022/03/09/business/economy/starbucks-union-vote-buffalo.html).

29. While these jobs cannot be offshored in the traditional sense, they may be filled by immigrant workers as one way to keep labor standards and wages down. French anthropologist Emmanuel Terray called this "*delocalization sur place*" or domestic outsourcing. Emmanuel Terray, "Le Travail des Etrangers en Situation Irrégulière ou la Délocalisation sur Place" in *Sans-Papiers: l'Archaïsme Fatal*, eds. E. Balibar, J. Costa-Lascoux, M. Chemillier-Gendreau, and E. Terray (Paris: La Découverte, 1999), 9–34.

30. There are an estimated 180,000 fast food workers in the state of New York, with more than one-third (over 60,000 individuals) working in New York City. Patrick McGeehan, "Board Hears Support for Raising Fast Food Workers Minimum Wage," *New York Times*, June 16, 2015, https://www.nytimes.com/2015/06/16/nyregion/board-hears-support-for-raising-food-workers-minimum-wage.html.

31. Official data in terms of the amount of funding or number of SEIU organizers working on the campaign have not been made public. Some sources, however, mention that SEIU is spending over $10 million to sustain the movement. See Steven Greenhouse, "Strong Voice in 'Fight for 15' Fast-Food Wage Campaign," *New York Times*, December 5, 2014, http://www.nytimes.com/2014/12/05/business/in-fast-food-workers-fight-for-15-an-hour-a-strong-voice-in-terrance-wise.html?ref=topics.

32. Center for Union Facts, "Exposing SEIU's Fake Fast Food 'Strikes,'" http://worker-centers.com/exposing-seius-fake-fast-food-strikes/; Richard Berman, "The Public is Catching on to Fast-Food Strikes," *Nation's Restaurant News*, April 18, 2014, https://www.nrn.com/opinions/public-catching-fast-food-strikes.

33. Jenny Brown, "Thousands Strike Fast Food, Picketing and Occupying," *Labor Notes*, August 13, 2013, http://www.labornotes.org/2013/08/thousands-strike-fast-food-picketing-and-occupying; Arun Gupta, "Fight for 15 Confidential," *In These Times*, November 11, 2013, available at https://inthesetimes.com/article/15826/fight_for_15_confidential. For a more general critique on the organizing strategies and shortcomings of SEIU, see Jane McAlevey, *Raising Expectations (and Raising Hell): My Decade Fighting for the Labor Movement* (New York: Verso, 2012).

34. Micah Uetricht, "Steven Greenhouse on Keeping the Labor Beat Alive," *In These Times*, February 18, 2015. http://inthesetimes.com/article/17634/keeping_the_labor_beat_alive.

35. See, for example, Milkman and Ott, eds., *New Labor in New York*.

36. Nathan Schneider, "From Occupy Wall Street to Occupy Everywhere," *The Nation*, October 31, 2011, http://www.thenation.com/article/163924/occupy-wall

-street-occupy-everywhere#; on the evolution of the Walmart campaign, see http://forrespect.org.

37. According to the Director of the NYCC, the $15/hour, roughly the U.S. median hourly wage, is considered something to aspire to and was decided upon when taking into account the long-term goals of the campaign.

38. See Steven Greenhouse, *Beaten Down, Worked Up: The Past, Present, and Future of American Labor* (New York: Knopf, 2019), 240–241.

39. On the 1963 march, see William P. Jones, *The March on Washington: Jobs. Freedom, and the Forgotten History of Civil Rights* (New York: W.W. Norton, 2013).

40. IUF, "Fast food workers from around the world come together to fight for their rights," August 5, 2014, http://www.iuf.org/w/?q=node/3340.

41. Steven Greenhouse and Jana Kasperkevic, "Fight for $15 swells into largest protest by low-wage workers in US history," *The Guardian*, April 15, 2015, http://www.theguardian.com/us-news/2015/apr/15/fight-for-15-minimum-wage-protests-new-york-los-angeles-atlanta-boston.

42. Sarah Jones, "McDonald's Wants to Reopen Its Dining Rooms, Workers Say Not So Fast," *New York Magazine*, May 20, 2020, https://nymag.com/intelligencer/2020/05/workers-say-that-mcdonalds-still-isnt-protecting-them.html.

43. Daniel Wiessner, "McDonald's Settles Lawsuit with U.S. Franchise Workers for the First Time Ever," *Time*, November 1, 2016, https://time.com/4552835/mcdonalds-settlement-labor-law-california/.

44. Associated Press, "McDonald's Agrees to $26M Settlement with California Workers over Wages, Work Conditions," KPIX-CBS, November 25, 2019, https://sanfrancisco.cbslocal.com/2019/11/25/mcdonalds-california-workers-lawsuit-26-million-settlement/.

45. David Yaffe-Bellany, "McDonald's Lawsuit Targets 'Pervasive' Culture of Sexual Harassment," *New York Times*, November 12, 2019, https://www.nytimes.com/2019/11/12/business/mcdonalds-harassment-lawsuit.html?smtyp=cur&smid=tw-nytimesbusiness.

46. Justin Wise, "Workers File Class-Action Lawsuit against McDonald's over Coronavirus Precautions," *The Hill*, https://thehill.com/homenews/498676-workers-file-class-action-lawsuit-against-mcdonalds-over-coronavirus-precautions.

47. The 2015 Browning-Ferris NLRB Decision significantly softened the test for determining joint-employer status. Under this decision, franchisors might be considered joint employers of a franchisee even if they don't exercise direct control over the company. If that decision would have been upheld, collective bargaining could have become a viable option within the fast food sector. Under the Trump administration, however, the traditional, preexisting standards for determining joint-employer status were restored and the definition of "employer" was again narrowed (Elmore and Griffith 2020). At the time of writing, it seems possible that the Biden administration will revoke the Trump-era standard (https://news.bloomberglaw.com/employee-benefits/biden-dol-preps-joint-employer-rule-after-trump-version-blocked).

48. Over 50% of the fast food workers are white, with just almost 20% black or Latino. However, in large metropolitan areas, the majority of the fast food workers are people of color. See Schmitt and Jones, "Slow Progress for Fast Food Workers"; Rosemary Batt, Jae Eun Lee, and Tashlin Lakhani, "A National Study of Human Resource Practices, Turnover, and Customer Service in the Restaurant Industry," January 15, 2014, https://archive.ilr.cornell.edu/sites/default/files/National-Study-of-Human-Resource-Practices-High-Turnover-and-Customer-Service-in-the-Restaurant-Industry.pdf.

49. See, for example, Savage, "Geographies of Organizing."

50. See, for example, Steve Lopez, *Reorganizing the Rust Belt: An Inside Study of the American Labor Movement* (Berkeley: University of California Press. 2004).

51. Some cities, such as Seattle, have pushed for the right to organize, rather than the right to unionize, as the workers realize the limitations and challenges to form a traditional union in the sense of the NLRA. Using this broader narrative opens the door to new, experimental forms of worker organizations.

52. See http://forrespect.org.

53. See http://nyworkersrising.org.

54. Felstead, *The Corporate Paradox*.

55. Julie Jargon, "After Complaints, McDonald's Franchisee to Sell Restaurants," *Wall Street Journal*, March 14, 2013, http://online.wsj.com/news/articles/SB10001424127887324532004578360613867975552.

56. Kathy Tomlinson, "McDonald's Foreign Worker Practices Face Growing Investigation," CBCnews, April 17,2014, http://www.cbc.ca/news/canada/british-columbia/mcdonald-s-foreign-worker-practices-face-growing-investigation-1.2607365.

57. Weil, *The Fissured Workplace*.

58. National Employment Law Project, "Impact of Fight for $15: $68 Billion in Raises, 22 Million Workers, Data Brief, https://www.nelp.org/publication/impact-fight-for-15–2018/.

59. Steven Greenhouse, Larry Mishel, Katherine V.W. Stone, and David Weil, "The Future of Real Jobs: Round Two," *The American Prospect Blogs*, May 29, 2019, https://prospect.org/labor/future-real-jobs-round-two/.

60. David Rolf, *The Fight for $15: The Right Wage for a Working America* (New York: The New Press, 2016); Chris Rhomberg, "$15 and a Union: Searching for Workers' Power in the Fight for $15 Movement," in *No One Size Fits All: Worker Organization, Policy, and Movement in a New Economic Age*, ed. Janice Fine, Linda Burnham, Kati Griffith, Minsun Ji, Victor Narro, and Steven Pitts (Ithaca: Cornell University Press, 2018), 251–270.

61. Presentation by Jonathan Westin at Cornell University, April 9, 2014.

62. See, for example, Michael Pollan's website for a list: http://michaelpollan.com/resources/politics-policy/#faqstart.

63. For more details on Fight for $15's intersectional organizing, see Maite Tapia, Tamara L. Lee, and Mikhail Filipovitch, "Supra-Union and Intersectional Organizing: An Examination of Two Prominent Cases in the Low-Wage US Restaurant

Industry," *Journal of Industrial Relations*, 59, no. 4 (2017): 487—509. This also brought internal challenges as key strategists and organizers of Fight for $15 had to resign or were fired because of sexual misconduct or abusive behavior. See Cora Lewis, "A Top Labor Executive Has Been Suspended after Complaints about His Relationships with Female Staffers," *Buzz Feed News*, October 19, 2017, https://www.buzzfeednews.com/article/coralewis/seiu-suspension and "The Organizing Director of the Fight for 15 Has Resigned amid Harassment Investigation," *Buzz Feed News*, November 2, 2017, https://www.buzzfeednews.com/article/coralewis/seiu-new-york-director-of-the-fight-for-15-resigned; Rachel Abrams, 2018. "McDonald's Workers across the U.S. Stage #MeToo Protests," https://www.nytimes.com/2018/09/18/business/mcdonalds-strike-metoo.html.

64. Steven Greenhouse, "Fast-Food Workers Claim Victory in a New York Labor Effort," *New York Times*, January 9, 2018, https://www.nytimes.com/2018/01/09/business/economy/fast-food-labor.html.

65. Steven Greenhouse, "'We're Organizing to Improve Lives': New York Fast-food Workers Push to Unionize," *The Guardian*, September 30, 2019, https://www.theguardian.com/us-news/2019/sep/30/new-york-chipotle-mcdonalds-union-fight-for-15.

66. Dave Jamieson, "Labor Critic Claims Union behind the 'Fight For $15' Cut Funding for Fast-Food Campaigns," *Huffpost*, April 3, 2018, https://portside.org/2018-04-01/union-behind-fight-15-cuts-funding-fast-food-campaign.

PART III

Global Influence and Its Challenges

8

Renewing Union Practices and Strategies

A Case Study of SEIU's Sweet $16 Campaign in Ontario, Canada

LAURENCE HAMEL-ROY AND YANICK NOISEUX

Since the turn of the millennium, union renewal has been a subject of interest for civil society organizations, trade unions, think tanks, and labor scholars. Faced with increasing nonstandard employment relations and unions' declining membership numbers and social power, unions are devising new strategies to mobilize and pursue collective action.[1] One of the pressing challenges unions face is how to reimagine strategies and campaigns to include the longtime ignored workers in the "non-union zone,"[2] while taking into account the deleterious changes in the labor markets in Western countries. It is with this in mind that we examine SEIU Local 1's Sweet $16 campaign in Ontario, Canada, to illustrate the challenges inherent to unionization at the margins of the labor market, while also highlighting the Local's concrete actions in tackling these challenges to organize vulnerable workers.

Launched in 2014 with the aim to improve the working conditions of Ontario's personal support workers (PSWs), the Sweet $16 campaign targeted the Ontario government with four main demands: "1) a raise [to] the minimum wage for home care from $12.50/hour to $16/hour (as a first step toward wage parity with PSW working in long-term care); 2) [access to] retirement security through a good pension plan; 3) [the] declaration of home care [as an] essential service; and 4) [. . .] access to standardized and ongoing continuing education and specialized training opportunities to meet the evolving needs of home care clients."[3] In less than two months, an agreement was reached raising hourly wages in laborly funded agencies to $16.50/hour, an increase larger than SEIU's initial bid.[4] Yet to be met were the three remaining demands.[5]

This chapter uses the case study of the Sweet $16 campaign to demonstrate Local 1's successful strategies in tackling the specific challenges of home care service work in the province of Ontario, Canada.[6] In doing so, it considers more broadly union reinvention in advanced capitalism. Our analysis attributes the campaign's success to: 1) its strong accountability for home care services particularities, and 2) its strategic and well-crafted public stance in the debate on home care services quality. The first part of the chapter introduces the Ontario home care services structure and its impact on the workforce regarding working conditions. Part two and three describe the organizing difficulties faced by unions in the home care sector and the strategies developed by SEIU to overcome them. The chapter ends with a discussion of research issues raised by this case study and relevant to a broader reflection on collective action to tackle nonstandard employment relations, experience, and status.[7]

SEIU Healthcare and Home Care Workers

SEIU Healthcare history[8] starts with the Building Services Employees Unions (BSEIU) founded in Montreal and Vancouver in 1943. In 1944, hospital workers in the Toronto General Hospital organized, leading to the establishment of BSEIU's first charter in Ontario. The BSEIU changed its name to the Service Employees International Union (SEIU) in 1968 and over the last five decades continues to build its membership through certification campaigns across the province, starting with hospitals and soon followed by nursing home and home-based health workers. In 2003, six SEIU locals merged, creating SEIU Local 1, which rebranded itself as SEIU Healthcare in 2013. The union now represents over 55,000 frontline healthcare workers throughout Ontario, among which more than 12,000 are in the home care and community service subsectors. Three-quarters of its membership is female and many are immigrants from Eastern Africa, the Caribbean, the Indian subcontinent, and South Asia. It is one of the fastest-growing unions in Ontario as 10,000 new members—accounting for almost one fifth of the total membership that joined the union between 2004 and 2013. SEIU Local 1 contributes to the shaping of healthcare policy by running public campaigns and lobbying the Ontario government with tactics and strategies corresponding to the changing political and economic landscape in the province. In the early 1990s the Local collaborated with the Neo-Democrat government (NDP) to try and ensure the right to strike for "essential workers." To achieve its goals, the union regularly mobilized its members' individual power to elect or defeat representatives and policy makers working in the interests of union members, care recipients, and their families.[9]

In March 2014, the union held a Home Care Summit where the foundation of the Sweet $16 campaign was envisioned. Assessing that the additional $100 million budget investment by the government in the sector in 2016 was insufficient regarding the growing needs of the sector in the coming years, the union called on members and the general population to "Rise for Home Care" and launched a specific campaign targeting the income inequality between home care and long-term institution PSWs.[10]

In Canada, as in most Western countries, an aging population combined with the decreasing availability of family members to provide care in the home of their elderly parents—largely owing to women's growing participation in the labor market—means continued growth in the need for home care services.[11] In 2015, more than 100,000 PSWs were active in Ontario with roughly 34,000 employed in the home and community services,[12] of which less than 25% are represented by a union.[13] As with most care professions, women are overly represented in this sector and a high proportion of the workforce is immigrant and/or racialized.[14] In Ontario, these workers are providing home care services—a broad range of activities seeking to help aging and disabled people live in their own homes—to 1.5 million people.[15] As the "backbone"[16] of home healthcare, PSWs perform an extensive variety of tasks crucial to care recipients' well-being and their families. Their tasks include personal care (bathing, grooming, dressing), help with transportation, housekeeping, groceries, meal preparation, and general assistance.[17] Because they mostly work with the frail and elderly in their home, the PSWs personalize their interventions, bring moral support, and deliver important emotional work.[18]

The home care sector is one of the fastest growing employment sectors in Canada.[19] Indeed, the expected "apocalyptic demography"[20] change translates into the elaboration of strategies seeking cost-effective means of care, among which is an increased tendency toward the provision of home care services.[21] In Ontario as elsewhere, governments prefer home care over care in institutional settings, nesting their decisions on a discourse of fiscal crisis and debt reduction.[22] As the need for care rose dramatically, the implementation of austerity measures through the "Common Sense Revolution" by the Conservative government of Harris in 1995—legitimated by the drastic reduction of the Canadian Health and Social Transfer by the federal government[23]—resulted in market-driven policy-making at the cost of the partial dismantling of Ontario's welfare state: in the 1990s, while the need for home care was booming, public-private partnerships (PPPs) involving "for-profit" agencies were "experimented" alongside reductions in social spending in the sector. And in 1996, the Ontario government decentralized home care services to deliver it through "not-for-profit" community services. In a so-called quest to derive benefits (and cost reduction) from free-market competition,[24] fourteen Community Care Access Centres (CCAC) (now responsible for the coordination and management of "community and home care services" in their respective territories) were created, and a bidding competition process involving 160 service providers and more than 1,000 agencies throughout the province ensued.[25]

The process by which the government actively sustains competition between providers follows the delusion that managerial techniques and neoliberal policies result in greater efficiency and savings.[26] Coming from sectors where work is objectified and subjected to time measurement, these "lean management" techniques include guidelines seeking reduction in the intervention time and the promotion of a "one-size fits all" plan. Because care work isn't something to be easily subjected to that exercise—as the changing and variability of situations compel different responses that cannot be either predicted with high certainty, neither standardized—the shift to cost-effective managing policies means services delivered do not reflect care recipients' specific needs.[27] This shift also equates with negative effects on service availability,[28] especially in rural areas,[29] all of which contribute to escalating levels of insecurity for care recipients. This increases the burden on informal caregivers, mostly in-laws, usually women, as they then become the ones "filling the gap" when needs are not met.[30] Recognizing the fact that austerity politics has primary negative consequences for women—as workers and as caregivers—underscores the gendered roots of the neoliberal project.[31]

The PSWs workplace is the house or the flat of the care recipient. And, because "home" still carries ideologies of intimacy, privacy, and care, it resists traditional considerations as a "worksite."[32] In this setting, home care PSWs wage is indeed lower than their counterparts performing similar duties in hospitals and nursing homes, even though the workload and flexibility expected in the private household is higher and the opportunities for upward mobility scarce and limited.[33] Data sources obtained from SEIU[34] indicate that 70% of its home care PSWs members work part-time for an average annual income of $21,957. The average salary for full-time workers is $33,436 per year.[35]

Although the Ontario Ministry of Health states that PSWs play a "vital" role in healthcare,[36] much of the educational material produced by SEIU demonstrates how the Ministry of Health does not uphold this standard. The video series "Walk-a-day in the shoes of a PSW,"[37] for example, exposes the high workload imposed on PSWs, their extended schedules (both on a daily and weekly basis), and the transportation hassles they have to deal with. More importantly,

PSWs testify about the need for "help, support and security" to keep doing their jobs. These videos highlight the PSWs sense of social usefulness and the genuine bonds they build with people receiving their care. They also expose, again through testimonies, how care work, as "women's work," is a site of intense struggle for dignity and against exploitation but also one of genuine attachment and personal reward.

Following the Harris government's large-scale adoption of austerity measure, the restructuring of the home care system took place and focused on managed competition and expenditure containment, as well as putting pressure on service providers now subject to uncertain funding and bankruptcy threats.[38] Many service providers' agencies that offered quality employment opportunities exited the market following the implementation of the bidding process. This breakdown of the industry created the condition for higher turnover, low wages, job insecurity, high risks of health hazards, and high levels of stress—all now key characteristics of the sector.[39] Work intensification also means rationalization of the time previously spent on personalizing care and stirred a loss of satisfaction. In other words, PSWs could not accomplish what they consider "good care" anymore.[40]

Challenges and Difficulties Faced by SEIU Healthcare

Even though unfavorable working conditions for PSWs can largely be attributed to public policies, the union's delayed interest in engaging with jobs at the margins of the labor market were also part of the equation. The home care sector has historically been out of the "union zone" largely because of its resemblance to domestic work. It became the target of more aggressive union campaigns only in the late 1980s as unions increased their commitment to organize workers who had been left behind, and in hope of constraining union density decline among standard employment.[41] Care workers, and more specifically the home care workforce, have then become part of some of the most significant mobilizations in the United States despite the fact that they represent only a small portion of unionized wage earners and that their work structuration hampers collective organization.[42] In addition to Ontario's political context (detailed earlier) and the challenges that context posed in terms of decreased power advantage, three characteristics of the home care sector deserve special attention in understanding the difficulties raised by home care workers' organizational strategies: 1) the socio-demographic profile of the workforce; 2) their work environment; and 3) the nature of duties performed.

Women account for 90% of PSWs members of SEIU Local 1,[43] with a large portion being racialized and/or immigrant.[44] Care professions—and especially those that provide care in the home—are often coined a "female ghetto" because they constitute an "easy" entry to the labor market for women, while keeping them captive in less financially rewarding sectors of the economy.[45] This poses several challenges not only for the workers but also for union organizing, since unions have been accustomed (and comfortable) to deal with white male breadwinners while women and people of racialized and ethnic backgrounds were believed to be uninterested in political and union involvement or deemed insufficiently equipped to do so.[46] Furthermore, union internal spaces have been identified as poorly suited to deal with sexist and racist practices, contributing to the exclusion of potential activists.[47] As a consequence, executive positions are often predominantly occupied by white male workers, even in female-dominated sectors.[48] This can reinforce the gap separating "the base" from union leaders, thus making it more difficult to achieve membership integration and address rank-and-file concerns.[49] In the end, the lack of diversity in union representation impacts on women workers' ability to integrate, whether in terms of their formal participation in action groups or union engagement more generally. Another challenge related to the feminization of the labor force arises from the "second shift"[50] for women who still bear most of the household chores and parental responsibilities despite their increased participation in the labor market.[51] The reduced availability and flexibility of women are barriers that bring into question the organizational ability of unions to accommodate women's needs in order to foster their participation. This is most obvious in terms of scheduling of meetings and events and the persistence of a gendered division of labor within unions.[52]

Union campaigns targeting PSWs in the home care service sector must also contend with their isolation and dispersal into an individual's home. With few opportunities to gather and share their respective experiences—a process that would allow them to build solidarity—PSWs are then prone to repress acting upon and defending their self-interests. With PSWs subject to assume that their problems are individual matters, rather than collective issues, workers' isolation complicates collective mobilization strategies.[53] The consequences for unions and worker atomization thus depends on unions' ability to reach their membership and disseminate information about labor rights, collective agreement protections, health and security hazards, and client responsibilities.[54] In sum, worker distribution in atomized workplaces and duties performed in isolation can hamper the development of collegial relationships and the solidarity that face-to-face relationships make possible. This situation brings the need to reflect on alternative channels to support workers' efforts to come together and fight a common cause.[55]

Home care service history is one of commodification of domestic labor provided free of charge by spouses, daughters, sisters, and other women; this promotes the naturalization of its gendered assignation. Taking caring and domestic techniques and abilities as "natural" ignores PSWs' skill development experiences, both in the course of their professional career and in their intimate life as caregivers.[56] Unfavorable labor policies in the home care service sector then persist as PSWs work is seen as vocational or an extension of women's gendered identities and duties. Furthermore, this tends to validate the idea that women care workers can always "do more with less" in the name of "love," as if the satisfaction of helping others is a sufficient compensation beyond the salary earned.[57] This logic intersects race, class and gender oppression, as care work simultaneously often draws from a vulnerable pool of racialized workers.[58]

From this point of view, insufficient recognition of PSWs' skills and efforts justifies meager compensation. The general public (and even the workers themselves) are not immune to such prejudices, a situation that complicates union efforts to deal with home care issues.[59] For one thing, PSWs themselves do not always feel a sense of injustice, caught as they are in conflicts of identity and interest crystallized through the population's expectations and their ability to meet these expectations.[60] This is an important point because a sense of injustice has been identified as a key element in mobilization.[61] Moreover, it is clear that people in Ontario are not familiar with what PSWs do, making it difficult for them to support their fight.[62] As a result, an enormous amount of education and consciousness-raising is necessary for unions to achieve a critical mass of supporters and slow the neoliberalization of home care services.

Because service providers depend on government funding, lack of resources—and this is especially true in time of austerity—justifies poor job quality[63] as was the case when *Red Cross Care Partners*[64] and SEIU were renegotiating their collective agreement in 2013. This led the union to launch the Justice4PSWs campaign denouncing the agency's corporative turn and unfair treatment of its employees.[65] Despite quick actions leading to a two-week strike during Christmas and disclosures aimed at tarnishing the agency's reputation (calling out the agencies' "greed and selfishness"), SEIU failed in raising wages substantially and in negotiating travel allowances.[66] The negotiations ended in arbitration. But the decision was not favorable to the demands of PSWs because of the so-called *Red Cross Care Partners* dependency on government funding (even if the agency is for profit). To overcome the union's undermined power leverage in a public-private partnership context, six SEIU Healthcare PSWs met with then Premier Kathleen Wynne in January 2014 to seek support from her government to improve working conditions by "fixing" the home care system.[67] This meeting aimed to seek solutions to support frontline workers by bargaining at the political level instead of doing so through collective agreement. Even though it was difficult to assess the outcome of this strategy in the long term, it highlighted the shortfall of traditional labor board mechanisms when it comes to three-party negotiations involving the government and its subcontractors.

The Campaign: Practices and Strategies

Earlier in the chapter we showed how gendered dimension of home care points toward an explanation for job devaluation and organizational difficulties. We also discussed how the reorganization of the Ontario home care services sector both structures the labor market and influences job quality and union campaigns, a dynamic that impacts workers at the "rough ends" of the labor market. Despite the consensus that unions must renew themselves by moving beyond merely defending their gains, precisely how and by what means this should be pursued remains a matter of debate.

According to our analysis, Sweet $16 success is due to its focus on strategic adjustments toward the relevant sector's gendered characteristics. Interestingly, the campaign sought new benefits for PSWs by moving beyond previous gains. In addition to articulating home care sector's unique characteristics, it seems that the Sweet $16 "public" campaign weakened the curbing effects of PPPs on potential avenues for collective action. Renewing its practices, SEIU found new footing by running a "public" campaign challenging the government (instead of employers) by building alliances with Ontarians over their concern about home care quality.[68] By doing so, the Sweet $16 campaign spoke to issues beyond workers' self-interest and aimed at tackling the effects of government neoliberalization especially on care work.

As stated by our informants, the success of the Sweet $16 campaign owes much to its focus on overcoming four main factors hindering PSWs organizing: 1) a female labor force whose profile and specific needs are shaped by women's social position and the difficulties in mobilizing them; 2) the dispersion of workplace and worker isolation; 3) insufficient recognition of skills and effort required for the job by the general population; and 4) particular challenges created by the Ontario government's neoliberal management practices.

FOCUSING ON SPECIFIC CHALLENGES

Merely acknowledging the presence of women, immigrants, and racialized persons is insufficient to ensure their full inclusion in formal and informal union activities or even to generate unions' sense of belonging; there is a need for concrete practices. In this regard, the fact that the informants we interviewed vigorously relayed SEIU's efforts to increase diversity among its union stewards and union representatives was a first step in getting beyond an abstract rhetoric of commitment to minorities.[69] As for Sweet $16 campaign advocacy role, our informants reported the use of proactive outreach methods with people coming from diverse sociodemographic background recruited directly in the field (starting with activists who were actively involved in the Justice4PSWs campaign against the *Red Cross*).[70] SEIU also offered regular union training sessions through its Member Leadership and Action Program (MAPE) to not only tutor a cohort of activists, but also to bolster their confidence and create a sense of legitimacy among them regarding their actions.[71] Travel allowance and childcare reimbursements for participating in union activities helped offset the lack of time and resources many workers faced, especially single moms—reflecting the union's consideration of the specific needs of its members.[72] Following its quest for diversity, SEIU also created in 2015 "new positions [. . .] on the Executive Board that reflect the growing diversity of the membership and Ontario."[73]

The campaign likewise attempted to overcome the considerable challenge of worker isolation. Because the dispersal of the workplace into multiple homes of the care recipients is one of the sector's inherent characteristics, SEIU used diverse communication channels to disseminate educational and awareness material to the PSWs who would be otherwise difficult to reach because of the home care structure.[74] During the Justice4PSWs campaign, for example, the union created the J4PSWSBLOG, an online website which kept the members informed of the different actions and posted regular blog entrees supporting the strikers on the picket line. Building on the strike's momentum, this strategy was pushed further by increasing the union's reliance on social media[75] and through the multiplication of calls to "join the conversation." The "Healthaholic Blog," Youtube and Vimeo channels, a Facebook page, and a Twitter account were used to create a virtual network of organized PSWs. In doing so, SEIU hoped to bring PSWs into social media activism.

According to our informants, the sharing and reposting of the union's videos constituted effective tools for raising members' awareness.[76] Unable to rely on face-to-face networking and collective awareness, SEIU briefed its members by sharing videos within which workers recognize the precarity of their status and ready themselves with tools needed to denounce the situation.[77] Through them, the union was thus able to accomplish the crucial task of coaching its members, initiating collective reflection, and rousing the sense of injustice about their condition.[78] Awareness-raising proved to be a critical step because it allowed PSWs to recognize their experiences of unfair treatment.

Considering that during the Justice4PSWs campaign the union framed its public narrative in regard to higher wages as a way to obtain justice against the management practices of *Red Cross Care Partner* elite executives, the Sweet $16 Campaign departed from this strategy and chose to focus its discourse on dignity. This new strategy sought to increase the social value associated with home care work and gain public support regarding a raise of the PSWs' wage to $16 per hour. To do so, SEIU built on the vocational narrative put upfront by PSWs when speaking about their work and articulated it with the lack of consideration they receive from the general population.[79] The wage hike they requested was thus argued as a way to merely ensure that the PSWs could "continue [to do] their job." This realignment of the narrative reflected the view that a "decent" wage was a matter of dignity and not a greedy demand from the workers. Moreover, in the union's series of videos, SEIU highlighted the "professional" standing of PSWs by portraying them as experienced, multitasking, and caring workers,[80] and put emphasis on technical aspects of home care PSWs' job and on the emotional support workers provided to care recipients and their family. In sum, the PSWs' job depiction was stripped from the devaluated dimensions of care work such as the "dirty work," the physical strain and the emotional exhaustion associated with home care work. Instead, the focus was set on the professional standing of PSWs, the altruistic values that motivate them and the genuine care they feel toward the clients and their families. Doing so was not a question of completely denaturalizing these workers' skills or challenging the feminine trope, but somehow reversing PSWs' depreciation by putting upfront the skills needed while highlighting the vital work PSWs perform in society.[81]

RENEWING UNIONS: GOING PUBLIC

If we take a step back and try to understand the context in which the Sweet $16 campaign unfolded, we must keep in mind that in a previous campaign the *Red Cross Care Partners* benefited from arbitration by pleading the "lack of resources." Indeed, subsidies for the home care services sector has been declining since the mid-1990s in Ontario at a time when the government's promotion of home as the go-to health and community care setting increased with the number of home care services recipients. The creation of CCAC and PPPs followed in order to contain expenditures and derive benefits from the market. By complicating employer-employee relations, this resulted in severely limiting unions' operational capabilities and put at the forefront their need to renew their practices and move beyond strategies inherited from the industrial era and its factory organizing type of context. With this in mind, the Sweet $16 campaign tried new strategies to overcome issues stemming from subcontracting and underfunding of home care.

In addition to strategies aiming at overcoming internal power issues regarding diversity, worker isolation, and job depreciation, the Sweet $16 campaign was characterized by what informants called a "public" design. Concerned with labor-related legislative frameworks rather than targeting collective agreements, as in Justice4PSWs, the SEIU ventured on activism beyond workplace issues and called over multiple actors to join together and campaign for the PSWs' cause.[82] Because of the specific position of PSWs within the PPPs framework, the Sweet $16 campaign sought to convince the provincial government to bestow the funds required to raise the PSWs' minimum wage from $12 to $16 an hour. As we have seen, the Sweet $16 campaign was a success within less than two months when Ontario's 2014–2015 Health and Long-term Care budget passed. It included "a promise to raise home and community care wages by $4 across the board," which was an increase of 32% affecting all PSWs working in publicly funded agencies.[83]

The campaign also insisted on warranting the involvement of elected officials as a way to ensure that the Ontario government's budget could support the wage increase. As early as January 2014 and taking advantage of the post-Justice4PSW momentum (and before the launching of the Sweet $16 campaign), a team of six PSWs and SEIU officers met with Premier Wynne and Minister of Health and Long-Term Care, Deb Matthews. This meeting, involving rank-and-file members as a way to personify the demands, argued urgency for injecting funds into the home care system as a way to support PSWs' retention.[84] A rally around the campaign followed in March 2014 with eighty PSWs coming from across Ontario to "share their work story."[85] Meanwhile, Ontario's population was encouraged to write directly to their Member of the Provincial Parliament and impress upon them concerns about home care's future and the necessity of the Sweet $16 campaign for this purpose. People were reached through social media and traditional advertising in newspapers.[86] Pre-filled forms were available on the union's website to facilitate the process as much as possible.[87] Parliamentarians were especially targeted as SEIU "[. . .] know[s] the government is hearing [its] members loud and clear, so [the campaign is now] the time to keep up the pressure and get real commitments."[88] And then when Tim Hudack—then head of Ontario's Conservative Party and Leader of the Official Opposition—threatened to undermine the union's gains if elected, SEIU's political engagement was bolstered by arguing that he represented a threat to the future of home care services, and a "Stop Hudack, Save Healthcare" campaign blitz was immediately launched to encourage the public to cast strategic votes for either the Liberal Party or the New Democratic Party in the upcoming election.[89]

In the course of its lobbying activities, not only did SEIU enter the political stage, but it also positioned itself to fight to enhance people's lives beyond its own membership. Not only did all PSWs working in publicly funded agencies feel the wage increase (and not just SEIU Healthcare members), but the union also demanded the recognition of home care as an essential service. Furthermore, the reduction in staff turnover promised better quality service for care recipients and their families. By highlighting the links between PSWs' working conditions and quality of service the union thus distanced itself from traditional union battles focused on worker interests, giving the campaign a political spin.[90] Transforming worker demands into social rights claims means defending issues of citizenship and dignity, rather than focusing on employer-based claims as salaries and benefits.[91] There is little doubt that this type of framing of the issue of PSWs' salaries in the public sphere made it possible to avoid negative perceptions often associated with unions.[92] And in so doing, SEIU gained support from a larger pool of people—namely all PSWs (not only the ones working in public settings), beneficiaries (or future care recipients), and their families.

Even if many strategies were used to encourage member involvement—as discussed in the previous section—the campaign also mobilized nonunion member partners to increase pressure on the government by pressing them to write to their elective representatives and by voting against the Conservative Party of Ontario. One way to mobilize union members and nonmembers is to draw on identity concerns to raise awareness about issues shared by a variety of groups in contact with those making the original claim.[93] Following this, the Sweet $16 campaign evoked identity in two ways. First, a video series and commercials presented the occupation's professional characteristics. The subtext of these videos was to tug at the public's ethical sensibilities by trying to build empathy with the PSWs' difficult situation.[94] Second, the campaign reminded everyone of their dependence on PSWs, whether as family members providing home care services or as potential future service users.[95] In sum, by incorporating subjectivities into the campaign, SEIU aimed and succeeded in stimulating civil society actors' political involvement and influence provincial social policy.

This development of SEIU's campaign, which participants qualified as "public," found inspiration in several social movements. It benefited from expertise developed in the United States, including efforts led by SEIU Locals in California, Oregon, and Illinois, as well as the better-known Justice4Janitors campaign.[96] The Sweet $16 campaign strategy to rely on care recipients or their families—something that can also be seen in the Rise for Home Care campaign that followed—reflects the particularity of American home care services sector campaigns.[97] They were based on coalition building with user advocacy groups to present a common front demanding recognition and redistribution of income. Closer to Ontario, SEIU was also inspired by the narratives of the 2012 "Maple Spring" student protests in Quebec.[98] Using this struggle's social component—a large population of nonstudents joined this movement by taking to the street—the union focused on linking austerity, decreased public funding, and their impact on underprivileged populations. As our informants put it, SEIU was inspired by different campaigns with components of community unionism and/or social movement unionism and seen as a way to better achieve its goals through an increased customization of the campaign. The insistence of the Sweet $16 campaign on "dignity and social justice issues," rather than limiting itself to "bread-and-butter" issues is, furthermore, consistent with what we found in other case studies on "nonstandard" workers collective organization in Quebec and Nova Scotia.[99]

Finally, our informants insisted on the degree of organization and planning the campaign required. When asked about their roles in the campaign, informants emphasized coordination, bringing together key actors, and collaboratively establishing objectives and timelines.[100] Not only did this approach allow the campaign to achieve the observed scope, but it also increased the number of unionized members. In fact, it is reasonable to assume that SEIU's visibility during the campaign explains the union's reported 17% increase in membership.[101] From this perspective, organizing new members, and therefore increasing union density in Ontario, resulted from the campaign's specific structure and reveals itself as a significant piece of information regarding the "crisis" of unionism.

Conclusion

The neoliberalization of the Ontario home care system has strongly deteriorated service quality and PSWs working conditions. The interconnection of these two concerns was put forward by SEIU's in framing the Sweet $16 campaign "to fix the home care system." Nevertheless, home care work still carries the ideology of not fully "work" that does not deserve fair compensation because it is performed in the nexus of the intimate life and the tasks performed align "naturally" with women's skills. This discourse is no stranger to home care historical ties with women's work that harden ongoing workers' struggles for recognition and fair compensation. Our analysis shows that the campaign's success owes much to the recognition of these difficulties inherent to the home care services sector. Presented here in three categories, these difficulties in fact represent three components of the gender division of labor associated with women who perform these tasks, where this work takes place, and the nature of the duties. To address this, SEIU adopted measures to encourage member participation by recognizing obstacles specific to women, attempted to create alternative spaces for consciousness-raising outside of isolated, atomized workplaces, and presented a counter-discourse to the delegitimization of personal support work.

That being said, the success of the Sweet $16 campaign lies not only in recognizing the home care service sector's particularities, but in handling them effectively. In addition to shaping working conditions, as demonstrated above, the organization of home care service markets also determines what kind of collective action is necessary. Fighting for better working conditions while facing challenges created by the outsourcing of public services, SEIU developed strategies to make the campaign a public issue; it also focused on partnerships to move beyond corporate interests and bring about legislative change. More concretely, the campaign encouraged the population to exert pressure on elected officials to adopt a provincial budget capable of supporting an increase of the minimum wage for Ontario PSWs, a measure meant to ensure quality services for all. Still, although avenues opened by campaigns like Sweet $16 seem attractive because of their wide-reaching impact on hard-to-mobilize groups, researchers cannot overlook or ignore their limitations.

Although the Ontario government did not implement all of the Sweet $16 campaign's recommendations (retirement security, recognition of the essential nature of home care work, and standardized training), the Liberal government did concede to some demands. In this context, the campaign is significant in light of the dismantlement of the Welfare State and the "austerity turn" in the province. The $4.50 wage increase ($0.50 higher than the initial recommendation) has given PSWs improved working conditions, and a "better" standard of living. The importance of this gain must be underlined as it is particularly beneficial for women and other marginalized workers in the home care industry. This is especially interesting given the campaign's clear vision: to present a realistic picture of women PSWs and engage with workers "at the margins."

Notes

The research findings presented in this article are drawn from a series of case studies funded by the Social Sciences and Humanities Research Council of Canada (SSHRC). The authors wish to thank the executive representatives of SEIU for their generous collaboration.

1. Marie-Josée Dupuis, "Renouveau syndical: proposition de redéfinition du projet syndical pour une plus grande légitimité des syndicats en tant que représentants de tous les travailleurs," CRIMT, 2004; Yanick Noiseux, *Transformations des marchés du travail et innovations syndicales au Québec* (Québec [Canada]: Presses de l'Université du Québec [PUQ], 2014); Joseph B. Rose and Gary N. Chaison, "Unionism in Canada and the United States in the 21 St Century: The Prospects for Revival," *Relations Industrielles/Industrial Relations* 56, no. 1 (2001): 34–65.

2. Kate Bronfenbrenner and Dorian T. Warren, "Race, Gender, and the Rebirth of Trade Unionism," *New Labor Forum* 16, no. 3/4 (2007): 142–148; Larry Haiven, "Expanding the Union Zone: Union Renewal through Alternative Forms of Worker Organization," *Labor Studies Journal* 31, no. 3 (2006): 85–116; Charlotte Yates, "Expanding Labour's Horizons: Union Organizing and Strategic Change in Canada," *Just Labour* 1, (2002): 31–40.

3. SEIU Healthcare, "'Sweet $16' Campaign Seeks Wage Hike for All Homecare PSWs," SEIU Healthcare (blog), March 14, 2014, http://www.seiuhealthcare.ca/_sweet_16_campaign_seeks_wage_hike_for_all_homecare_psws.

4. The 2014–2015 Health and Long-Term Budget proposed a $1.50 per hour wage increase for the coming year, an additional $1.50 in 2015–2016 and finally a $1.00 increase in 2016–17, see Ministry of Finance of Ontario, "Improving Home and Community Care for Ontario Seniors," news.ontario.ca, April 2014, https://news.ontario.ca/mof/en/2014/04/improving-home-and-community-care-for-ontario-seniors.html.

5. The situation in Ontario has changed since the research was conducted. Under Premier Doug Ford and leader of the Conservative Party, the province embraced austerity measures, reduced front-line services for seniors and promoted, to some degree, the privatization of home care services.

6. In Canada, healthcare and services fall under provincial jurisdiction, which means that each province has its own system, funded through transfer payments from the federal government. However, despite variation between provinces, issues regarding the Ontario health and social service system described in this chapter are quite like those in other Canadian provinces.

7. Data for this case study draw on press releases available on SEIU Local 1 website and local newspaper articles. For in-depth understanding of the province's home care services, we also consulted and reviewed reports, public policy documents, and press releases published by the Ontario government. Finally, three informants in Local 1 were interviewed about their role in the unfolding of the campaign.

8. SEIU Healthcare website: http://www.seiuhealthcare.ca/.

9. In a letter addressed to Ottawa's three main political leaders before the 2015 federal election, SEIU states that it will encourage members to volunteer in coming election and insisted that "Before any of our members advocate for you, they need to know that you will advocate for them." SEIU Healthcare, "Showing Justin Trudeau Hands-on Personal Support Work," SEIU Healthcare (blog), September 21, 2015, http://www.seiuhealthcare.ca/showing_justin_trudeau_hands_on_personal_support_work.

10. SEIU Healthcare, "Ontario Homecare Gets a Booster Shot," SEIU Healthcare (blog), juillet 2016, http://www.seiuhealthcare.ca/ontario_homecare_gets_a_booster_shot.

11. Pamela Doty, "Family Care of the Elderly: The Role of Public Policy," *The Milbank Quarterly* 64, no. 1 (1986): 34–75; Arlie Russell Hochschild, *The Commercialization of Intimate Life: Notes from Home and Work* (University of California Press, 2003); Peter C. Coyte and Patricia McKeever, "Home Care in Canada: Passing the Buck," *Canadian Journal of Nursing Research Archive* 33, no. 2 (2001): 11–25.

12. Ministry of Finance of Ontario, "Improving Home and Community Care for Ontario Seniors."

13. CUPE, "Sector Profile: Health Care," Canadian Union of Public Employees (blog), October 17, 2016, https://cupe.ca/sector-profile-health-care.

14. Jane Aronson and Sheila M. Neysmith, "'You're Not Just in There to Do the Work': Depersonalizing Policies and the Exploitation of Home Care Workers' Labor," Gender & Society 10, no. 1 (1996): 59–77; Sara Charlesworth, "The Regulation of Paid Care Workers' Wages and Conditions in the Non-Profit Sector: A Toronto Case Study," *Relations Industrielles/Industrial Relations* 65, no. 3 (2010): 380–399; Kim England, "Home, Work and the Shifting Geographies of Care," *Ethics, Place & Environment* 13, no. 2 (2010): 131–150.

15. Ministry of Health and Long-Term Care of Ontario, "Patients First; A Roadmap to Strengthen Home and Community Care," 2015, http://www.health.gov.on.ca/en/public/programs/lhin/roadmap.pdf.

16. Jane Aronson and Sheila M. Neysmith, "The Retreat of the State and Long-Term Care Provision: Implications for Frail Elderly People, Unpaid Family Carers aid Home Care Workers," *Studies in Political Economy* 53, no. 1 (1997): 37–66.

17. Isik U. Zeytinoglu et Margaret Denton, Catherine Brookman, Sharon Davies, and Firat Sayin, "Health and Safety Matters! Associations between Organizational Practices and Personal Support Workers' Life and Work Stress in Ontario, Canada," *BMC Health Services Research* 17 (June 21, 2017): 427.

18. Aronson and Neysmith, "You're Not Just in There to Do the Work."

19. Janice M. Keefe, Lucy Knight, Anne Martin-Matthews, and Jacques Légaré, "Key Issues in Human Resource Planning for Home Support Workers in Canada," *Work* 40, no. 1 (2011): 21–28.

20. Robert G. Evans, K. M. McGrail, S. G. Morgan, M. L. Barer, and C. Hertzman, "APOCALYPSE NO: Population Aging and the Future of Health Care Systems," *Canadian Journal on Aging/La Revue Canadienne Du Vieillissement* 20, no. S1 (2001): 160–191.

21. Aronson and Neysmith, "'You're Not Just in There to Do the Work.'"

22. Kim England and Joan Eakin, Denise Gastaldo and Patricia McKeever, "Neoliberalizing Home Care: Managed Competition and Restructuring Home Care in Ontario," in *Neoliberalization: States, Networks, Peoples,* ed. Kim England and Kevin Ward (Malden, MA: Wiley-Blackwell, 2007), 169–194; Aronson and Neysmith, "The Retreat of the State and Long-Term Care Provision"; Pat Armstrong and Hugh Armstrong, "Women, Privatization and Health Care Reform: The Ontario Case," in

Exposing Privatization: Women and Health Care Reform in Canada, ed. Pat Armstrong et al. (University of Toronto Press, 2001), 163–204.

23. Allison M. Williams, "Restructuring Home Care in the 1990s: Geographical Differentiation in Ontario, Canada," *Health & Place* 12, no. 2 (2006): 222–238.

24. Anne Wojtak and Linda Stark, "'Uberizing' Home Care in Ontario," *Healthcare Management Forum* 29, no. 4 (2016): 149–152.

25. P. C. Coyte and P. McKeever, "Home Care in Canada: Passing the Buck"; Margaret Denton, Isik Zeytonoglu, Karen Kusch, and Sharon Davies., "Market-Modelled Home Care: Impact on Job Satisfaction and Propensity to Leave," *Canadian Public Policy* 33, no. Supplement 1 (2007): S81–99.

26. Aronson and Neysmith, "You're Not Just in There to Do the Work"; England et al., "Neoliberalizing Home Care"; Charlesworth, "The Regulation of Paid Care Workers' Wages and Conditions."

27. Jane Aronson and Sheila M. Neysmith, "Obscuring the Costs of Home Care: Restructuring at Work," *Work, Employment and Society* 20, no. 1 (2006): 27–45.

28. Susan A. McDaniel and Neena L. Chappell, "Health Care in Regression: Contradictions, Tensions and Implications for Canadian Seniors," *Canadian Public Policy/Analyse de Politiques* 25, no. 1 (1999): 123–132.

29. Denise Cloutier-Fisher and Alun E. Joseph, "Long-Term Care Restructuring in Rural Ontario: Retrieving Community Service User and Provider Narratives," *Social Science & Medicine* 50, no. 7 (2000): 1037–1045.

30. Denise Guerriere, "Predictors of Caregiver Burden across the Home-Based Palliative Care Trajectory in Ontario, Canada," *Health & Social Care in the Community* 24, no. 4 (2016): 428–438; Marianne Kempeneers, Alex Battaglini, and Isabelle Van Pevenage, "Chiffre les solidarités familiales" (Montréal: Centre de recherche et de partage des savoirs InterActions, 2015); Nancy Guberman and Jean-Pierre Lavoie, "Politiques Sociales, Personnes Âgées et Proches Aidant-e-s au Québec: Sexisme et Exclusion," Canadian Woman Studies 29, no. 3 (2012): 61–70; Aronson and Neysmith, "'You're Not Just in There to Do the Work.'"

31. Kate Bezanson and Meg Luxton, *Social Reproduction: Feminist Political Economy Challenges Neo-Liberalism*, First edition (Montreal: McGill-Queen's University Press, 2006).

32. England, et al., "Neoliberalizing Home Care"; Nancy Folbre and Julie A. Nelson, "For Love or Money—Or Both?" *The Journal of Economic Perspectives* 14, no. 4 (2000): 123–140; Danielle Chabaud-Rychter, Dominique Fougeyrollas-Schwebel, and Françoise Sonthonnax, *Espace et temps du travail domestique* (Paris: Méridiens-Klincksieck, 1985).

33. Christine Kelly, "Exploring Experiences of Personal Support Worker Education in Ontario, Canada," *Health and Social Care* 24, no. 4 (2017): 1430–1438; Allison M. Williams, "Restructuring Home Care in the 1990s: Geographical Differentiation in Ontario, Canada"; Margaret Denton et al., "Job Stress and Job Dissatisfaction of Home Care Workers in the Context of Health Care Restructuring," *International Journal of Health Services* 32, no. 2 (2002): 327–357.

34. Data provided by email in 2018.

35. For comparison, Ontario's average full-time salary, all sectors combined, is $50,061.96/year.

36. Ministry of Health and Long-Term Care of Ontario, "Estimates Briefing Book 2016–17," 2016, 42, http://www.health.gov.on.ca/en/common/ministry/publications/plans/ppar16/.

37. We are here making a reference to a four-video series "Walk-a-day in the shoes of a PSW" that aimed to raise awareness about PSWs' daily life and work. See "SEIU Healthcare Presents: Walk a Day," SEIU Healthcare (blog), October 22, 2013, http://www.seiuhealthcare.ca/seiu_healthcare_presents_walk_a_day.

38. England, et al., "Neoliberalizing Home Care"; Aronson and Neysmith, "Obscuring the Costs of Home Care: Restructuring at Work"; Jane Aronson, Margaret Denton, and Isik Zeytinoglu, "Market-Modelled Home Care in Ontario: Deteriorating Working Conditions and Dwindling Community Capacity," *Canadian Public Policy/Analyse de Politiques* 30, no. 1 (2004): 111–125.

39. Zeytinoglu, et al., "Health and Safety Matters! Associations between Organizational Practices and Personal Support Workers' Life and Work Stress in Ontario, Canada"; Denton, et al., "Job Stress and Job Dissatisfaction"; Margaret Denton, Isik Zeytonoglu, Karen Kusch, and Sharon Davies., "Market-Modelled Home Care: Impact on Job Satisfaction and Propensity to Leave," *Canadian Public Policy* 33, no. Supplement 1 (2007): S81–99 "; England, et al., "Neoliberalizing Home Care"; Aronson, Denton, and Zeytinoglu, "Market-Modelled Home Care in Ontario."

40. Margaret Denton, Isik Zeytonoglu, Karen Kusch, and Sharon Davies., "Market-Modelled Home Care: Impact on Job Satisfaction and Propensity to Leave," *Canadian Public Policy* 33, no. Supplement 1 (2007): S81–99); Aronson and Neysmith, "You're Not Just in There to Do the Work."

41. Clare L. Stacey, *The Caring Self: The Work Experiences of Home Care Aides*, 1 edition (Ithaca, NY: ILR Press, 2011); Nari Rhee and Carol Zabin, "Aggregating Dispersed Workers: Union Organizing in the 'Care' Industries," *Geoforum, Labouring Geography: Negotiating Scales, Strategies and Future Directions* 40, no. 6 (2009): 969–979.

42. Eileen Boris and Jennifer Klein, *Caring for America: Home Health Workers in the Shadow of the Welfare State* (Oxford University Press, 2015); Premilla Nadasen, *Household Workers Unite: The Untold Story of African American Women Who Built a Movement* (Boston: Beacon Press, 2015); Kate Bronfenbrenner, "Organizing Women: The Nature and Process of Union-Organizing Efforts among U.S. Women Workers Since the Mid-1990s," *Work and Occupations* 32, no. 4 (2005): 1–23.

43. Data shared by email.

44. Interview #1, August 10, 2016.

45. Pat Armstrong and Hugh Armstrong, *The Double Ghetto: Canadian Women and Their Segregated Work* (McClelland & Stewart, 1993).

46. Rolande Pinard, *L'envers du travail: Le genre de l'émancipation ouvrière* (Montréal: Lux, 2018); Bronfenbrenner, "Organizing Women"; Tania Das Gupta, "Racism/

Anti-Racism, Precarious Employment, and Unions," in *Precarious Employment: Understanding Labour Market Insecurity in Canada*, ed. Leah F. Vosko (McGill-Queen's Press—MQUP, 2006), 318–334; Charlotte Yates, "Challenging Misconceptions about Organizing Women into Unions," *Gender, Work & Organization* 13, no. 6 (2006): 565–584; Linda Briskin, "Victimisation and Agency: The Social Construction of Union Women's Leadership," *Industrial Relations Journal* 37, no. 4 (2006): 359–378.

47. Louise Birdsell Bauer and Cynthia Cranford, "The Community Dimensions of Union Renewal: Racialized and Caring Relations in Personal Support Services," *Work, Employment and Society* 31, no. 2 (2017): 302–318; Bronfenbrenner and Warren, "Race, Gender, and the Rebirth of Trade Unionism"; Gill Kirton, "Sustaining and Developing Women's Trade Union Activism: A Gendered Project?" *Gender, Work & Organization* 6, no. 4 (1999): 213–23; Yates, "Challenging Misconceptions about Organizing Women into Unions."

48. Gill Kirton and Geraldine Healy, "Commitment and Collective Identity of Long-Term Union Participation: The Case of Women Union Leaders in the UK and USA," *Work, Employment and Society* 27, no. 2 (2013): 195–212; Dorothy Sue Cobble, "Rethinking Troubled Relations between Women and Unions: Craft Unionism and Female Activism," *Feminist Studies* 16, no. 3 (1990): 519–548; Edna E. Raphael, "Working Women and Their Membership in Labor Unions," *Monthly Labor Review* 97 (1974): 27–33.

49. Bronfenbrenner and Warren, "Race, Gender, and the Rebirth of Trade Unionism"; Dupuis, "Renouveau syndical."

50. Arlie Russell Hochschild and Anne Machung, *The Second Shift: Working Families and the Revolution at Home*, Revised ed. edition (New York: Penguin Books, 2012).

51. Interview #1.

52. Heidi Gottfried, "Why Workers' Rights Are Not Women's Rights," *Laws* 4, no. 2 (2015): 139–63; Charlotte Yates, "Expanding Labour's Horizons"; Kirton, "Sustaining and Developing Women's Trade Union Activism: A Gendered Project?"; Cobble, "Rethinking Troubled Relations between Women and Unions: Craft Unionism and Female Activism."

53. Christelle Avril, *Les aides à domicile : Un autre monde populaire* (Paris: La Dispute, 2014); Rhee and Zabin, "Aggregating Dispersed Workers."

54. Louise Boivin, "Réorganisation des services d'aide à domicile au Québec et droits syndicaux : de la qualification à la disponibilité permanente juste-à-temps," *Nouvelles Questions Féministes* 32, no. 2 (2014): 44–56; Rhee and Zabin, "Aggregating Dispersed Workers"; Denton, et al., "Market-Modelled Home Care"; Hélène David, Esther Cloutier, and Sara La Tour, "Le recours aux agences privées d'aide à domicile et de soins infirmiers par les services de soutien à domicile des CLSC" (Montréal: l'Institut de recherche Robert-Sauvé en santé et en sécurité du travail [IRSST], 2003).

55. Interview #2, January 12, 2017.

56. Joanie Sims-Gould, Kerry Byrne, Catherine Craven, Anne Martin-Matthews. and Janice Keefe, "Why I Became a Home Support Worker: Recruitment in the Home

Health Sector," *Home Health Care Services Quarterly* 29, no. 4 (2010): 171–194; Magalie Bonnet, "Le métier de l'aide à domicile: travail invisible et professionnalisation," *Nouvelle revue de psychosociologie*, no. 1 (2006): 73–85; Beverly Skeggs, *Formations of Class & Gender: Becoming Respectable* (London: Sage Publications, 1997).

57. Denton et al., "Market-Modelled Home Care"; Donna Baines, "Caring for Nothing: Work Organization and Unwaged Labour in Social Services," *Work, Employment and Society* 18, no. 2 (2004): 267–295; Folbre and Nelson, "For Love or Money—Or Both?"

58. Evelyn Nakano Glenn, *Forced to Care: Coercion and Caregiving in America* (Cambridge, Mass.; London: Harvard University Press, 2012); Hochschild, *The Commercialization of Intimate Life*; Rhacel Salazar Parrenas, *Servants of Globalization: Women, Migration, and Domestic Work*, First Edition (Stanford, CA.: Stanford University Press, 2001); Elsa Galerand, "Quelle conceptualisation de l'exploitation pour quelle critique intersectionnelle?" *Recherches féministes* 28, no. 2 (2015): 179–197.

59. Interview #2.

60. Stacey, *The Caring Self.*

61. Caroline Murphy and Thomas Turner, "Organising Precarious Workers: Can a Public Campaign Overcome Weak Grassroots Mobilisation at Workplace Level?" *Journal of Industrial Relations* 58, no. 5 (2016): 589–607.

62. Interview #2.

63. This is true whether the agencies providing the workforce in the sector invest all their government subsidies in operations—as with not-for-profits agencies—or provide a return to their shareholders (as with "for-profit agencies), balancing the budget largely depends on transferring the financial burden onto their workforce.

64. *Red Cross Care Partners* is a home care agency that provides traditional support services, nursing, and therapists. It was created in 2012 by merging nonprofit Red Cross Society agency and for-profit company CarePartners. It is the largest agency in Ontario and employs more than 4,500 PSWs SEIU Healthcare, "Why Is Red Cross Care Partners Exploiting Personal Support Workers?" SEIU Healthcare (blog), November 12, 2013, http://www.seiuhealthcare.ca/why_is_red_cross_care_partners_exploiting_personal_support_workers.

65. SEIU Healthcare.

66. Interview #1.

67. SEIU Healthcare, "Ontario Homecare Announcement Gives Hope to PSWs," SEIU Healthcare (blog), January 27, 2014, http://www.seiuhealthcare.ca/ontario_homecare_announcement_gives_hope_to_psws.

68. Informants used the expression "public campaign" to refer to what were considered key components of the Sweet $16 campaign: political engagement, noncorporatist demands, and attempts to establish alliances with civil society actors.

69. Interviews #1 and #2.

70. Ibid.

71. Interview #2.

72. Interview #1.

73. SEIU Healthcare, "Changing the Union to Reflect Our Membership," SEIU's Newsletter (blog), September 4, 2015, https://cld.bz/bookdata/m1BbQCu/basic-html/page-6.html#. However, the actual union's officers and executive board—composed predominantly of mostly (white) males—illustrates the existence of a "glass-ceiling" for aspiring activists.

74. Interview #1.

75. See, for example, SEIU Healthcare, "What Do We Want? Sweet $16! When? THIS MONTH!" SEIU Healthcare (blog), April 2014, http://www.seiuhealthcare.ca/what_do_we_want_sweet_16_when_this_month.

76. Interview #2.

77. Ibid.

78. At the end of the campaign, however, questions emerged about the extensive use of virtual spaces, specifically in the context of unequal access and participation to virtual networks by members and their supporters. Given the rapid development of communications technologies, this might be less of a concern in 2019.

79. Interview #1.

80. Interview #2.

81. Interview #1.

82. Ibid.

83. SEIU Healthcare, "It's Official: First Ask of Sweet $16' Campaign Achieved," July 2014, http://www.seiuhealthcare.ca/news-events/news/press-release/256-it-s-official-first-ask-of-sweet-16-campaign-achieved.

84. SEIU Healthcare, "Ontario Homecare Announcement Gives Hope to PSWs."

85. SEIU Healthcare, "'Sweet $16' Campaign Seeks Wage Hike for All Homecare PSWs."

86. SEIU Healthcare, "Sweet $16: Hot off the Press!" SEIU Healthcare (blog), March 20, 2014, http://www.seiuhealthcare.ca/sweet_16_hot_off_the_press.

87. Interview #1.

88. SEIU Healthcare, "What Do We Want?"

89. SEIU Healthcare, "Healthcare Union Members Elated by 'Stop Hudak' Success," SEIU Healthcare, June 2014, http://www.seiuhealthcare.ca/healthcare_union_members_elated_by_stop_hudak_success. This kind of practice echoes SEIU's strategies of counting on its members (and extensively the population) for specific votes, indeed encouraging citizenship participation.

90. Interview #1.

91. Guy Bellemare, Anne Renée Gravel et Alain Vallée, "Syndicalisme et mouvements sociaux: Voie de renouvellement des théories du syndicalisme et de l'action syndicale efficace? Le cas des services de garde," *Économie et Solidarités* 36, no. 2 (2006): 192–218; Paul Johnston, *Success While Others Fail: Social Movement Unionism and the Public Workplace* (Cornell University Press, 1994); Paul Johnston, "The Resurgence of Labor as a Citizenship Movement," in *Rekindling the Movement: Labor's Quest for Relevance in the*

Twenty-First Century, ed. Lowell Turner, Harry C. Katz, and Richard W. Hurd (Ithaca, NY: Cornell University Press, 2001), 27–58.

92. Dupuis, "Renouveau syndical."

93. Bellemare et al., "Syndicalisme et mouvements sociaux: voie de renouvellement des théories."

94. Interview #2.

95. Interview #1.

96. Interview #2.

97. For a more complete review of the several campaigns led by SEIU in the US in the home care services, see Linda Delp and Katie Quan, "Homecare Worker Organizing in California: An Analysis of a Successful Strategy," *Labor Studies Journal* 27, no. 1 (2002): 1–23; Keith Kelleher, "Growth of a Modern Union Local: A People's History of SEIU Local 880," *Just Labour* 12 (2008): 1–15; Mareschal, Patrice M. "Innovation and Adaptation: Contrasting Efforts to Organize Home Care Workers in Four States," *Labor Studies Journal* 31, no. 1 (March 2006): 2549; Stacey, *The Caring Self*.

98. Interview #2.

99. Rachel K. Brickner and Meaghan Dalton, "Organizing Baristas in Halifax Cafes: Precarious Work and Gender and Class Identities in the Millennial Generation," *Critical Sociology* 45, no. 4–5 (2019): 485–500; Yanick Noiseux, *Transformations des marchés du travail et innovations syndicales au Québec*.

100. Interviews #1, #2, and #3. Interview #3 was conducted on October 11, 2016.

101. Data provided by email.

9

The Global Career of Justice for Janitors and the Limits of Institutional Permeability

LUÍS LM AGUIAR

Is Justice for Janitors (J4J) the new form of organizing cleaners for global unionism in the 21st century? What, if anything, does J4J offer global organizing campaigns focused on cleaners in particular? Can this model really define the organizing of low-wage service workers in this century? These are ambitious and perhaps even presumptuous questions to pose and pursue. And yet, given the effectiveness of J4J in the United States in the midst of the fragmenting and splintering nature of neoliberalism, the unprecedented rise in inequality, the continuous growth in low-wage service work, and the task of organizing increasingly marginalized and vulnerable workers, the questions merit examination. The pursuit of these questions is not, however, without caution and controversy.[1] This chapter maps the global topography of J4J to understand the transnational relationships SEIU knitted together for organizing purposes to improve the lives of cleaners and their families. In conducting this research, I found the stitching of partnerships between SEIU and other unions served to excite, refocus, and in some cases redefine unions organizing workers differently in the face of the greatest obstacles to workers' rights and unionization since the early 20th century.[2]

The impact of J4J is differently felt in different locations due to the extent of its adoption, the rigor by which it continues to be (or not) pursued and its ability to connect with allies and the greater public.[3] The global ambitions of SEIU unfolded through scale jumping across national borders and resource stretching as it attempted to forge a new model of global union campaign using J4J as its vehicle. But the result was not a transnational campaign coherently coordinated and operating seamlessly across borders in organizing cleaning in the face of global cleaning capital. Instead, the findings reveal the implementation of nation-based J4J campaigns within national borders simultaneously occurring with changing national unions and traditions, inspired by shifts to the organizing model of union activities and identity. In this chapter I discuss the partnerships between SEIU and unions in Western Europe and then summarize the findings common to the different unions partnered with SEIU through J4J.

J4J Migrating across Borders

Neoliberalism is a double-edged sword. It assaults and claws back most workers' gains achieved in the post-war period. At the same time, the severe impacts of neoliberalism provide an impetus for unions to reinvigorate their efforts in globalizing their structures, strategies. and campaigns. Four examples stand out: One, by joining global labor organizations such as the Union-Network-International (UNI) for political action;[4] Two, by establishing and working through Global Unions Federations (GUFs) for coordinated action against a common company operating globally;[5] Three, by developing solidarity links with unions and NGOs elsewhere to organize workers across borders in the same industry or with the same employer (for example, to push for codes of conduct, independent monitoring, or worker rights petitions);[6] and Four, via grassroots internationalism connecting rank-and-file workers and their activism across borders and outside formal union structures.[7]

Peter Evans argued the time is right for labor to globalize since developments in new technologies facilitate communications across borders even as globalization fosters "the emergence of a globally-shared culture and everyday practices to create new potential for building solidarity across even the widest geographical divides."[8] Luce too sees advances in new technologies and communications as a means to connect activists across borders to develop global unionism in this period of neoliberalism.[9] Few contributions to this literature follow the transferability of an organizing model for marginalized workers—visible minorities, women, and undocumented workers—across different places, spaces, and scales and watch it unfold.[10] My work builds on this more recent research by examining how SEIU proposed to organize cleaners globally by exporting J4J worldwide and working with unions to anchor this campaign in specific geographical locations. Globalization, the transnationalization of the cleaning industry, ownership, and working conditions, as well as social reproduction issues, are the impetus for J4J organizing. SEIU, an adventurous union, has taken upon itself to change, challenge, and move the labor movement out of its doldrums.[11] In the US labor landscape, J4J reroutes unions previously reliant on an interventionist state for legislative changes to challenge their internal cultures and leaders to rethink how to improve workers' lives through street theatre protests, civil disobedience, and militancy.[12] What then does an investigation of the globalizing of J4J add to our understanding of organizing transnationally? What does J4J promise in organizing globally? These questions are tackled in the remaining sections of this chapter.

There are four main reasons J4J migrated across borders: (1) Countries are in the grips of aggressive economic restructuring, though experiencing it in different intensities.[13] Unions such as SEIU and its partners are seeking best strategies[14] to respond to government policies, and shrinking union density, which in France is approximately 11%,[15] 14% in Australia,[16] 18% in the Netherlands,[17] and 24% in Ireland.[18] (2) The restructuring was especially evident in the cleaning industry across the developed world. The industry fragmented; the deregulation of the labor market became pervasive—as did contracting-out and privatization—and risk was shifted to the individual and away from business and government, while also intensifying women's unpaid domestic work, social reproduction, and women's work generally.[19] (3) Unions in different countries were searching for innovative ways to stem membership decline in the face of economic restructuring while at the same time growing union members through new organizing strategies, and the J4J model seemed to provide an answer to their problems. For instance, the Howard government (defeated in 2007 by Kevin Rudd's Labour Party) pushed through in Australia "enterprise unionism," while the labor movement's adoption of "Organizing Works" failed to stem the decline in union membership.[20] In France, different socialist governments over the last forty years did little to improve workers' lives, and union density remained abysmally low.[21] Not surprisingly, the success of J4J in the US attracted attention in Australia, France, and elsewhere where organizers were struggling to revitalize their unions. (4) The mobility of models and campaigns across borders intensified with globalization, which compressed time and distance and pushed activists to take advantage of organizing experiences in other national contexts, reworking innovative "models, methods, and mutations" in place-specific ways. If corporate and government policies were "on the move" in the neoliberal era, so too were organizing models like J4J.[22] The latter drew attention from labor movements across the globe driven in part by the missionary zeal of SEIU, a union that was in constant search of partnerships and coalitions to organize the industries it had chosen to target.

As J4J evolved, scaled up, and went transnational, it implemented change differently depending upon the existing history and practices of SEIU's partner unions and the different industrial relations regimes within which they operated—regimes which, despite their diversity, were all, according to Marginson, "fracturing" due to the "weakening" of the "institutional pillars" of industrial relations owing to the declining influence and increasing incoherence of the European social model.[23] In this context, SEIU and its partners faced a key question: should the J4J model be flexible, malleable, and adaptable to these changes, or should it be implemented in a uniform way in every setting in order to be effective?

Partnerships and Institutional Permeability

In the difficult and challenging political and economic context of the collapse of the postwar social contract,[24] the deconstruction of the male standard on employment relationship and the feminization of employment,[25] the rise of economic restructuring, rapidly declining union density in western countries,[26] and SEIU controversies within the American Labour Movement,[27] SEIU remained defiantly independent and one of the most aggressive forces in organizing workers anywhere.[28] Many of its successes are attributable to the ideas, tactics, and strategies embedded in the union's J4J campaigns. These include: a direct approach to organizing workers; a focus on alternative forms of organizing to bypass the National Labor Relations Board; grassroots methods of gathering strength and resiliency often through civil disobedience;[29] public shaming of building owners and managers; a focus on immigrant and visible minority workers as organizable;[30] the national union's use of trusteeship to impose the J4J approach in reluctant locals,[31] employer neutrality, and a focus on women workers and social reproduction as critically important to organizing gains.[32] The success of J4J elevated the status of the campaign to the "ideal model" for organizing workers in the enfolding neoliberal economy of late capitalism where small workplaces proliferate, culturally diverse workforces are the norm, capital contracts-out and de-regulates, and antilabor legislation is omnipresent. The development and unfolding of J4J raised important criticisms regarding over-reliance on a "militant minority" of activists to organize and run campaigns. This has consequences for workers' democratic participation in campaigns to organize their own workplace and industry. Moreover, its top-down approach alienates some workers and coalition members such as social movements who organize in a nonhierarchical fashion and see participation as empowering rather than as opportunistic.[33] Yet, for all SEIU's militancy, the union tended to be mostly regionally grounded,[34] and the union's national strategy had only taken shape in the late twentieth century.[35]

In spite of the features outlined earlier, SEIU "jumped scale" by going global shortly after the turn of the century. In 2004 it marked out a blue-print for the future including developing "global strength" by establishing partnerships with unions in other countries to unite workers doing the same job (for example, cleaning or security) and often for the same employer. The nature of SEIU's alliances with other unions around the world remains little explored despite the breadth and number of these "global partnerships." These included an alliance with the Liquor, Hospitality & Miscellaneous Workers' Union (LHMU, now United Voices) in Australia;[36] another in Ireland with Services Industrial Professional and Technical Union (SIPTU);[37] one in Holland with the then FVN Bondgenoten;[38] relationships with the Solidaires, Unitaires, Democratiques (SUD-Rail) union federation[39] and the French Democratic Confederation of Labour (CFDT) in France;[40] and with the Centro de Trabajadores de la Limpieza and other Mexican workers' rights groups such as PODER.[41]

The strategic importance of these partnerships to SEIU's global ambitions in the Stern era was underlined by its appointment of key staff members to building and maintaining a network of global relationships. Stern named Debbie Schneider as head of the union's "Global Strength" effort.[42] Michael Crosby was named organizing director for the union's Global Partnerships effort for Australia and Pacific Rim countries;[43] Nick Allen was dispatched as a special envoy to Paris; Liz O'Connor was charged with exploring relationships in Mexico City; David Chu, Valery Alzaga, and Andrea Staples staffed the Change to Win (CtW) organizing office in Utrecht, The Netherlands; and Christy Hoffman went to head up the property services division of the Geneva-based Union-Network-International (UNI), in which SEIU played a major role. (Hoffman would go on to become Deputy General Secretary of UNI in 2010 and then General Secretary of the organization in 2018.) As they dispersed around the world, these SEIU staffers sought to partner with local unions to implement J4J in an effort to stymie union decline, inject momentum into cleaners' campaigns, and target marginalized and immigrant workers for organizing. They found willing partners and advocates in each of these locations. These included Louise Tarrant (LHMU/United Voices) in Australia,[44] Eddy Stam in the FNV Bondgenoten in The Netherlands,[45] Ethel Buckley of SIPTU in Ireland, and assorted activists from the Centro de Trabajadores de la Limpieza in Mexico City who worked with Liz O'Connor.[46] The progress of the J4J model as a global undertaking is traceable in these personalities and the relationships they built between SEIU and its partners.

Veterans of SEIU organizing initiatives and campaigns played a central role in the Change to Win office in Utrecht. Their work helped turn SEIU from an uninvolved and disengaged observer of global events into a union establishing partnerships and institutionalizing new practices and mechanisms at the global level. Some of them—Crosby and Schneider, for example—remained steadfast for the long haul, while others eventually grew disappointed with the work for reasons to be discussed later.[47] Table 9.1 details the country, the time-line, key supporters of the partnership, and the reception of J4J by the local union.

Partnership is not a concept usually applied to unions for it evokes a corporate connotation, such as neoliberal public-private partnerships overseen or legitimated by the state (the so-called 3Ps). Unions are more likely to use the term *collaboration* to capture the common ideal or solidarity they seek in a particular initiative or campaign. Nonetheless, SEIU sought partnerships with like-minded unions across the globe to coordinate strategies to address global capital and, in particular, cleaning capital and security capital, which was everywhere tied to commercial real estate capital. Wary of their own union's history during the Cold War,[48] SEIU officials made it a point to visit potential partners to candidly discuss SEIU's history and open dialogue about its new approach and direction as it sought to knit together long-term relationships capable of countering the power of capital.[49] Once this consulting period was complete, the union announced its intentions to establish partnerships at its 2004 convention.

Thereafter the union "scale-stretched" resources to the global with a new vision and purpose. As Kieran Allen put it, "instead of a haphazard approach

TABLE 9.1 The Global Career of J4J

Country	Australia	Holland	Ireland	Mexico	France
Field visit	2007	2008	2012+2015	2012	2008
Partner	LHMU	FNV B	SIPTU	Centro	CFDT
Advocates	Tarrant	Stam	Buckley*	Activists	?
Reception	On board	Skeptical/ lukewarm	On board with reservations	Folded	Shadowing unionists
Personnel	Crosby	Alzaga	Chu/Staples	O'Connor	Allen
Support network	SEIU +	SEIU/CtW/UNI	CtW/UNI/SEIU	SEIU/PODER	CtW

* In the case of SIPTU, Jack O'Connor (General President of the union 2003–2017) and Joe Cunningham who at the time of the interview (August 20, 2015) was the Head of the Strategic Organizing Department since the restructuring of the SIPTU in 2010. Cunningham is now General Secretary of the SIPTU. Buckley (interviewed June 21, 2012) was supported in her work by these union leaders. Today, Buckley is Deputy General Secretary to the SIPTU.

to organizing," SEIU "systematically targeted particular industries" where it sought "to have a high union density in order to gain leverage."[50] The point was to "create institutional structures to solidify and reproduce the partnerships established with various unions so as to sustain a presence in workplaces and industry across different borders and spaces."[51] Jaime McCallum styles this approach "institutional internationalism."[52] That term suggests an institutional permanency that is more fluid and haphazard in actual practise. Moreover, the concept of institutional internationalism, with its connotations of structures, mechanisms, and practices, can obscure the extent to which paternalism was embedded in the power imbalances between partnered unions. These imbalances often were the source of resentment that hindered SEIU's partnerships with "weaker" unions and meant that in many cases the steps partners took to consolidate the partnership were occasionally taken ambivalently or even reluctantly.[53] This was the case across the studies described here, as country-specific advocates, staff, and activists grew uncomfortable with the assertiveness of American "colleagues," and as they came to question the imposition of a model that too often seemed to disregard or marginalize the relevance of a partner union's history.

Rather than institutional internationalism, "institutional permeability" seems a more appropriate term to describe how J4J worked when it was at its most effective. Successful J4J campaigns outside of North America were largely contingent on the strength of local agents, histories, practices, and ideas and on how well these were incorporated into the design, implementation, and unfolding of the cleaners' campaign. While SEIU and partner unions were cognizant of different national industrial relations systems and their attendant corporative frameworks, these were less an obstacle to the achievement of common objectives than was gaining local internal union leadership support for SEIU-inspired changes which in turn depended upon SEIU's ability to listen and adapt.[54]

Having described both the reasons for organizing internationally and the opportunities and pitfalls inherent in forging partnerships around J4J, let us turn to the actual process by which J4J was adopted, implemented, transformed, and critiqued.

Globalizing J4J

The effectiveness of J4J in organizing cleaners across the US attracted desperate unions in other nations that were looking to organize against the growing power of capital and seeking new ways of organizing and resisting capital.[55] The potential transferability of the J4J model intrigued them. But could J4J deliver new hope in organizing cleaners across the globe? Did it possess the dynamics necessary for inspiring and transforming organizing cultures in global unions keying on resisting global capital? Jaime McCallum writes that just as the organizing model in which J4J occupied a central place was failing in the United States, "it was gaining popularity around the world." He argues that its origin and development within the unique American industrial relations regime made J4J "non-transferable."[56] Yet while there are clear and significant differences between the American and European industrial relations regimes, the common experiences regarding the consolidation of the cleaning industry, its increasingly homogenous workplace experiences, and the growing impact of neoliberalism on the industry in country after country encouraged both SEIU and its partners to believe that the J4J model could scale globally.[57] Indeed, the very concept of neoliberalism encouraged this belief. As David Harvey notes, neoliberalism is space-specific.[58] Yet it shares enough features to enable not only transnational study but transnational strategy. Ultimately, it was workers' experience with neoliberalism—and its impact on the alarming decline of union density across Western Europe—that encouraged J4J's transnational extension. There was then a push-pull factor in this process. SEIU pushed across borders through a concerted effort to coordinate organizing with partnered unions that would give it leverage against its adversaries in capital. At the same time, partnered unions sought to pull SEIU's successful organizing model into to their geographies to organize the growing service economy and stymie rapidly declining union density.

Despite its attraction, there were obstacles to J4J's transnational spread. The most significant was the suspicion that adhered to J4J's tactics and analysis among many of its partners.[59] Within the European union's adopting J4J model, discussions emerged about how much of the union resources should be dedicated to the unfolding of J4J and the extent to which local unions were willing to receive instruction on adopting a model developed by a US union with an unsavory history of labor internationalism. A further consideration was a trepidation about accepting US boorish attitudes in promoting and imposing an American model of organizing, while paying lip service to local histories, initiatives, ingenuity, and actors. For this reason, it was important that an Australian (and not an American) initially approached the union partner (e.g., Ireland's SIPTU) intending to explain how to implement the organizing model.[60] In fact, an Australian SEIU-connected official produced a forensic study of the SIPTU indicating the ways by which the union went about shifting from a service to an organizing model.[61] The internal reorganization of SPITU, the report argued, could use J4J as the organizing approach for bringing new workers into the union.[62]

In addition to the suspicion that often clouded potential partners' views of SEIU, the spread of J4J was hampered by the sidelining of its architect just as the transnational project was gaining traction. Stephen Lerner, the architect of J4J, was forced to resign from SEIU shortly after Mary Kay Henry defeated Anna Burger, whom Andy Stern attempted to install as his successor when he stepped down from the union's presidency in April 2010 (see Lerner interview in this volume). Following Lerner's departure from SEIU, some prominent union insiders concluded J4J's time was over and relegated it to the status of a mere symbol of a bygone era of organizing.[63] Others questioned its utility in developing strategies and tactics transferable to other settings such as commodity chains.[64] Yet supporters of J4J remained within SEIU, especially in its organizing department. Indeed, despite McCallum's remark above, J4J and its global ambitions persisted in the post-Lerner era.

How did J4J partnership-building proceed? Having established a partnership and putting aside resources, the next step for partner unions was to implement J4J onsite. A first step was to rename the J4J campaign to ensure traction and appeal to people and workers in the countries where J4J landed. Table 9.2 identifies the partner unions, names the local campaign, defines the degree of commitment made by the local partner, and the extent to which it embodied J4J principles and practices.

So J4J in Sydney was baptized "Clean Start," in Amsterdam "Cleaners for a Better Tomorrow," (also "Schoon Genoeg"—"Clean Enough"), in Dublin "Fair Deal for Cleaners," and in Mexico City "Brillando con Justicia" ("Shining with justice/Justice shines").[65] In addition to each of these locations devising a place-specific slogan to capture workers' experience to resonate with the larger

TABLE 9.2 The Global Career of J4J

Union	LHMU	FNV B	SIPTU	Centro/SEIU	CFDT/SUD*
Slogan	Clean Start	Schoon Genoeg	Fair Deal	Brillando con Justicia	none
Commitment	Yes	Lukewarm	Yes, but	Exploratory	none
Model	Organizing	Pilot	Organizing	Exploratory	none
J4J	"Pure J4J"	"Not J4J Enough"	"J4J sans politics"	"J4J miscarried"	none
City	Sydney	Amsterdam	Dublin	Mexico City	Paris

* Most of the column here is blank since there was no coherent articulation of partnership between CtW/SEIU and the French unions. Interview with Nick Allen, May 25, 2011, Washington, D.C. Also, while these campaigns originally sought to organize cleaners in the entire country, the stretch on resources, people, and time consumption reduced most of the organizing activities to the capital cities.

community, each demonstrated greater or lesser degrees of flexibility (or not) of the J4J model as in different locations shaped by diverse social, economic, and political forces. Each of the campaigns was inspired by J4J and the mentorship and received the advice and instruction of SEIU personnel seconded across the globe to work with trade unions on how to mount, develop, organize, and sustain campaigns where activism, union leadership, and street theatre performance were all rolled into the new identity of the unionist as (community) organizer. At the start this was not always an easy task since unions elsewhere were unaccustomed to militating on the street, having learned to bargain within state-sponsored corporatist structures.[66] However, as the state deregulated, decentralized, privatized, and turned its back on past practices and workers, unionists increasingly questioned past faith in the state and demonstrated a willingness to try SEIU's model.

One of the attractions of SEIU's approach was its ability to make invisible workers visible. Invisibility is a powerful metaphor to capture the experiences of cleaners. Because cleaners usually work at night, the "regular" workforce in an office building is gone and does not see them or even realize they have been present unless their offices are not cleaned or are cleaned poorly. In this case, office occupants (the "regular" workforce) complain to the cleaning contractor, who then puts pressure on cleaners to intensify their work and increase the standard of cleanliness. In addition, cleaners often use separate entrances into their workplaces, and are instructed by employers to make themselves visually "scarce," thereby furthering their invisibility. In large cities like Toronto, cleaners use the subway and underground walkways to get to work. In so doing, they "escape" the eye of the onlooker as they walk hidden passages and corridors, climb steps, or use elevators rarely encountering the 9–5 workforce or anyone else except perhaps security guards. In some cases, they hide in plain view.[67] Also hidden from view are their working conditions and experiences. Because no one is around, no one can witness their work performance and the conditions under which they work.

Part of making cleaners visible entailed naming their campaigns in a way that gained attention and sympathy.[68] As Canadian transit union local leader Scott Lovell has argued, the right slogan identifying a campaign or strike action is key to garnering public support and encouragement.[69] For this reason, organizers in each of the locations studied chose different slogans and campaign names appropriate to their settings. For example, in Australia "Clean Start" identified the campaign. In Australia, as in other settings outside of the United States, organizers did not refer to janitors, since that term was not used to describe people who clean office buildings for a living. Nonetheless, Michael Crosby reported that the strategy in Australia was "pure J4J." What did Crosby mean by "pure J4J"? Essentially, he meant that SEIU's model was transferred in toto. According to Crosby, several organizers from SEIU US moved to Australia to train and coordinate the campaign there. In addition, SEIU helped fund the campaign, including staff salaries. At its high point, a team of thirty organizers and five researchers, including both LHMU and SEIU staff, were dedicated to the Clean Start campaign.[70]

These staff members coordinated an effort that closely resembled J4J in the United States, including its combination of worker recruitment and public-shaming employers. As with J4J's American campaigns, Clean Start focused on making cleaners visible and demanding recognition of their work and contributions to Australian society.[71] This wholesale adoption and implementation of J4J in Sydney also entailed bringing on board the limitations in the model critics have pointed out and which I summarized earlier, including a tendency toward staff-driven strategy and tactics.

The campaign in Ireland unfolded differently. There, SIPTU adopted the organizing model and collaborated with CtW/SEIU in the mid-2000s but did not cede as much control over strategy and message to their American colleagues as the Australians had done.[72] SIPTU mounted and coordinated a "Fair Deal" for cleaners' campaign targeting metropolitan Dublin. The campaign's name implicitly spoke to the injustice Dublin's cleaners endured on the job even as it highlighted the agency of the union in pushing for equity. After all, who in Irish society could be openly against "fairness"? In taking this name, the Irish union attempted to turn neoliberalism's promise of fair reward for hard work back on itself. In arguing for a fair deal, cleaners signaled that they were not after any advantage or privilege but simply sought an equitable reward for their hard work and sacrifices; they simply wanted to extend to cleaners neoliberalism's "deliverable" on fairness and reward for hard work and dedication.[73] Over the years SIPTU worked closely with CtW and SEIU in both the development of the campaign and, more importantly, in transforming the structures of the union from service to organizing.[74] This entailed numerous visits by parties from both unions to and from Dublin. In addition, staff from the Change to Win office in Utrecht shepherded the mounting of the original campaign and remained regularly in touch with SIPTU staff and activists.[75]

The strong collaboration between SIPTU and SEIU/CtW waned over time, however. I observed this in two visits to SIPTU headquarters in 2012 and 2015 during which it became clear that the work of transforming the union to SEIU's organizing model had stalled and, in some cases, had begun to encounter internal opposition.[76] It appears that growing trepidations within SIPTU about the changes required by the organizing model led to a retreat in the campaign for organizing cleaners. Initially when J4J was dropped into Dublin and SIPTU people, resources, and even the entire basement of SIPTU's headquarters, Liberty Hall, were dedicated to the Fair Deal for Cleaners campaign, staff were excited and believed they had become part of something bigger with prospects of making significant impact in the lives of low-waged Irish workers. Meetings with cleaners were frequent and the latter's participation was organic to the unfolding of the campaign. Cleaners' Forum brought together workers across Dublin and nearby cities to join, socialize, and discuss their common experiences. A social bond between participants developed and they saw the gathering as both a formal assembly for union business and an informal opportunity to bond and share where even the shyest member felt at ease to participate. Potlucks were welcome, and plays were mounted by cleaners displaying their creativity.[77]

But during my last fieldwork visit to SIPTU organizing office in August 2015, the mood in the room had changed along with the personnel and leadership of the campaign. The numbers of staff assigned to the campaign had been significantly reduced, and organizers were now tied to their desks, quite a different practice from what I had observed in my visit three years before. During interviews, some unionists complained about feeling overextended because of understaffing. Others were disappointed the Cleaners' Forum had ended since it had done much to build solidarity among cleaners.[78] Unionists who had taken part in the original organizing moved on to other positions and campaigns within the union, while others left the union altogether in frustration with the re-direction of the campaign and focus.[79] Discouraged interviewees expressed concern that more staff reductions were likely. One summarized for me the more radical and disappointing changes the campaign was undergoing, including a change of leadership in the organizing department and the campaign, which impacted creativity and diminished aspirations and expectations on organizing. This individual, "Pat," had been involved in the original cleaners' campaign but by 2015 had moved into another campaign in another floor of Liberty Hall. I recorded our conversation in my fieldnotes.

> Pat thought that perhaps the most important change related to the politics of solidarity whereby cleaners from different locations came together to share stories, meet one another and make common cause. The original campaign had a politics of consciousness raising and a kind of insurgency attached to the work and the people involved. This is no longer the case in the organizing department with respect to cleaning. The department is moving away from the grassroots

> too, and as a result, issues and ideas increasingly come from the top. Pat said this leads to a distancing between the work of unionists and cleaner activists.

Pat believed this change was a result of personnel substitutions and personality conflicts within the organizing division.

> Pat believes that some of the reasons for this shift are due to personality conflict between key figures in the organizing division. As a result, re-assignments happen for workplace "peace." Pat believes the current head of the organizing campaign is career unionist without social movement credentials and possibly put in place to manage the current approach rather than re-invent a more militant direction to organizing cleaners.[80]

According to Pat, recruitment replaced activist campaigning through worker solidarity building and identity.

It is not uncommon for personality conflicts to emerge within organizations or for leaders to shift people around to get the most out of them while working in a tense climate.[81] It is not unusual for activists to feel frustrated by the slow pace or redirection of a campaign. Most disappointing for Pat was the lack of substance and sustenance to the campaign. Like most other initiatives within a union, campaigns face time constraints and must meet specific goals on defined timetables. Clearly, the Fair Deal campaign had fallen off the curve and its once bustling office had lost its excitement and energy.[82] J4J in Ireland was in contraction. I observed staff members at their desks using their phones to reach out to contacts. While they were hard at work, the initial excitement I had witnessed in my first visit was gone. The posters, slogans, charts, photos, tables, paper, testimonials, and expansive "war room" in the basement of Liberty Hall had disappeared and been replaced by three desks behind which organizers did their work. Although organizing visits to workplaces was still exciting and rewarding when they happened, they had become infrequent and were now undertaken on an individual organizer's initiative, rather than as a large-scale team effort. What had promised to be an industry-wide assault on organizing devolved into an effort by individual organizers to respond to members' inquiries, recruit members. and grow the union. My observations suggested that the effort in Ireland had devolved into what Melanie Simms and Jane Holgate describe as efforts to improve the "toolbox" of organizing approaches that stress techniques over substance.[83]

It is worth noting that between my first and second visits to SIPTU offices, SEIU's efforts in the United States had moved increasingly away from investing in the J4J model and toward a new and different direction. In January 2011, under the leadership of Mary Kay Henry, SEIU launched the Fight for a Fair Economy, a $50 million drive by the union to mobilize low-wage workers impacted by the Great Recession and deepening austerity. By the fall of 2012 that effort had in turn spawned organizing among fast food workers in New York City, which led to a symbolic one-day strike by SEIU-supported activists on November 29 of that year. Over the course of 2013, the fast food workers' movement spread beyond New York and took on a name: the Fight for $15. By the time I returned to SIPTU headquarters in 2015, the Fight for $15 had displaced J4J as SEIU's signature campaign in the United States. Even as far away as Dublin, one could sense that J4J no longer captured the same degree of SEIU's investment or enthusiasm.

The same diminution of energy that I witnessed in SEIU's partnership with SIPTU was replicated in its collaborations in Amsterdam and Mexico City and its search for a partner in Paris. In each of these locations, the campaigns lost momentum after promising beginnings.[84] Most of SEIU's initial partners scaled down their national ambitions to city-based efforts because of stretched resources and the unwillingness of union leaders to invest the time, money, and personnel necessary to let the campaign germinate. In some cases, organizers assured me that no time limit was attached to their campaign. Yet, subsequent research visits revealed that this was not the case; the results-based union leadership had lost patience with the slow unfolding of campaigns.[85]

As these efforts showed, J4J could not be simply "up-scaled" in "pure" form since scale is not just another level where organizing takes place but is complicated by different and often more powerful and particular local forces.[86] Up-scaling across global spaces with different histories, social actors, models of organizing workers, labor relations systems, gender histories, and scales of action and intervention proved difficult.[87] The scale of organizing depended on several factors. There was an initial and ambitious campaign to organize cleaners nationally in each setting, putting pressure on employers across the country and organizing them simultaneously, with the goal of winning similar wages, benefits, and working conditions. This initial excitement soon met reality, however. For most campaigns, a time line was set to have the campaign prove itself. This period is not always rigidly imposed but organizers knew intimately that they needed results and success in order to maintain the campaign operating with the vigor, breadth, and scale it had initially defined. Unfortunately, even the best plans can come up against harsh realities, as was the case in Ireland and other settings. That SEIU's priorities began to shift toward the Fight for $15 at precisely the moment when these global efforts were attempting to gain traction only compounded the problems campaigns ran into on the ground in Europe and Australia.

Conclusions

Did SEIU and the partner unions that attempted to implement its Justice for Janitors model ever hold the best roadmap to organizing low-wage workers across Western Europe and Australia? While much fanfare and excitement emerged regarding the potential of J4J to deliver a new way to organize cleaners in particular, my research casts doubts on its transferability. My findings suggest some of the most significant criticisms of J4J in the US also reared their heads in Europe, where tensions emerged between worker-empowering democratic processes and campaign-driven structures, goals, and timetables.[88] When these problems were combined with the difficulties of transferring the J4J model into widely divergent settings and the shift of SEIU's priorities away from J4J, these factors together ensured that J4J fell far short of its initial promise.

Yet, my research also suggests a more hopeful conclusion. While J4J is no longer seen as central to the story of the revitalization of the labor movement in the 21st century, it lives on in reincarnated form in new campaigns to organize low-waged. racially marginal, and immigrant workers.[89] It therefore behooves today's labor movement activists and organizers both inside and outside SEIU to, as another contribution to this volume puts it, "ponder the evolution of Justice for Janitors" and ask whether its "final fruits have yet to be harvested."[90] It would be unfortunate indeed if a model once so exciting, innovative, and militant was to be relegated to the status of a mere symbol, the signature campaign of a bygone era of SEIU organizing.

Notes

I presented an early version of this chapter at the Confronting Global Capital Conference, McMaster University, Hamilton, Ontario, October 12–14, 2017. For their insightful questions and comments on this paper, I thank the participants in the session "Organizing Transnationally." I also thank Joe McCartin for his edits and advice on making this a more cogent chapter. The research for this paper is part of a larger project on the J4J and Globalization funded by the Social Sciences and Humanities Research Council of Canada (SSHRC), grant # 410-2010-1530.

1. Jaime McCallum, *Global Unions, Local Power: The New Spirit of Transnational Labor Organizing* (Ithaca, NY: ILR Press, 2013); Melanie Simms, Jane Holgate, and Edmund Heery, *Union Voices: Tactics and Tensions in UK Organizing* (Ithaca, NY: ILR Press, 2013); Bill Fletcher Jr. and Fernando Gapasin, *Solidarity Divided: The Crisis in Organized Labor and the New Path Toward Social Justice* (Berkeley: University of California Press, 2008).

2. Andreas Bieler et al., (eds.), *Labour and Transnational Action in Times of Crisis* (New York: Rowman & Littlefield, 2015); Philippe Crevier, Hubert Fortier, and Samuel

Trepanier (eds.), *Renouveller le Syndicalisme pour Changer le Quebec*, (Montreal, QC: Ecosociete, 2015); and Kim Moody, *Workers in a Lean World: Unions in the International Economy* (New York: Verso, 1997).

3. Heather Connolly, Stefania Marino, and Miguel Martinez Lucio, "'Justice for Janitors Goes Dutch': The Limits and Possibilities of Unions' Adoption of Organizing in a Context of Regulated Social Partnership," *Work, Employment and Society* 31, no. 2 (2017): 319–335; Russell and McCartin, "Persistence, Militancy, and Power," in this book.

4. Andrew Herod, *Geographies of Globalization: A Critical Introduction* (Malden, MA: Wiley-Blackwell, 2009).

5. Richard Croucher and Elizabeth Cotton, *Global Unions Global Business: Global Union Federations and International Business* (London: Middlesex University Press, 2009).

6. Ralph Armbruster-Sandoval, *Globalization and Cross-Border Labor Solidarity in the Americas: The Anti-Sweatshop Movement and the Struggle for Social Justice* (New York: Routledge, 2005).

7. Noel Castree, "Geographic Scale and Grass-Roots Internationalism: The Liverpool Dock Dispute, 1995–1998," *Economic Geography* 76, no. 3 (2000): 272–292.

8. Peter Evans, "Is It Labour's Turn to Globalize? Twenty-First Century Opportunities and Strategic Responses," *Global Labour Journal* 1, no. 3 (2010): 357.

9. Stephanie Luce, *Labor Movements: Global Perspectives* (Malden, MA: Polity, 2014), 175.

10. Adrien Thomas, "The Transnational Circulation of the 'Organizing Model' and Its Reception in Germany and France," *European Journal of Industrial Relations* 22, no. 4 (2016): 317–333.

11. For an example of this, see SEIU's role in creating the Change to Win labour federation in Ruth Milkman and Kim Voss, "New Unity for Labor?" *Labor: Studies in Working-Class History of the Americas* 2, no. 1 (2005): 15–25.

12. Simms, Holgate, and Heery, *Union Voices*; Edward Webster, Rob Edward, and Andries Bezuidenhout, *Grounding Globalization: Labour in the Age of Insecurity* (Malden, MA: Blackwell, 2008).

13. Chris Howell, "The State and the Reconstruction of Industrial Relations after Fordism: Britain and France Compared," in *The State after Statism*, ed. Jonah D. Levy (Cambridge: Harvard University Press, 2006), 139–184; Shaun Ryan and Andrew Herod, "Restructuring the Architecture of State Regulation in the Australian and Aotearoa/New Zealand Cleaning Industries and the Growth of Precarious Employment," *Antipode* 38, no. 3 (2006): 486–507.

14. Renaud Damesin and Jean-Michel Denis, "SUD Trade Unions: The New Organisations Trying to Conquer the French Trade Union Scene," *Capital & Class* 29, no. 2 (2005): 17–31.

15. https://www.worker-participation.eu/National-Industrial-Relations/Countries/France/Trade-Unions.

16. https://www.abs.gov.au/statistics/labour/earnings-and-work-hours/trade-union-membership/latest-release. Union density in Australia in 1986 was just short of half at 47.3%.

17. https://www.worker-participation.eu/National-Industrial-Relations/Countries/Netherlands/Trade-Unions.

18. https://www.worker-participation.eu/National-Industrial-Relations/Countries/Ireland/Trade-Unions.

19. Kate Bezanson and Med Luxton (eds.), *Social Reproduction: Feminist Political Economy Challenges Neo-Liberalism* (Montreal/Kingston: McGill/Queen's University Press, 2006); Leah Vosko, *Temporary Work: The Gendered Rise of a Precarious Employment Relationship* (Toronto, ON: University of Toronto Press, 2000).

20. G. Griffin, R. Small and S. Svensen, "Trade Union Innovation, Adaptation and Renewal in Australia," in *Trade Unions in Renewal: A Comparative Study*, ed. Peter Fairbrother and Charlotte A.B. Yates (New York: Routledge, 2003), 78–101.

21. Dominique Andolfatto and Dominique Labbe, "The Future of the French Trade Unions." *Management Revue* 23, no. 4 (2012): 341–352. On the ability of French workers to use militancy to compensate for low density, see https://www.aljazeera.com/features/2016/8/1/just-how-powerful-are-frances-labour-unions *and* https://jacobinmag.com/2020/1/france-strikes-trade-unions-gilets-jaunes.

22. Jamie Peck and Nik Theodore, "Mobilizing Policy: Models, Methods, and Mutations." *Geoforum* 41, no. 2 (2010: 169–174.

23. Paul Marginson, "European Industrial Relations: An Increasingly Fractured Landscape?" *Warwick Papers in Industrial Relations*, no. 106, University of Warwick, Industrial Relations Research Unit, Coventry, 2017.

24. Isabella Bakker, *Rethinking Restructuring: Gender and Change in Canada* (Toronto, ON: University of Toronto Press, 1996); William Carroll, "Introduction: Social Democracy in Neoliberal Times," in *Challenges and* Perils, ed. William Carrol and R. S. Radner (Halifax, NS: Fernwood, 2005), 7–24; and David Harvey, *The Condition of Postmodernity* (Malden, MA: Blackwell, 1989).

25. Vosko, *Temporary Work.*

26. Rebecca Gumbrell-McCormick and Richard Hyman, *Trade Unions in Western Europe* (New York: Oxford University Press, 2014).

27. Dan Clawson, *The Next Upsurge: Labor and the New Social Movements* (Ithaca, NY: ILR Press, 2003); Kim Moody, *US Labor in Trouble and Transition: The Failure of Reform from Above, the Promise of Renewal from Below* (New York: Verso, 2007); and Carl Winslow, *Labor's Civil War in California: The NUHW Healthcare Workers' Rebellion* (Oakland, CA: PM Press, 2010). See also Fletcher and Lichtenstein, http://inthesetimes.com/article/5309/seius_civil_war.

28. Steven Henry Lopez, *Reorganizing the Rust Belt: An Inside Study of the American Labor Movement* (Berkeley: University of California Press, 2004); and Roger Waldinger, et al., "Helots no More: A Case Study of the Justice for Janitors Campaign, in *Organizing*

to Win, ed. Kate Bronfenbrenner, et al. (Ithaca, NY: Cornell University Press, 1998), 102–119.

29. Lydia Savage, "Geographies of Organizing: Justice for Janitors in Los Angeles," in *Organizing the Landscape*, ed. Andrew Herod (Minneapolis: University of Minnesota Press, 1998), 225–252.

30. Ruth Milkman, *L.A. Story: Immigrant Workers and the Future of the U.S. Labor Movement* (New York: Russell Sage, 2006).

31. Rick Fantasia and Kim Voss, *Hard Work: Remaking the American Labor Movement* (Berkeley: University of California Press, 2004), 136.

32. Lydia Savage, "Justice for Janitors: Scales of Organizing and Representing Workers." In *The Dirty Work of Neoliberalism*, ed. Luis LM Aguiar and Andrew Herod (Malden, MA: Blackwell, 2006), 214–234.

33. Luis LM Aguiar, "Sweatshop Citizenship, Precariousness and Organizing Building Cleaners," in *Neoliberal Capitalism and Precarious Work: Ethnographies of Accommodation and Resistance*, ed. Rob Lambert and Andrew Herod (London: Edward Elgar, 2016), 255–276; and Jane McAlevey, *Raising Expectations (and Raising Hell): My Decade Fighting for the Labor Movement* (New York: Verso, 2012).

34. Jeremy Anderson, "Labour's Lines of Flight: Rethinking the Vulnerabilities of Transnational Capital." *Geoforum* 40 no. 6 (2009): 959–968; and McCallum, *Global Unions*.

35. See Eaton, Fine, and Porter in this collection.

36. Luis LM Aguiar and Shaun Ryan, "The Geographies of the Justice for Janitors," *Geoforum* 40, no. 6 (2009): 949–958.

37. Gumbrell-McCormick and Hyman, *Trade Unions*; Kieran Allen, "Trade Unions: From Partnership to Crisis," *Irish Journal of Sociology* 18 no. 2 (2010): 22–37.

38. Aguiar, "Sweatshop Citizenship;" Connolly, Marino and Lucio, "'Justice for Janitors Goes Dutch.'"

39. Damesin and Denis, "SUD Trade Unions."

40. Interview with Nick Allen, Washington, D.C. 2011.

41. Interviews with SEIU's Liz O'Connor September 12, 2012, and local community organizers, September 13, 2012. Mexico City, Mexico.

42. Interview with Debbie Schneider, May 25, 2011, Washington, D.C.

43. Michael Crosby, *Power at Work: Rebuilding the Australian Union Movement* (Sydney, Australia: Federation Press, 2006).

44. At the time, Tarrant was the National Secretary for the LHMU. Today she is a board member of Greenpeace Asia Pacific and the Climate Action Network and Chair of the Australia remade Secretariat. After LHMU, she carried on her role as National Secretary but now in United Voice, which was created in 2011. https://www.greenpeace.org.au/bios/louise-tarrant/.

45. In 2014, FNV Bondgenoten, along with two other unions, joined the Federatie Nederlandse Vakbeweging (The Federation of Dutch Trade Unions). See https://en.wikipedia.org/wiki/Federatie_Nederlandse_Vakbeweging. Eddy

Stam led the campaign to organize cleaners in Holland. In 2006, he had a stint at SEIU Baltimore learning SEIU organizing methodologies. https://rocketreach.co/eddy-stam-email_58745610. Today Stam heads the properties services department at UNI Global. https://www.uniglobalunion.org/news/uni-property-services-welcomes-new-president-biggest-ever-sector-meeting.

46. Interview with Ethel Buckley June 21, 2012, Dublin, Ireland. Interview with Liz O'Connor, September 12, 2013. Tarrant joined me for lunch along with Michael Crosby and Shaun Ryan in Sydney, Australia, in Fall 2007.

47. Interviews with union officials in Local 1 in Chicago and SEIU headquarters in Washington, D.C., 2011.

48. Beth Sims, *Workers of the World Undermined: American Labor's Role in US Foreign Policy* (Boston, MA: South End Press, 1992).

49. Interviews with Nick Allen and Debbie Schneider, May 25, 2011, Washington, D.C.

50. Allen, "Trade Unions: From Partnership to Crisis," *Irish Journal of Sociology* 18 no. 2 (2010): 22–37, quoted in Aguiar, "Sweatshop Citizenship," 261.

51. Aguiar, "Sweatshop Citizenship."

52. McCallum, *Global Unions*, 102.

53. John Stirling, "Global Unions: Chasing the Dream or Building the Reality?" *Capital & Class* 34 no. 1 (2010): 107–114.

54. See Thomas, "The Transnational Circulation of the 'Organizing Model'"; and Allen, "Trade Unions: From Partnership to Crisis."

55. Milkman, *L.A. Story*; Connolly, Marino and Lucio, "'Justice for Janitors Goes Dutch"; McAlevey, *Raising Expectations*.

56. McCallum, *Global Unions*, 58 and 55.

57. Russell Landsbury, "Work and Industrial Relations: Towards a New Agenda." *Relations industrielles/Industrial Relations* 64 no. 2 (2009): 326–339; Carola Frege and John Kelly, "Union Revitalization Comparative Perspective," *European Journal of Industrial Relations*, 9 no. 1 (2003): 7–24.

58. David Harvey, *A Brief History of Neoliberalism* (New York: Oxford University Press, 2005).

59. Interview with SEIU official, Washington, D.C. 2015; see also Taipe and Lakhani in this book.

60. Interviews with union officials in Sydney 2007 and Amsterdam in 2008.

61. Interview with Joe Cunningham, SIPTU, August 20, 2015, Dublin, Ireland. Michael Crosby examined the structure of the SIPTU with an eye to recommending ways to restructure the union according to a flexible, organizing model. See C. Higgins, "Commission on SIPTU's Future Sets Out Radical Changes." *Industrial Relations News* 29—https://www.irn.ie/article/old/13736.

62. Allen, "Trade Unions."

63. Interview with SEIU official, Chicago 2011.

64. Interview with SEIU official, Washington, D.C., 2011.

65. Interview with Liz O'Connor and local social activists, Mexico City, 2012.

66. Leo Panitch, *Working Class Politics in Crisis: Essays on Labour and the State* (New York: Verso, 1986). For a discussion of the corporatist Pollar model in the Netherlands, see Aguiar, "Sweatshop Citizenship."

67. For an example of cleaners "learning" to make themselves "invisible," see Jane Hood, "From Night to Day: Timing and the Management of Custodial Work," *Journal of Contemporary Ethnography* 17 no.1 (1998): 86–116. For the social and pop cultural construction of cleaners' in/visibility, see Luis LM Aguiar, "Cleaners and Pop Cultural Representation," *Just Labour* 5 (Winter 2005): 65–69.

68. Michael Crosby, "Cleanstart—Fighting for a Fair Deal for Cleaners," in *The Future of Organizing: Building for Tomorrow*, ed. Gregor Gall (London: Palgrave 2009), 131–149.

69. Scott Lovell, guest speaker, Globalization and Cross-Borders Organizing Sociology Class, February 2017.

70. Ryan and Herod, "Restructuring," 77.

71. Crosby, "Cleanstart."

72. Allen, "Trade Unions."

73. Aguiar and Ryan, "The Geographies."

74. Mary Hyland, "Rising to the Occasion? Trade Union Revitalization and Migrant Workers in Ireland" (Ph. Diss., Dublin City University, 2015).

75. Interviews, summer 2015, Dublin, Ireland.

76. Interview with "Pat", Dublin, August 17, 2015.

77. Interviews with union officials, summer 2012, Dublin, Ireland.

78. Interviews, August 2015, Dublin, Ireland.

79. Interviews with union officials, August 2015, Dublin, Ireland.

80. Field notes, Monday August 17, 2015. Dublin, Ireland.

81. Fletcher Jr. and Lichtenstein, "SEIU's Civil War."

82. Field notes on meeting with Pat, August 17, 2015, Dublin, Ireland.

83. Melanie Simms and Jane Holgate, "Organizing for What? Where Is the Debate on the Politics of Organizing?" *Work, Employment & Society* 24, no. 1 (2010): 157–168.

84. Aguiar, "Sweatshop Citizenship."

85. Aguiar and Ryan, "The Geographies."

86. Savage, "Justice for Janitors."

87. Jennifer Jihye Chun, *Organizing at the Margins* (Ithaca, NY: ILR Press, 2011); Amanda Tattersall, *Power in Coalition: Strategies for Strong Unions and Social Change* (Ithaca, NY: ILR Press, 2010); and Tattersall, "Labor-Community Coalitions, Global Union Alliances, and the Potential of SEIU's Global Partnerships," in *Global Unions: Challenging Transnational Capital through Cross-Border Campaigns*, ed. by Kate Bronfenbrenner (Ithaca, New York: ILR Press, 2007), 155–173.

88. Savage, "Justice for Janitors"; Allen, "Trade Unions."

89. Interview with SEIU official at union headquarters, Washington, D.C. See also Taipe and Lakhani in this collection.

90. Russell and McCartin in this collection.

10

Organizing Strategies without Borders

The Case of Brazil

EUAN GIBB AND LUÍS LM AGUIAR

The union renewal literature has been full of innovative organizing and base-building strategies for decades.[1] However, clear examples of rapid growth in union density that lasts are uncommon.[2] Instead, stories about unions are usually about the opposite: decreases in membership, and erosion of workers' desire and incentives to become active trade unionists—stories that are remarkably consistent across rich, poor, northern, and southern countries. Brazil often reinforces this global pattern where successful organizing drives are rare.[3] It is a country with high and increasing unemployment, an informal sector that includes over half of Brazilian workers, and a media-driven public sphere dictating that workers' rights and high salaries are the main problem blocking a return to the high economic growth rates of the early 2000s.[4] This argument is also commonly expressed by Brazilian right-wing think tanks and organic intellectuals pushing, since the early 2000s, for the removal of Lula and his Partido dos Trabalhadores (PT) from governing or even contesting the running of the country.[5] Some of the challenges the PT faces have been self-inflicted. Given the number of unionists appointed to important posts within PT governments and the scandals associated with leaders of the party, unions and their leaders have been tainted with a poor public image.[6]

Yet one positive example stands out in this otherwise grim period of defeated Lulismo and crisis in trade unionism in Brazil.[7] The union Siemaco-SP[8] representing urban cleaners and maintenance workers in the city of São Paulo increased its membership from 30% to 43% in less than two years. These density numbers are far above the national average of 14.4%.[9] The increase in the representation of "marginal" workers identified above is largely the direct result of an international solidarity project between Siemaco-SP and the US-based Service Employees International Union (SEIU). The aim of this chapter is to describe and discuss this solidarity project by placing it within the historical trajectory of Brazilian labor law and evolving trade unionism activism in the country. This Siemaco-SP–SEIU partnership occupies the second half of the chapter.[10] First, though, a brief summary of Brazilian labor law and its consequent challenges to labor unions is in order. This is followed by a look at the work of the Siemaco-SP.

Labor Law and the Limiting of the Activities of Unions

Historically, labor legislation has been unkind to Brazilian workers. A persistent adverse environment to workers and their rights embedded trade unions in "bureaucratic, corporatist and patronising" structures, challenged only in the second half of the 1970s.[11] Then, protests and movements for a democratic Brazil led to, among other developments, the emergence of "novo sindicalismo" which included pushes for union freedom and autonomy from government interference, as well as the right to workplace organizing, enhanced collective bargaining rights and features associated with the "broad right to strike."[12] According to Gay Seidman, this "new unionism" arose in the workplace amid changing labor processes and fissures within the bourgeoisie, while also reaching into workers' communities demanding resolution to broader class issues such as housing, transport, and industrial citizenship.[13] These gains and initiatives to improve workers' lives were pushed back with the rise of neoliberalism in the 1980s and 1990s. In this era, trade union politics adopted a defensive posture even if the new Constitution of 1988 gave workers some rights in law including the recognition of the right to strike in the private sector, the unionization of civil servants (but not their right to strike), the elimination of mechanisms of government intervention in trade unions, and greater freedom for collective bargaining and trade union elections.[14] The Central Unica dos Trabalhadores (CUT)[15] played a key role in this campaign for a new labor code until defeated by neoliberalism and the changing allegiance of its former campaign partner, Força Sindical. The resulting deregulation of labor rights and the flexibilization of work along with increased insecurity "produced an extremely unfavorable environment for workers."[16] Deregulation of labor and the flexibilization of labor markets continued under the "left neoliberalism" of Lulismo's "greater legitimacy of the state" while constraining trade union activists by coopting them into the existing bureaucratic structures of the state. Some on the left criticized Lula for reinstating a corporatist trade unionism befitting his economic development model and fiscal plans for the country.[17] This development was held together by a precarious hegemony based on "'passive' consent of the subaltern classes and the 'active' consent of the trade union bureaucracy."[18]

The labor legislation model governing Brazilian industrial relations rests on constructs from the 1930s. Few significant changes were made over the decades. As in most other countries, the basic regulatory framework and legislation was not simply offered by an altruistic and forward-thinking state, but rather as a direct response to successful union organizing by anarchists, socialists, and communists.[19] Union security and legal legitimacy was a product of organized struggle. Legal structures managing labor relations were introduced during the presidency of Getúlio Vargas, twice Brazilian president and one-time dictator. Vargas governed for a combined total of 18 years during important formative periods both economically and politically. He was a nationalist populist that came to be known as the "father of the poor."[20] Commentators commonly attribute Vargas's inspiration for the legal structures governing trade unions and labor relations to the Italian fascist, Benito Mussolini.[21]

The shape labor law took was particularly contradictory for unions. In this specific case, the orientation of the state was to organize class harmony to ensure smooth economic development (or the related emerging processes of urbanization and industrialization) of the country.[22] The resulting framework for both social and individual rights was created and understood since the beginning to be particularly authoritarian.[23] Characteristics included "obligatory singularity" with resulting sectoral and territorial fragmentation and forced adaptation to economic and professional categories defined and advanced by the state. This also served to structurally maintain a distance between the base of the union and its leaders, thereby weakening workplace-based structures and members' participation in their own unions. Labor regulation of this kind was a crucial component of a particular type of state that deals with economic, social, and political conflicts in a corporatist and authoritarian way. This long-standing system of national union regulation created an environment where false, yellow or "pelego" (in Portuguese) unions are common. There are many examples of unions that exist only on paper or "in a drawer" somewhere. Sometimes workers attempt to organize only to discover a union already represents them.

Until very recently, unions enjoyed a guaranteed source of funds. All legally registered (formal sector) workers (both union members and nonmembers) paid one day per year of their salary into a fund the federal government collected and administered to labor organizations. From this fund local trade unions received 60%, federations 15%, confederations 5%, and national trade union centrals 10%; the remaining 10% stayed with the Federal Labor Ministry to fund the ministry's work, and a separate court system for the interpretation and application of labor law. The value of this so-called "union tax" totaled more than R$35 billion in 2016, or just over $11 billion US.[24] This is precisely the pyramid imagined by Vargas, with the base of local trade unions at the bottom and spread out across the country and the government firmly situated at the top. Local unions (and the national/confederative organizations to which a union is affiliated) claiming to represent specific groups of workers are eligible to receive money collected by the national government without the need to build the union at the workplace.

Labor Reforms Designed to Extinguish Brazilian Unions

The Temer government came to power using illegitimate means and took[25] full advantage of the political momentum to reduce the power of Brazilian workers and their trade unions. A kind of "neoliberal revenge" is being carried out after thirteen years of Workers' Party (PT) rule.[26] Direct attacks on workers and their organizations began immediately after the 2016 parliamentary coup[27] that ultimately led to the election of the extreme-right government of Bolsonaro. The propaganda of the current government speaks of the need to "modernize" labor legislation. Both the national government and the most important business federation in the country (Federacao das Industrias do Estado de Sao Paulo—FIESP)[28] expound a logic that Brazilian labor laws are outdated, too costly for employers, and too generous to workers, and thus the fundamental reason for the current unemployment crisis. Despite ongoing political and institutional crises and a total lack of evidence to support this logic, the government is committed to increasing the flexibility of labor contracts and reducing workers' and trade union rights.[29]

This approach is consistent with other neoliberal "shock therapy" policies implemented around the world since the 1980s.[30] In addition to the labor reforms introduced in July 2017, funding for education and health has been constitutionally frozen for the next twenty years; large sections of the Amazon rainforest are being handed over to foreign mining companies, while the policing of illegal logging is largely abandoned.[31] In addition, funding for government and NGOs working to protect the rights of indigenous people has been cut, rights to develop known oil reserves are being sold to the highest (foreign) bidder, while inequality, murder of land-rights activists, violence against the

LGBTQI community, and modern slavery all increase with a vengeance. The most consistent component of all of the examples of these policies is the passing of risks and costs to those who have the least capacity to bear them—the working class.[32]

The labor legislation reforms carried out in 2017 were the most extensive and meaningful since 1943. More than one hundred clauses were modified by taking advantage of a new legal environment to "reappraise collective bargaining," deregulate the national labor market, and modify trade union funding system by eliminating the union tax, thereby jeopardizing unions' financial survival.[33] This dismantling of historic protections for formal workers coincided with the rise of precarious employment. Data for Brazil in 2018 indicates that 22% of workers with formal employment were outsourced, or roughly 10 million workers out of 45.7 million workers with formal employment.[34] Despite the fact that formal/informal is often a crucial categorical difference for Brazilian workers and their possibility to have their basic workplace rights respected, formal employment is no guarantee of a quality job. This is particularly the case for workers with formal contracts that are outsourced. Most formal outsourced jobs continue to be lower paid, precarious, and have worse working conditions than non-outsourced. Workers can be and are easily fired without just cause.[35] Siemaco-SP organizes to combat these features.

Siemaco-SP

Every day more than 100,000 workers clean the public streets, parks, private commercial buildings (factories, stores, offices, malls, supermarkets, and so forth), residential buildings, hospitals, schools, banks, bus terminals, train and metro stations and public buildings including libraries, museums, and theatres in the city of São Paulo, the largest city in the southern hemisphere. A massive group of more than 12,000 workers are mobilized daily to collect garbage and clean the streets of this massive metropolis of more than 20 million inhabitants. One of the most remarkable characteristics of this group of workers is that almost none of them have direct employment contracts with the city of São Paulo. Almost every single one of these workers is outsourced, or "terceirizada/o" in Portuguese, which literally translates to English as "thirded."[36] The "third" in this case are the companies that hire and then organize these workers to undertake this essential work. These companies are third parties in the employment relationship.

Despite the high number and diversity of employers in the sector and the complexity of employment relationships, all of these workers are represented by a single trade union—Siemaco-SP. The union was founded in 1958 and today represents more than 100,000 workers spread across almost 40,000 workplaces; the union is present in every single neighbourhood of São Paulo. The union is an active affiliate of relevant state (regional), national, and international organizations, as well as an important affiliate of the second largest (after the CUT) Brazilian national trade union central, the União Geral dos Trabalhadores (UGT).[37] Given the diverse cultural, regional, racial, educational, and ideological base of Siemaco-SP, the union has never affiliated to any political party.

The workers are divided across four principal areas; garbage collectors, building cleaners and maintenance workers (property services), street cleaners, and gardeners. Approximately 60% of the workers in cleaning and maintenance inside buildings are women, whereas more than 90% working in the streets and parks are men. Many of those women (more than half) are heads of families and have children. Almost three-quarters of workers self-identify as black or colored.[38] Many workers are new immigrants from other countries. Almost two-thirds have primary school (or part thereof) as their highest level of formal education. Thus, the vast majority never entered high school, with most finishing their formal education before turning thirteen years old. Of workers who entered high school, 43% didn't finish. According to staff journalist Adriana do Amaral, "our membership is made up [of] many excluded populations; black workers, women, workers with disabilities, immigrants—both internal and external—and youth."[39] Extensive concrete work with new immigrants and refugees is organized by Siemaco-SP. A Portuguese language literacy workbook was published and distributed to these newly arrived workers. In order to combat racism and discrimination, the union has given a prominent profile for these workers in events and in their own publications, explaining where these workers come from and why.[40] The union recently hired an organizer from Haiti to help build the union in that community of workers.

Wages in Brazil are calculated on a monthly basis. The legal minimum wage is currently set at R$1,100 Brazilian Reis (Rs) per month (roughly $200 US). More than half of these workers live in families with a household income of a little more than this legal monthly minimum wage. Two-thirds earn up to R$1200 per month. According to an internal union study, workers understand and believe their wages to be too low.[41] Almost two-thirds never access the internet in a country where more than half the population has access. This statistic is directly related to income. The most recent national census indicates that 95% of the rich have access to the internet.

These workers maintain a deeply held conviction that they are not valued or recognized for the crucial work that they perform every single day.[42] One need only imagine what any major institution or building like an airport or a hospital would be like after one day without property services staff to understand how essential these workers are.[43] One worker stated that "sometimes you work for years in the same place and the people there don't even know your name. They say 'hey come here . . . hey cleaner.' Because of this we understand that we are not valued, we are treated like things."[44] They are a group of workers that suffer humiliation and disrespect every day, from managers, people in the streets, even neighbors, friends, and family. Almost 90% report that it's because of their job and perhaps more alarmingly, 20% claim that they suffer such consistent and widespread disrespect due to personal characteristics, indicating an intimate understanding of how racism works.[45] Many times, these workers are not only invisible, but are what many in the union call "*invisibilized*." The noun describing a state of being transforms to a verb that describes a process. A social process. This is an important distinction that shows a consciousness on the part of trade unionists that invisibility is not a permanent or natural state and that it is created and imposed on their members. These are workers that are *made* to be invisible by/to others. This process of making workers invisible is profoundly linked to the still-present cultural, economic, social, and political leftovers of slavery and the ways that misogyny and racism work in Brazil and more specifically, in the massive and diverse metropolis of São Paulo.[46]

Siemaco-SP has spent a lot of time, money, and energy experimenting with and developing the concept of a "sindicato cidadão" or "citizen union" whereby a union fundamentally integrates the understanding that the role of the union goes beyond the workplace and understands workers as citizens active in society. In part, this role is linked to the tendency toward "assistencialismo."[47] This idea was developed and implemented long before it appeared in North American and European union renewal literature that argued for a widening of the understanding of workers as community members with the consequent legitimacy that unions maintain when intervening in wider community issues beyond the workplace.[48]

Popular culture plays an integral role in the practice of this model of trade unionism. As detailed below, the base of membership of Siemaco-SP has little formal education. In contrast, this same base is extremely rich in popular culture. Historically, almost every union meeting or event ended with music and dancing, usually a forró, a popular musical style for the North East of Brazil. An ex-president of Siemaco-SP even became a president of one of the city's samba schools.

The longest standing president, José Moacyr Pereira, held the position from 1993 to 2020. The development of the variety of expression of the concept of "sindicato cidadão" were expanded continuously under his leadership. Since 1999, workers have had access to a benefit known as "Solidarity in life and death." This is a negotiated clause in the collective agreement that pays funeral costs for family members in cases of death. Additionally, two large "cesta básicas"[49] are sent to members' families on a monthly basis for a year after a member dies. Many of these workers are internal migrants from the less-developed North East for whom family support is extremely important.[50] The state has historically been absent for the majority of these workers. They are working in São Paulo far from their families and many times the union can provide this basic and essential solidarity function.

The system of "cesta básicas" has largely been substituted by a credit card that is replenished monthly by the employer. Often, workers have two cards, one accepted at supermarkets and another that is used at restaurants. In the case of Siemaco-SP members, the value of these cards can make up to 40% of a base salary. Workers that voluntarily join the union pay a membership fee of R$10 per month. Members gain access to many benefits that nonmembers do not. In the historical context of both trade union "assistencialismo" and a weak or absent state, the union has negotiated benefits to substitute and go beyond services commonly offered by other states. The union also runs its own daycare with up to sixty places for the children of members. And six medical clinics are spread throughout the city where the highest concentrations of workers are. These clinics are either free for members or they charge a nominal fee. Services provided to members include general medical clinics, dermatology, gynecology, allergist, pediatrics, nutritionist, psychology, orthopedics, and dentistry. Free legal services are also provided. These services are extensive and very popular with workers. This brings thousands of workers into contact with the union every month. In addition, the union provides leisure avenues for workers by maintaining a beach resort with vacation apartment buildings for members to rent at low cost. It reaches out to them by running workers' help centres spread throughout the city with courses on technical and political training for union representatives.

Siemaco-SP makes systematic and ongoing attempts to increase the confidence and pride of these workers and to converse with the public in order to make these workers more visible and increase respect for their work. In 2011, the leadership of the union decided to pay the costs of reforming an abandoned public square in the center of São Paulo, near the union's central office. The union commissioned a local artist to build four life-sized bronze statues of the primary categories of workers that are represented by Siemaco-SP, including a worker serving coffee, a gardener, a building cleaner, and a garbage collector.

Preservation and maintenance of the square is organized and paid for by the union until today. During the inauguration event, the State level secretary at the labor ministry, David Zaia, claimed that the monument brings anonymous workers into the light, which brings them both dignity and includes them in citizenship whereas, "all the other monuments that we have represent the elite of society including politicians, professionals of some kind or military figures."[51] Workers are particularly proud of these statues and regularly pass through the square to take pictures with these statues that so clearly and publicly highlight the importance of their work.

Siemaco-SP-SEIU Relationship

Brazil is deeply integrated into global supply chains.[52] Multinational corporations are present in all sectors of the economy via transplanted offices and operations or in the acquisition of local Brazilian companies. In this context, organized labor pursues various forms of activities including: participating in global compact agreements with multinationals (though company participation is voluntary); responding to globalization by trying to find a way to insert themselves in the process, believing this to be the best way to address the issue arising from globalization and the displacement of workers; doing nothing as a wait-and-see approach to see how globalization unfolds; and resisting and devising alternative approaches to globalization. In addition, trade unions in Brazil are devising new forms of organizing. These are: (1) sharing information and opening dialogue with unions and federations including those of different ideological orientations; (2) organizing national networks with common goals and approaches to change; and (3) developing and elaborating a strategy to engage unions at the international scale. Siemaco-SP exhibits examples of some of these approaches, especially in its turn toward international solidarity and partnership with SEIU under the latter's Global Partnership Campaign.[53]

The leadership of Siemaco-SP has shown consistent commitment to innovative and creative strategies to build the union at the base in this time of economic restructuring and globalization. One of the examples of this commitment is this joint international base-building and organizing project with SEIU. In 2013, the leadership of Siemaco-SP made a commitment to build and strengthen the base of the union, experimenting with a variety of techniques. Interestingly, some of the strategies adopted have been imported from the United States and translated directly into a Brazilian context by veterans of the U.S. labor movement who had spent decades base-building in the USA. Techniques include a focused development of education resources, systematization, professionalization and recording of the interactions between trade unions and workers and the establishment and strengthening of steward-like representatives at the level of the workplace. While some Brazilian unions have developed strong workplace-based structures over the years, particularly the strong and independent unions in core sectors of the economy,[54] this had not been the case at Siemaco-SP.

The leaders of Siemaco-SP have had a relationship with the Service Employees International Union since at least the early 1990s.[55] Despite their histories in different continents, the unions have a lot in common. Both unions have large numbers of property services and maintenance workers as important constituents of their bases. Many members and potential members of both Siemaco-SP and SEIU are poorly paid, classified as less-skilled, and are intensely exploited in highly labor-intensive jobs. A high proportion of these workers are women and/or are racialized and immigrants. They all work in industries with exceptionally high turnover rates, thus complicating the task of union building in both countries.

It was precisely in the mid-1990s that newly elected SEIU president Andy Stern dismantled the International Affairs department of the union and dedicated resources to efforts to "globalize" an organizing model of union building. Throughout the rest of the 1990s and the first decade of the millennium, important joint projects were organized between SEIU and trade union partners in Australia, New Zealand, the UK, the Netherlands, and Germany. Organizing initiatives have included SEIU strategies of building community support, strong communications and public relations, and worksite mobilization.[56]

This Brazilian example differs from the more well-known and analyzed international experiences. Similar to other Brazilian trade union leaders, former Siemaco-SP president Jose Moacyr's extensive international experience allowed him to see first-hand the strengths and weaknesses of other models of trade unionism. According to the SEIU staff representative stationed in Brazil, Joe Simões, Moacyr "has really built strong international ties in the last few years."[57] These ties are essential to get any kind of joint international work off the ground. Simões believes "Moacyr gets credit for starting this . . . he understood that he needs to build a stronger union and that the only way to do that is to have more leaders and more members involved." In the absence of a strong history of membership development at the workplace level and a trajectory of enduring bureaucratic legal structures that intentionally disincentivize the building of strength at the base of a union, Moacyr reached out to access resources and experiences beyond his direct context. With the choice to engage in this project, it is clear he adopted a vision for the future of the union that centralizes and prioritizes membership involvement. According to Simões, "he has that vision and his directors share it. If the leadership isn't ready, it doesn't work in any union. Siemaco gets the necessity . . . they're willing to experiment."

A crucial difference between this project and most other examples, particularly those of SEIU analyzed elsewhere, is the near total absence of trade union structures at the workplace level. Stewards structures that are familiar in many other workplaces were completely absent. So, this joint international solidarity project focused on resolving the specific problems linked to this weakness. It was essentially the joint effort of the unions in developing an extensive organizing program, the building and strengthening of workplace representative capacities, and a professionalization of the interactions between staff, elected and appointed trade unionists, and workers. Before the formal beginning of this organizing initiative, Siemaco-SP did dedicate resources to organizing new members. However, progress was slow and mixed. The union has a base of more than 100,000 workers spread across more than 40,000 worksites in the largest city on the continent. All of this in sectors with an average turnover rate of 70%. Consequently, the union was basically maintaining its voluntary membership density of 30% without any growth.[58]

Therefore, multiple strategies have been adopted in order to fulfill the primary goals of building workplace representative capacities and a professionalization of the interactions between staff, elected and appointed trade unionists, and workers in order to grow and build strength throughout the union. The initial work was about understanding where the union was, in terms of members at the workplace, and where Siemaco-SP wanted to get to. Compilation of basic information can be extremely challenging for Brazilian unions. Getting lists of workers and worksites is difficult, particularly in the sectors where Siemaco-SP operates. It requires a lot of groundwork. This type of information is crucial to understand where the union is strong or weak, and where and how it needs to build a plan with measurable results.

The union needed to develop a system to do this. It sought to create a growth program based on data. Some of this work includes the oldest and most common organizing tactics like workplace mapping. Mapping includes developing a frank and updated assessment of strength in numbers and in terms of leaders. None of this data existed before the project. Basic information about where and who workers are and what their schedules are had to be built from the ground up. For example, Siemaco-SP mapped out where the bank cleaners are and then contacted the companies to organize meetings to talk to those workers. While union access is negotiated and guaranteed in the collective agreement, organizers reported that "for some workplaces, even large ones, access is very difficult at times. In these cases, we go to the doors to meet workers at shift change or meal times."[59] In addition to negotiated meetings, the union now takes better strategic advantage of the opportunity offered by legally required new member orientation meetings and annual health and safety meetings that include workers. The union needed to know how close they were to 50% + 1 at as many workplaces as possible. Siemaco-SP needed to expand the staff component of their organizing department. They went from six to ten with plans to hire two more to have a dedicated team of twelve organizers. The union pays for this staff and all of the implementation costs of the project while SEIU pays Simões's salary. While he spent a lot of time on the street and has physical space at Siemaco-SP where he spent 2–3 days a week, he did not work exclusively on this project. Simões explains the initial contact with Brazilian unions and issues needing to be addressed:

> To this day as many times as I been to Brazil, there is a desire in Brazil about wanting to learn, unlike other country [who] look at us and say you Americans "what you going to do? What you can offer us? You are already dying! Why should we listen to you?" There was also a lot of mistrust from unions elsewhere in South America given the role of the American Labour Movement in supporting local dictators. But we were very clear about staying away from the political. We are not here representing anyone but SEIU.

Simões goes on to describe the Brazilian appetite for J4J:

> The Brazilians wanted to talk to us. They wanted to learn how we went from a union of one union million members to a union of 2 million members. They wanted to know about the justice for janitor; they wanted to know how we organized in sectors; they wanted to know how we thought about creating [a] campaign that clients were strategic. They really wanted to learn. [So we started at] the beginning [on] how you identify workers, how to spread out, let's figure out how we get recognition out of management right because that is the different globally, is that our model, the way we behave with workers we are exploring everywhere, you can see it in Brazil. And they will tell you, yea, Wal-Mart is organizing in Brazil but is extremely difficult because management behavior the same way in they do in the U.S. [. . .] The idea is to put our resources together and figure out how to develop work that we can do together.[60]

These organizers and the many union directors that spent time on the streets and at workplaces with members worked collectively to understand what kinds of strategies would resonate in the different sectors where the union maintains a base. Simões was able to integrate this, "listening to who was in the street and experience sharing," in order to build the bridges necessary between a traditional US-style organizing program and something that could work in concert with and maintain respect for this completely different context with a markedly different history and traditions.[61] The organizing program included weekly development and numerical goals that are reported by email using the very popular communication app WhatsApp.

Several durable changes have come out of these efforts. First, directors and organizers have become good at identifying, recruiting, and communicating with workplace leaders. The hard work of developing some basic trade union structures at the workplace has followed the implementation of the more basic organizing. Strategic and targeted leader identification, mentoring, and nurturing was not common in Siemaco-SP before this project. Almost none of the existing workplace leaders organized or tried to recruit new members, even at their own places of work. Directors and organizers have jointly developed common criteria on what leaders are, what their roles should/can be, and what can be asked of them in concrete and practical terms.

Second, almost every trade unionist now knows how to talk to workers about joining the union, the essential work of building direct relationships with workers. After receiving and integrating feedback from the street, "there has been a real shift in the rap," according to Simões. Directors, members, and almost all of the union staff have been trained on what to say to workers. Workers' responses have been tracked and fed back to the organizers. Directors and organizers have helped to create and experiment with the tools to talk confidently about the union. More than 80% of people that have contact with the members have gone through internal trainings.[62] Training has included role playing scenarios focused on how to encourage, train, and mentor workers based on one-on-one conversations.

The strong history and traditions of service provision in the Brazilian labor movement has led most unions to focus on health and dental care and the many other services provided to members detailed earlier when talking to workers about the importance of membership. Trade unionists commonly "sell" the union to potential members with a cost-benefit analysis focused exclusively on (extensive) service provision. Siemaco-SP has substituted the focus on service provision for a focus on the importance of the collective agreement and broader working-class issues. Every trade unionist that has gone through the trainings now knows how to talk to workers about the importance of collective bargaining and strong contracts with the employers. This discussion includes providing basic facts about the process of negotiations and explaining to workers that employers don't simply provide wage increases, but that this is negotiated by the union and that, in order to strengthen the negotiating position of the union, more workers need to be members and participate in the union. Collective bargaining is presented as the most important work of the union and the provision of benefits comes after. Workers have been brought directly into the process of bargaining in a more systematic manner. For example, the street cleaning sector recently organized forty workplace meetings all over the city to debate and decide bargaining priorities.[63]

Young workers' secretary Daniela Sousa comments, "historically unions have been too timid in attempts to convince workers to join. We should be proud of our work and should want to tell everyone about it."[64] She has been through the training and has become convinced that this strategy is strengthening the union. In addition to the focus on bargaining, Sousa has organized several events that bring workers together to talk about issues that directly affect them, what she refers to as "real, concrete conversations" about important issues. Most recently, Sousa organized collective discussions about proposed labor reforms, why these proposals are arriving now, what their impacts are, and what workers and unions can do to try to reduce the (intended) negative impacts of the legislation.

The president himself makes the case directly to workers that the benefits of membership are broad and go far beyond narrow service provision. In his 2017 New Year's message, Moacyr argued for Siemaco's efficacy: "We took part in important public demonstrations in the country, demanding effective actions from our leaders regarding the maintenance of jobs for thousands of workers, particularly in the category of street cleaners in the capital. We are fighting violence against women, against precarious work and now, regularizing outsourced workers, one of our main demands. So, I ask each of you to do your part, helping us to increase our representativeness, observing our work; invite your colleagues to be part of the Siemaco-SP family."[65]

The third related result of this project is the rapid growth in the number of workers that voluntarily affiliate to Siemaco-SP. Membership has gone from 30% to 43% in less than two years, far above the national average of 14.4%. The trend from the early phases of implementation through 2017 was steady growth. When interviewed, Siemaco-SP's young workers' secretary had a 15cm tall pile of union membership forms on her desk. Asked about why she was working on data entry for new member information, she responded that she was, "helping out the department that enters this info so that they don't fall behind."[66] The union is running to keep up with the demand for membership. That is an extremely rare situation. Sousa also understands the reciprocal consequences of building strength at the base. As the union is built and strengthened at the workplace, the capacity to solve problems increases. Consequently, the "result of good work is increasing membership."[67] This dramatic increase in membership density reflects the initial goal, not the goal itself. The original goal was to build strength at the base. Capacity to reach this goal has increased dramatically. Workplace leaders are now quickly identified, supported, and developed. Siemaco-SP has organized committees that are familiar with setting goals, sharing experiences, and measuring their progress. They now have a much richer experience with clear structures. The union wants to be able to reach the point where workers can organize and lead an action at the workplace. Siemaco-SP is showing that with a rigorous focus on the development of this kind of structure, the union can get results.

SEIU staff member Joe Simões notes that a couple of other similar projects have recently been initiated outside of Siemaco-SP. SEIU first met with the health workers' union SindsaudeSP more than ten years ago. He remembers that, "Sindsaude was very much opposed to the idea of building union structures at the workplace. They thought leaders build the union but now understand that's not enough."[68] The union has recently hired five new organizers. Nobody in the union was doing any kind of organizing work prior to this. While this project was halted when the country entered into a crisis six months after having been launched, similar results to the Siemaco-SP experience were already coming in despite the much more complex problem of union access to workplaces that is made more difficult by the public bureaucracy. These innovative experiments are being implemented in, and partly as a response to, a particularly unstable political-economic period in Brazil.

Conclusion

The history of the Brazilian labor movement is quite remarkable. Organized labor has survived dictatorships, authoritarian rule, neoliberalism, and now populist fascist leaders. Along the way, it has moved from an organization tied to and defined by the government not only for its rigid operations but for its basic survival due to government control of its union dues and membership contributions. And in this context, it developed the now influential modus operandi of union work known as "new unionism" or, more popularly, recently transformed into social movement unionism. It appears that whatever context and political regime one wants to understand about the operation and functions of organized labor, Brazil can be sourced for an example. This is increasingly the case when global changes constrain and potentialize labor, as well as the global sharing of labor ideas, strategies, cultures, and motivations. It is in this latter vein that SEIU and Siemaco-SP joined forces to initiate innovative approaches to organizing, training, education, and mobilizing union leaders, members, and workers to gradually enhance the Siemaco-SP from a service union to an organizing one. SEIU's experience in transforming internal union structures played out prominently in Brazil, especially in its cooperation with Siemaco-SP. As a result, Siemaco-SP's prioritization of the building of workplace-based structures and power means that no matter what the results of these reforms, this union is already much better prepared to survive and even continue to grow despite the declared intentions of employers and government to weaken unions. Employers in the sector will no longer be dealing with trade union leaders with a weak, fragmented, uninformed, and unengaged base when they enter negotiations.

One of the most radical things that any trade union or trade unionist can do is to go to the roots of how and why unions were first organized, to build independent power at the workplace, to help build the capacity and confidence of workers to fight back together, and then to build the links between these workers and others in the same sector, city, country, and eventually economic system. As in all trade union work, there never have been and never will be short cuts. Siemaco-SP has understood this and has undertaken to implement a plan based on the deep understanding that without strength and power at the base, the union doesn't really exist. Its resurgence and reinvention coincided with a partnership with SEIU as the latter offered expertise and initiatives regarding mobilizing the rank and file, revamping traditional union structures, and professionalizing union work.

Notes

1. On this literature, see: Gregor Murray, "Union Renewal: What Can We Learn from Three Decades of Research?" *Transfer* 23, no. 1 (2017): 9–29; Peter Fairbrother, "Rethinking Trade Unionism: Union Renewal on Transition," *The Economic and Labor Relations Review* 26, no. 4 (2015): 561–576; CM Frege and John Kelley, "Unions' Revitalization Strategies in Comparative Perspectives," *European Journal of Industrial Relations* 9, no. 1 (2003): 7–24; Pradeep Kumar and Gregor Murray, "Canadian Union Strategies in the Context of Change." *Labor Studies Journal* 26, no. 4 (2002): 1–28; MR Serrano, "Between Accommodation and Transformation: The Two Logics of Union Renewal," *European Journal of Industrial Relations* 20, no. 3 (2014): 219–235; Adalberto Cardoso, "Sindicatos no Brasil: Passado, Presente e Future," in *Trabalho: Horiozonte 2021,* ed. Antonio David Cattani (Porto Alegre, Brasil: Escritos), 121–145; Eduardo Noronha, "Cicloe de Greves, Transicao Politica e Estabilizacao: Brasil 1978–2007," *Lua Nova* 76 (2009): 119–168; and Roberto Veras, "Brasil em Obras, Peoes em Luta, Sindicatos Surpreedido," *Revista Critica de Ciencias Sociais* 103 (2014): 111–136.

2. But see Mark Anner, *Solidarity Transformed: Labor Responses to Globalization and Crisis in Latin America* (Ithaca, NY: Cornell University Press, 2001).

3. Adalberto Cardoso, *A Decada Neoliberal e a Crise dos Sindicatos no Brasil* (Sao Paulo, Brasil: Boitempo, 2003). See also Gay W. Seidman, *Manufacturing Militance: Workers' Movements in Brazil and South Africa, 1970–1985* (Berkeley: University of California Press, 1994).

4. Renato Raul Boschit and Carlos Eduardo Santos Pinto, "Crisis and Austerity: The Recent Trajectory of Capitalist Development in Brasil," *Contemporary Politics* 25, no. 3 (2019): 292–310; Andreia Galvao e Paula Marcelino, "The Brazilian Union Movement in the Twenty-First Century: The PT Governments, The Coup, and the Counter-reforms," *Latin American Perspectives* 47, no. 2 (2020): 1–17; Alfredo Saad-Filho, "Mass Protests under 'Left Neoliberalism': Brasil, June-July 2013," *Critical Sociology* 39, no. 5 (2013): 657–669.

5. Saad-Filho, "Mass Protests under 'Left Neoliberalism,'" 657–669.

6. Andre Singer, *O Lulismo em Crise: Um Quebra-cabeca do Periodo Dilma* (2011–2016) (Sao Paulo, Brasil: Companhia das Letras, 2018); Jose de Lima Soares, "As Centrais Sindicais e o Fenomeno do Transformismo no Governo Lula." *Revista Sociedade e Estado* 28, no. 3 (2013): 541; Ruy Braga and Sean Purdy, "A Precarious Hegemony: Neo-Liberalism, Social Struggles and the End of Lulismo in Brazil." *Globalizations* 16, no. 2 (2019): 201–215.

7. Adalberto Cardoso, "Dimensões da Crise do Sindicalismo Brasileiro," *Caderno CRH* 28, no. 75 (2015): 493–510.

8. Siemaco-SP 'Sindicato dos trabalhadores em empresas de prestação de serviços de asseio e conservação e limpeza urbana de São Paulo'—Union of workers at companies that provide cleaning, maintenance and urban cleaning services in the city of São Paulo.

9. On falling union density in Brazil, see https://agenciadenoticias.ibge.gov.br/en/agencia-press-room/2185-news-agency/releases-en/22957-ores-brasileiros-cai-para-14-4-a-menor-desde-2013,

10. This chapter is based on interviews with fourteen workers in the streets of São Paulo, the Siemaco-SP staff representative responsible for communications, elected youth chair Daniela Sousa, and SEIU staff member Joe Simões, all of whom agreed to be quoted in this chapter.

11. Roberto Veras de Oliveira, "Brazilian Labour Reform in Historical Perspective," *Global Labour Journal* 9, no. 3 (2018): 323.

12. Ibid., 324.

13. Seidman, *Manufacturing Militance.*

14. De Oliveira, "Brazilian Labour Reform in Historical Perspective," 325.

15. On the origins and politicizing of the CUT, see Seidman, *Manufacturing Militance.*166–171.

16. De Oliveira, "Brazilian Labour Reform in Historical Perspective," 328.

17. Alfredo Saad-Filho, "Mass Protests under 'Left Neoliberalism,'" 657–669; Galvao and Marcelino, "The Brazilian Union Movement in the Twenty-first Century," 1–17.

18. Ruy Braga and Sean Purdy, "A Precarious Hegemony: Neo-Liberalism, Social Struggles, and the End of Lulismo in Brazil," *Globalizations* 16, no. 2 (2019): 202.

19. A. G. Campos, *Breve histórico das mudanças na regulação do trabalho no Brasil* (Rio de Janeiro: IPEA. 2015), 7.

20. Robert M. Levine, *Father of the Poor? Vargas and His Era* (New York: Cambridge University Press, 1988).

21. A. Chaves, *O fascismo no Brasil: A influência fascista na CLT no período Vargas.* JusBrasil: https://alexandrechavesadv.jusbrasil.com.br/artigos/313510871/o-fascismo-no-brasil. See also Seidman, *Manufacturing Militance*, 27, 49, 50.

22. Campos, *Breve histórico das mudanças na regulação do trabalho no Brasil,* 9.

23. M. Chaui, *Brasil: Mito Fundador e Sociedade Autoritária* (São Paulo: Perseu Abramo, 2000).

24. D. Junqueira, "Arrecadação sindical aumenta 57% em uma década e chega a R$ 3,5 bilhõe em 2016," *R7 Notícias*, February 14, 2017, http://noticias.r7.com/brasil/arrecadacao-sindical-aumenta-57-em-uma-decada-echega-a-r-35-bilhoes-em-2016-16022017.

25. A. Saad-Filho, "The Implosion of Brazilian Democracy—And Why It Matters," *Critical Sociology* 43 nos. 7–8, (2017): 979–983.

26. For the immediate attacks on labor rights, see www.estudosdotrabalho.org/xi_sem2018/artigos/NeivionSergioLopesdeSousaJunior.pdf.

27. For the coup leading to Bolsonaro's election, see https://muse.jhu.edu/article/713723/summary and https://link.springer.com/chapter/10.1007/978-3-030-03288-3 3.

28. Translated as The Federation of Industries of the State of Sao Paulo.

29. M. Verlaine, *De Temer à Bolsonaro, a lógica é reduzir ou liquidar direitos,* https://contee.org.br/de-temer-a-bolsonaro-a-logica-e-reduzir-ou-liquidar-direitos/.

30. Naomi Klein discusses neoliberalism as "shock doctrine" in her book *The Shock Doctrine: The Rise of Disaster Capitalism* (Toronto: Knopf Canada, 2007).

31. https://www.vox.com/world/2016/12/15/13957284/brazil-spending-cap-austerity.

32. On new labor legislation, see Davide Carbonai, "Labor Rights in Brazil, Politics and Sindicatos: Notes on the General Strike of 2017," *Journal of Politics in Latin America* 11 no. 2 (2019): 231–245.

33. The "union tax" is a dues system in which one day's wages per year were awarded to unions representing workers. See Carbonai, "Labor Rights in Brazil."

34. F Medeiros, "Terceirização aumenta em 2018, aponta pesquisa." Mazzini, https://www.mazzini.com.br/blog/terceirizacao-aumenta-em-2018-aponta-pesquisa/.

35. M. Teixeira, H. de Andrade, and E. Coelho, eds. *Precarização e Terceirização: Faces da Mesma Realidade* (São Paulo: Sindicato dos Químicos—SP, 2016), 20.

36. União Geral dos Trabalhadores, "Perfil dos trabalhadores da limpeza é lançado, em São Paulo," January 24, 2012, www.ugt.org.br/post/4329-Perfil-dos-trabalhadores-da- limpeza-e-lancado,-em-São-Paulo. 24/01/2012.

37. The UGT is a ten-year-old central with more than 1,300 unions, federations, and confederations affiliated, representing roughly 10 million Brazilian workers. It is a politically centrist labor central affiliated to the International Trade Union Confederation (ITUC).

38. Siemaco-SP 2011, 18–24.

39. Adriana do Amaral interviewed by the author, 2017.

40. Siemaco-SP, "*SIEMACO e Você: Seu Sindicato*," Nov/Dec 2016, www.siemaco.com.br/upload/publicacao/img2-novembro-dezembro-2016-4792.pdf.

41. Siemaco-SP, *Perfil dos Trabalhadores em Asseio e Conservação e Limpeza Urbana de São Paulo* (São Paulo: Siemaco-SP, 2011), 40.

42. Ibid., 9.

43. This has taken on unprecedented urgency with COVID-19!

44. Siemaco-SP, *Perfil dos Trabalhadores*, 8.

45. Ibid., 78.

46. For a discussion of the "invisibility" of cleaners, see Luis LM Aguiar, "Cleaners and Pop Culture Representation." *Just Labour* 5 (2005): 65–79.

47. "Assistencia" in Portuguese literally means to give help. The concept of trade unionism known as "assistencialismo" is to provide mutual assistance and help to workers without challenging the nature of employment relations. It is similar to a "servicing" model of trade unionism in the labour studies literature but provides a wider variety of services including courses, access to holiday properties, and union managed health and dental services.

48. On workers as community members and unions' extension of their reach into the (potential) members' community, see, among others, Andrew Herod, *Labor* (Medford, MA, Polity, 2018); Jennifer J. Chun, *Organizing at the Margins: The Symbolic Politics of Labor in South Korea and the United States* (Ithaca, NY: Cornell University Press, 2009); Kim Moody, *US Labor in Trouble and Transition: The Failure from Above, the Promise of Revival from Below* (New York: Verso, 2007); Kate Bronfenbrenner et al (eds), *Organizing to Win: New Research on Union Strategies* (Ithaca, NY: Cornell University Press, 1998); Jane F. McAlevey, *No Shortcuts: Organizing for Power in the New Gilded Age* (New York: Oxford University Press, 2016); Craig Heron, *The Canadian Labor Movement: A Short History* (Toronto, ON: Lorimer, 1996); and Seidman, *Manufacturing Militance.*

49. A closed package or "basket" of essential groceries including rice, beans, oil, sugar, coffee, and so forth, which remains commonly available in Brazilian grocery stores until today. In many different sectors these packages were commonly provided by employers on a monthly basis.

50. More than 60% of workers were not born in the city of São Paulo. Of those, 83% are internal migrants, predominantly from the poorer and less-developed North East region of the country.

51. União Geral dos Trabalhadores, "Praça Marechal Deodoro é revitalizada com homenagem aos trabalhadores," January 26, 2011, www.ugt.org.br/post/3682-Praca-MarechalDeodoro-e-revitalizada-com-homenagem-aos-trabalhadores.

52. Four hundred and twenty of the globe's largest five hundred corporations are present in Brazil.

53. This paragraph relies on Karina L. Pasquariello Mariano e Leila Zidan, "Novas Estratégias Sindicais: A Experiência das Redes Internacionais," *Estudos Sociologicos Araraquara* 16 no. 31 (2011): 363–385. On SEIU's Global Partnership Campaign, see Aguiar in this book and, among others, Andy Stern, *A Country that Works* (New York: Free Press, 2006) and Jeremy Anderson, "Labour's Lines of Flight: Rethinking the Vulnerabilities of Transnational Capital," *Geoforum* 40, no. 6 (2009): 959–968.

54. Some of the strongest unions in the country (metalworkers, construction workers, and education workers. for example) maintain workplace-based steward structures similar to those in the USA and Canada while many unions do not.

55. M. Roza, *SIEMACO, São Paulo: Documento e História* (São Paulo: Marco Direito, 2006), 110.

56. On SEIU globalizing, see Aguiar in this book; Luis LM Aguiar and Andrew Herod (eds), *Cleaners in the Global Economy* (Malden, MA: Blackwell, 2006); Stern, *A Country that Works*; Stephen Lerner, "Global Unions: A Solution to Labor's Worldwide Decline," *New Labor Forum* 16: (2007): 23–37; Jamie McCallum, *Global Unions, Local Power: The New Spirit of Transnational Labor Organizing* (Ithaca, NY: Cornell University Press, 2013); and Kim Moody, *Workers in a Lean World* (New York: Verso, 1997).

57. Joe Simões interview with Gibb, August 2017.

58. These numbers are based on unpublished internal union documents. The union is under no legal obligation to publish or report these numbers to governments.

59. Joe Simões interview with Gibb, August 2017.

60. Aguiar interviewed SEIU leader Joe Simoes at SEIU Headquarters in San Francisco, February 2, 2007.

61. Joe Simões interview with Gibb, August 2017.

62. Ibid.

63. Siemaco-SP, "Limpeza Urbana aprova pauta de reivindicações em quase 40 assembleias," http://www.siemaco.com.br/acoes/6186-Limpeza-Urbana-aprova-pauta-de-reivindicacoes-em-quase-40-assembleias//.

64. Gibb interview with Daniela Sousa, 2017.

65. Siemaco-SP, "*SIEMACO e Você*," www.siemaco.com.br/upload/publicacao/img2-novembro-dezembro-2016-4792.pdf.

66. Siemaco-SP, "SIEMACO e Você."

67. Gibb interview with Daniela Sousa, 2017.

68. Gibb interview with Joe Simões, 2017.

PART IV

Assessing the Legacy and Employing the Lessons of SEIU

11

The Legacy of Justice for Janitors and SEIU for the Labor Movement

An Interview with Stephen Lerner

JOSEPH A. MCCARTIN

Stephen Lerner[1] joined SEIU in the mid-1980s and immediately took on the role of designing and directing the union's most innovative and successful campaign of that era, Justice for Janitors. In this interview,[2] he traces his involvement with SEIU from that campaign until his departure from SEIU in 2011. He assesses both the campaign's and the union's strengths and weaknesses, responds to critiques that have been directed at both, explains the development of his own thinking, and assesses the legacy and implications for SEIU's story for today's labor movement.

JM: What career trajectory ultimately led you to SEIU? What drew you to labor and what experiences did you have before SEIU?

SL: When I was still in high school, I volunteered in the summer of 1974 to work on the grape and lettuce boycott of the United Farm Workers (UFW). I lived with two farmworker families that had left California to work on the boycott in NYC. Pablo Lopez and Danny Sanchez were strikers from White River Farms and they had moved to New York with their families to work on the boycott. I fell in love with the UFW and movement. I remember the UFW leaflet we gave out that had a headline that was something like "God Called a Strike Once." It described the story of Exodus as a strike of the Jews against being enslaved and exploited by Pharaoh. It compared the struggle of Farmworkers who struck and then left their homes to launch the boycott around the country and world to the story of Exodus and liberation of Jews from slavery. It brought to life and animated the story of Passover by connecting it to current struggles. It was the first time I thought of the UFW and unions as being about far more than better wages but instead being liberation movements. I went back to school for 11th grade but then dropped out to work on the boycott fulltime.

After the UFW, I worked as an 1199 member in housekeeping at Long Island Jewish Hospital among other jobs. Then I was hired by 1199 to go to Rhode Island as an organizer in 1976. Soon after I got there, I got caught in complicated internal politics and was laid off in less than a year by 1199. There was a leadership battle going on there. I was advised to stay out of it, as a new organizer. The long and short of it is new leadership came in and they dumped me because I hadn't supported them. The old leadership went to Laborers' International Union of North America (LIUNA) but they didn't take me with them because I hadn't supported them.

I had a new baby along with my wife, her two kids, and mother-in-law living with us and was now unemployed in Rhode Island. I went to work at a jewelry factory, A and H Manufacturing, as a plastic extrusion operator and I was fired from there for trying to organize a union. I was then hired by the International Ladies' Garment Workers Union (ILGWU) and moved to Charlotte, North Carolina, as an organizer. My southern organizing experience taught me that southern workers far from being anti-union correctly knew that joining the union meant you would be crushed by the employer and power structure. In one of my first house visits, one of the workers in a sewing shop told me that if you joined the union you could get machine gunned by the National Guard—they were referencing what happened during the textile general strike in the 1930s. At the time I was dismissive, saying "that was 40 years ago." I didn't understand that 40 years ago wasn't ancient history. Peoples' parents and grandparents experienced the National Guard crushing the strike and peoples' current experiences reinforced the idea that the entire power structure would crush you if you tried to form a union.[3] In my years organizing all over the south, almost every shop we organized shut down. We ran long strikes where we walked the scabs out multiple times—but never won. This got me thinking that a strategy based on workers alone was insufficient. Workers in large numbers won't organize if there isn't a strategy to win—and if there isn't a broader strategy to win beyond workers taking action, then when workers do organize they will be crushed.

I then went to work for Communication Workers of America (CWA) in 1982. My initial work focused on organizing workers in Indianapolis in what was then called the emerging High Tech industry. This campaign was launched in the early 1980s at the same time RCA and all the unionized industrial plants were closing. We tried a new non–National Labor Relations Board strategy in this campaign at Wavetek. Since employers' major weapon in addition to firings and threats was to grant improvements and say the union wasn't needed—our campaign was based on "shop floor struggle." We constantly campaigned over shop floor and economic issues instead of filing for an NLRB election. We built campaigns around a newsletter written by workers called *Wavetek Workers' Voice* and did constant shop floor agitation—and won huge gains for workers but the plug was pulled on the campaign before we could test whether a strategy based on winning victory on top of victory through shop floor struggle—pre-recognition—could both win over workers in a nonunion sector and prove so costly to the company that they would agree to negotiate a traditional collective bargaining agreement. In addition to the shop floor actions, we experimented with developing corporate pressure but did not have an effective campaign to put pressure directly on the company beyond the activity on the shop floor. From there, I did the university organizing in Ohio for CWA when public sector collective bargaining passed there in 1984.

SEIU hired me in 1985–86 after the CWA campaign in Ohio. After that campaign came to an end, SEIU recruited a number of folks who worked on it. Andy Stern hired me. SEIU had started very early work mainly on defensive campaigns in building services. There was a long strike in Pittsburgh resisting concessions just before I started.

JM: In your view, what made SEIU such a nexus of creativity in the labor movement in the 1980s? To what extent was it the leadership of John Sweeney or of Andy Stern as organizing director? What other factors helped make SEIU a nexus of labor movement energy?

SL: SEIU was going through a transition from a completely decentralized union, to creating a national program. Sweeney was expert in allowing creativity to flourish while still maintaining support of right wing and conservative elements. He hired Stern, and combined, they created the space to allow all sorts of innovations and creativity. SEIU was one of the few unions that would hire from outside the union. An infusion of new people, who were given space (and protected) by Sweeney and Stern, made it possible to experiment on a grand scale.

JM: What led to Justice for Janitors?

SL: SEIU was founded as a union of janitors. The union's roots were as building service workers. What was then called the building service division—the original roots of the union was dying—cities were going nonunion. The industry was getting contracted out and immigrant workers were increasingly dominating the industry. As the union expanded into the public sector and health care, there was less and less focus on janitors. In the 1980s, the union was dying around the country except in cities of historic union strength like New York, Chicago, and San Francisco. The Pittsburgh strike—which focused on Mellon Bank—gave hope that you could fight back and win, after years of accepting concessions in an attempt to protect union contractors from lower paying nonunion contractors. I was hired, in part, because most people had given up on organizing in the sector so it wasn't a big risk to bring someone new in. Sweeney was president of Local 32BJ before becoming the International president—so he was always invested in building service workers. Also, a key part of his political base were building service locals. Andy was then the new organizing director, he didn't know the private sector—he had been a social worker in Pennsylvania. The Pittsburgh strike intrigued folks because they won and I think it gave them some hope about the sector.

So, after I was hired we tried an experiment in Denver, Colorado, to organize the whole city at once, avoid the NLRB, and base the campaign in the Latino community. We organized 1,000 workers into a city wide master contract—most of the city in under a year—despite much of our organizing committee being deported early in the campaign. Denver is where we started experimenting with new strategies and tactics, from building occupations, civil disobedience, to using slow moving cars to blockade Denver's airport over the conditions of airport janitors. Our quick win in Denver created incredible excitement in the union and led to our expanding J4J campaigns all over the country.

JM: Was there resistance to the Denver experiment?

SL: Yes. In Denver the AFL-CIO regional director tried to get me fired, saying I was working with "communist" Latino groups. Externally, prior to our breakthrough, everybody said it was impossible to organize undocumented part-time workers. The issue was less external than internal. It was the janitor organizing that drove the debate in SEIU about the need to organize undocumented workers. Prior to J4J, many locals would call the INS [Immigration and Naturalization Service] to deport undocumented Latinos who worked for nonunion cleaning contractors. Locals saw undocumented workers as the enemy, and in turn undocumented workers hated the union for being pro-deportation.

In Denver, and then later in LA, we demonstrated that undocumented workers, far from being un-organizable, were willing to engage in militant direct action. By winning, and humanizing undocumented workers, we were able to get SEIU to officially adopt a position that we were organizing all workers—with or without papers—which then helped change AFL-CIO policy.[4]

JM: What was the key strategic innovation of J4J growing out of Denver and other early fights?

SL: Once we understood that building owners controlled the show, [that] they decided wages by how they bid [their building service] contracts—we needed to figure out how to pressure building owners. One part was embarrassing them, actions at buildings, strikes, disruption. The other was understanding where they get their capital. It turns out that most of their capital comes from public employee pension funds and Taft-Hartley funds.[5] We were able to get "responsible contractor agreements" signed by close to $1 trillion in pension capital. These agreements in essence said that mistreating and underpaying workers was bad for long-term investments. This meant when workers organized or went on strike, building owners knew that their future financing was threatened if they didn't settle. Key to this is the idea that workers' pension dollars—which is just deferred compensation—shouldn't be invested in companies that exploit workers.

JM: Not long after the Denver success, Justice for Janitors had a big failure as the movement tried to organize Atlanta janitors using the run-up to the 1988 Democratic National Convention in that city as a leverage point. What did you learn from J4J's failure in Atlanta?

SL: First, Atlanta was far from being a progressive city—it was corporate-controlled. It was liberal on race, but viciously anti-union. We totally misjudged how tied [Mayor] Andy Young and many civil rights leaders were to business community.[6] Then, we couldn't beat big national cleaning contractors without support of New York City, and when we tried to get that support it wasn't there. Local 32BJ refused to pressure their contactors to be union in Atlanta.

Our big compression point and chance to win was tied to disrupting the Democratic convention. A chief sponsor of the convention was John Portman, the biggest developer in Atlanta. After creating massive tension, disrupting events, getting national press, putting J4J t-shirts on the majority of convention delegates, etc., Sweeney cut a deal with Andrew Young behind the scenes canceling activity until after the convention with promise that the city and John Portman would negotiate a deal later that allowed janitors to organize. Obviously, with no leverage post-convention, negotiations failed. The union caved to Democrats. We weren't successful in organizing Atlanta's janitors but the campaign helped put J4J on the national map because of all of the press we received and the fight with John Portman that was conducted around the country. [The campaign] started to build our reputation among building owners and cleaning contractors about how expensive and damaging it was to be in a fight with us.

We made a huge mistake in believing that because Atlanta had black political leadership with roots in civil rights struggles that they would be supportive of our organizing. It was hard to run a campaign saying black workers were being screwed by the business community when the black power structure of the city was tied to the business community and weren't willing to use their power to take on the giant corporations who used minimum wage janitors employed by subcontractors. It wasn't the cost of cleaning union they feared but that a victory for janitors in their buildings would open the door to their own workers organizing.

JM: Did the campaign have to struggle to get the resources necessary to wage its fights?

SL: Our initial budget was tiny—I think Denver started off with a $50,000 budget. After winning Denver, we got significantly more resources, though it was always a battle [to get resources]. When the New Strength Unity program was established, which created industry organizing funds, this gave us much more freedom because there was specific money specified for organizing in each division.[7]

The tension I mentioned before was peoples' view that janitor organizing was so much more expensive than public sector organizing. You could do 10,000 public sector workers in one election and be almost guaranteed a contract. Janitors took more money and time. There were multiple levels of financial pressure. One was the call for cheaper short cuts to winning. The second was in accessing other union money beyond the [New Strength] Unity fund and where we faced folks who didn't support industry/sectoral organizing and thought the union should just organize where it was most cost effective without regard to building power. We argued we need to organize and build power to achieve industry density—gaining more members alone didn't increase workers' power.

JM: Were there times when you weren't sure that the J4J strategy would work? What were the most difficult moments for J4J?

SL: Our difficult moments all revolved around people becoming impatient with how long campaigns took and the threat of losing funding and support. In LA, the union was close to giving up before the breakthrough in Century City. [Washington,] D.C. was the most difficult campaign because it was so long and difficult. It was winning victories in other cities that allowed us to continue D.C. until we finally won.

As we started to win, there was enormous pressure to do quicker less expensive campaigns, and a questioning of why we had so many strikes. As I said earlier, there was growing tension between the idea that we should use our victories and newfound strength to leverage organizing all over the country and globally, versus the idea that our success now made it possible to have more traditional labor management relations which didn't require risking the organized base or taking the battles to cities that were now under citywide master contracts. Many of the difficult moments revolved around pressure to make deals and not to be as aggressive. I was in a constant battle with, and eventually lost out, to the view that we could win with less conflict, over longer periods of time, and less strikes.

We also were sued again and again, and each piece of litigation, including a major RICO [Racketeer Influenced and Corrupt Organizations Act] suit in the Group 4 campaign, led to pressure to moderate tactics. It is important to note that we didn't lose most of the litigation—it was the cost of the litigation, especially the RICO lawsuits, that caused concern.

JM: The civil disobedience campaign initiated in Washington, D.C., happened not long before John Sweeney announced his candidacy for the AFL-CIO presidency. What impact did the campaign have on Sweeney and how he was seen within the AFL-CIO?

SL: The D.C. civil disobedience and bridge-blocking polarized the labor movement in fascinating ways. Many unions privately and publicly said we were ruining [the] image of labor and opposed what we did. When Sweeney ran for President of the AFL-CIO, Tom Donahue said he was for building bridges not blocking bridges. Sweeney then embraced the bridge blocking and said he too was for building bridges—when employers let up on the mortar fire (that's not an exact quote)—but until they did let up he was for blocking them. It became a defining difference between him and Donahue.

JM: How important was J4J's breakthrough in the Century City campaign, and how did that come about?

SL: As I mentioned, some in the union were ready to give up on J4J prior to the Century City strike. Winning this strike and the global press we received after the police riot was the first proof that we could win and organize thousands of workers. If we hadn't won Century City, there might not have been a J4J campaign.

We made the choice to strike Century City over weeks, instead of a quick one-or-two-day strikes. It is where we proved we could run a traditional strike—with workers out for weeks—and a nontraditional strike in terms of tactics. It is also what put us front and center as a union fighting for immigration rights. It captured peoples' imagination and put J4J on the map.

It also took J4J global. One of the big cleaning contractors in LA was International Service Systems (ISS), which at the time was a Danish corporation. We had been in touch with the Danish Cleaners union about pressuring ISS to recognize the union. They were shocked by the police violence and became much more engaged in pressuring the company to go union, which they did. This all overlapped with the various mergers of Global Union Federations (GUFS) which created what is now called UNI [the UNI Global Union, formerly the Union Network International]. With UNI we established Justice for Janitors Day, on the anniversary of the police riot, and did actions around the world to commemorate the strike and police attack. This continues to this day.

This is when we started deepening our work with unions in other countries both to pressure European cleaning companies, pensions, and building owners to be union in the US and also to encourage janitor unions around the world to organize to avoid what had happened in the US—where a formerly unionized industry de-unionized. Over time we worked with unions in Australia, the UK, the Netherlands, and other countries to launch Justice for Janitors campaigns. We started to develop a theory of global service workers organizing that was greatly influenced by Saskia Sassen's book, *The Global City*.[8] The basic argument was there are series of global cities that operated around the world that were the command centers of global capitalism where the economy was first world for corporations and the rich but workers still had sub poverty wages. We developed the idea of a "rent to wage ratio"—meaning if rents in office buildings were the same as in developed countries why couldn't workers' wages mirror those in developed countries? The same building owners and cleaning contractors operate in many of these cities, the rents, their profits, and wages of the managers were all first world—just not the wages of janitors and other service workers. These cities, even if in developing countries, were all connected and had great wealth. We had a vision of building a real global union of janitors and security officers embedded in the key global cities. It was a global version of what we were doing in the US by leveraging our base in New York, Chicago, and other cities to organize where the union didn't exist yet.

JM: Some critics of SEIU and Justice for Janitors argue that staff dominated the union's campaigns and strategies and these were top-down affairs. How do you respond to those critiques?

SL: Almost all SEIU locals in the building service division were run by older white men—in some, leadership was handed from father to son, [and this] didn't reflect either the membership or workforce we were organizing. They ranged from decent folks who couldn't adapt to changes in the workforce and industry, to folks resistant to change, to mob-dominated locals. We had a unique window where we both had huge financial resources and internal political support to force change in these locals. Over the life of the campaign, we trusteed almost every local.[9] Almost all SEIU property service locals now have elected leaders who are people of color. Rocio Saenz, a Mexican immigrant who helped organize Los Angeles, went onto to be President of the Boston local, and is now the Executive Vice President for SEIU in charge of the property service division. We needed to change leadership to make organizing possible. There is no evidence that spontaneous rank-and-file movements could have won this kind of dramatic leadership change in such a short period of time.

One of the key successes of J4J was crafting a national strategy to fit a national industry, meaning contractors and building owners were all national, and it was insufficient to have just a local strategy. Interestingly, workers totally got the reason for a national strategy. It was local staff and leaders who were upset that they had to be connected to a national organizing and bargaining strategy—many liked playing the role, even if ineffective, of local dealmaker.

I think we did completely the right thing in driving "top down" forced change focused on leaders who totally controlled their locals, instead of waiting and hoping that rank-and-file movements would arise that would force a leadership change.

J4J organized more workers in the private sector in this period than any other union, [and they] ran huge and successful strikes. That wouldn't have happened if we didn't have a national strategy, significant financial and human resources, and an agreement that locals were required to put money into organizing and be involved in regional and national campaigns.

I originally proposed creating larger locals within geographic areas that mirrored how the industry was structured. Meaning, instead of multiple locals with overlapping jurisdictions in the New York metro area—in New York, Connecticut, and New Jersey—having one local that would deal with common employers. This idea was then expanded to create what are now called "mega locals." The whole east coast from Boston to Florida is now all in [Local] 32BJ. This has created giant locals that in some ways mirror building trades locals in that they align with the industry and oppose ideas like rent control because the industry opposes it. This was the political fight I lost in the union. I think the creation of the mega locals was a mistake—which cut the heart out of Justice for Janitors. Mega locals fell into operating as regional fiefdoms, focused and negotiating and organizing regionally [thereby] undercutting a national industry wide strategy.

I think our overall approach was right. But it is a fair question to ask what we could have done differently because the property service division has now become increasingly cautious and risk averse. In many ways we mirrored what happened earlier in much of the labor movement. The union's growth and increased power, which came from strikes and militant struggles, led many to believe we could now have a more "mature" relationship with employers, and didn't need to do all that "crazy" stuff that forced building owners and cleaning contractors to deal with us in the first place. In some ways we created the monster that consumed us.

JM: You mentioned that after Century City, J4J started to go global. How would you describe what happened as the union made alliances around the world?

SL: It came organically in the sense [that] we reached out to various unions and countries to get them to help us pressure cleaning contractors and building owners that operated globally. Many of the big cleaning contractors were European-owned. Once we built relationships and got engaged with these unions, it allowed us to start working with them and they got excited about our model and launched campaigns in their own countries. This is when we started to develop the theory of building worker power by focusing on key global cities that I described earlier. I wrote about this.[10]

We had a culture clash in Europe where some unions were so heavily invested in "social dialogue." We wanted to fight companies and they believed that social dialogue would lead to victory. We argued, and history has proved us correct, that the European labor movement was operating on the fumes of dying social democratic labor parties and that their countries' labor relations would come to mirror US labor relations.

JM: You left SEIU for a time in the 1990s. Why? What did you do then, and how did you end up coming back to the union and to the campaign you had designed?

SL: I quit SEIU in 1994 when it became clear to me that SEIU wasn't willing or able to make the changes necessary to take our work to the next level. A memo that I sent to Sweeney and Stern, that analyzed the work of the previous eight years said that, in part, absent of dealing with corrupt and bankrupt leaders of big locals, there was no way that we could truly organize on scale. In it, I specifically cited Local 32BJ and its corrupt leader, Gus Bevona.[11]

The memo included seven recommendations of changes that needed to be made if the building service division was to succeed. The summary was: "If we are not moving forward we will be forced into retreating. If we are not growing and on the offensive, we will end up on the defensive while we are shrinking."[12]

After leaving SEIU, I became assistant organizing director at the AFL-CIO when John Sweeney was elected president. Andy Stern, after an internal battle, became President of SEIU. While at the AFL-CIO, we launched the industry-wide strawberry worker organizing campaign with the UFW in California and other industry campaigns.[13] I was then recruited to became the national organizing director for the Building and Construction Trades Department of the AFL-CIO where we launched the Building Trades Organizing Project (BTOP) in Las Vegas.

In 1999, as Andy Stern prepared to trustee Gus Bevona and local 32BJ, he said he was now ready to implement many of the proposals I made in 1994 and asked if I would come back to SEIU to be the Division Director of the Building Service Division. This was a higher level job than my previous jobs as organizing director. With the resources of the New Strength Unity Plan, we dramatically expanded the program, with rolling strikes starting in LA in 2000 as part of moving towards national bargaining. In 2002, we trusteed Boston Local 254 after years of corruption. Rocio Saenz became president and we had a city wide strike in 2002. I was elected to the union's International Executive Board.

JM: Houston and Miami campaigns were the last big wins for J4J. How would you compare them to each other and to the earlier struggles?

SL: In some ways it was the best of times and the worst of times. Houston showed we could roll picket lines around country, use pension capital to pressure building owners, and win broad public support in a southern city.[14] We had spent years regaining the right to honor picket lines in janitor contracts and this language allowed us to spread picket lines from one city to another.

Even though we won the strike, it exposed all the internal politics and internal contradictions. We struck the whole city and told building owners we wouldn't settle with some owners until we had a citywide agreement. The idea was to force building owners we had leverage on to help bring others owners to [the] table. Mike Fishman, the President of [Local] 32BJ, at the request of New York building owners that had operations in Houston that we struck, tried to set up a smaller table, of those owners that would settle—but without other owners. This undercut our strategy. But since we were running the strike and the bargaining table, he was unsuccessful in forcing this. Stern [then SEIU's president], throughout the strike second-guessed the strategy, told us we were losing public support for the strike through our sit-ins and traffic blocking, and supported the Fishman position. Interestingly, after we won the strike and did post-strike polling of the general public, it showed overwhelming support for the union.

It is in this period where the two competing visions of what should happen in property service came into sharpest focus. Mike Fishman, who became President of SEIU Local 32BJ in New York after it was trusteed,[15] argued that New York [w]as the biggest janitors union and home to the real estate industry and should control the property service division. He didn't want to risk relationships with New York building owners and cleaning contractors by using New York's power to support organizing and strikes around the country. We had spent five years getting all the contracts to expire at the same time, to force national bargaining, and Fishman took New York off common expiration dates. At the same time, Stern increasingly wanted to find a new way to organize and grow that was faster, cheaper, and didn't involve intense struggle. In many ways it was an old labor movement story played out again. The very success of the union led them to believe they could have a different kind of relationship with the industry that no longer required pitched battles. We believed in using our base and power to try to build a mass movement and exponential growth. They believed in incremental gains and finding ways to show employers the union could be a good partner. It was often called "peace plus." Meaning the union needed to convince employers that not only did settling with the union bring "peace"—no strikes—but the settling with the union also meant we would be their ally on issues like zoning, rent control, etc.

Miami was different in that it was a strike against the University of Miami's contractor—UNNICO—not a city-wide strike. It was a more traditional campaign and strike in the sense that we focused on one contractor at one university versus trying to organize a whole city. The university and cleaning contractor ran an aggressive anti-union campaign. After multiple attempts to pressure and negotiate with [university president] Donna Shalala, we went on strike, setting up a tent city outside the university. As an escalation, workers decided to go on a hunger strike and live twenty-four hours a day in the tent city. All of this overlapped with Hillary Clinton's first presidential run. We focused on Shalala, and the obscenity that she, a former secretary of Health and Human Services in the Clinton cabinet, didn't provide affordable health insurance for janitors, who earned poverty wages, and ran an aggressive anti-union campaign. The hunger strike brought national attention to the strike and opened up behind the scenes negotiations facilitated by people in the Clinton world. The union became very nervous about the long hunger strike that workers undertook, which workers had to quit after being hospitalized. Workers were incredibly committed to the union and willing to take great personal risks. I was privately accused of endangering workers' lives by not calling off the hunger strike. They [the union leadership] didn't realize that workers had real ownership of the hunger strike, it wasn't up to us to call it off, and those who physically could go on didn't want to quit the hunger strike—they wanted to win[!] It was an odd moment after years of hearing people in the union romantically talk about the risks workers used to take to win the union in the 1930s, they were really nervous when these workers took similar risks in Miami. On the ground, and throughout the country, there was tremendous support and excitement for the strike—which we won—but it increased the feeling among Stern and others that J4J fights were too hard and too expensive.[16] These were the last big J4J campaigns before I was taken out of the [building services] division and moved into the private equity campaign. The irony is we won two huge victories in the South and these were the swan song for J4J.

JM: How did J4J morph into organizing security workers? What was the thinking that went into it?

SL: When we started Justice for Janitors, janitors were the lowest paid workers and primarily immigrants, and security officers were higher paid and African American. Over time the janitors' wages and benefits passed security officers' as we continued to organize. Janitors made more and had better benefits than security. This created real interest among security workers in organizing. As janitorial companies expanded, many of them started offering security services in addition to janitorial. There was also a huge consolidation in the security industry with a Swedish company Securitas buying up Pinkerton and other American companies.

Security organizing came out of an industrial analysis of the property service sector and a strategy of building black/brown unity in key cities. In LA, linking Latino janitors and black security officers was a conscious decision to build an urban political base.

Jono Shaffer was the long-time advocate for organizing security. There was internal debate on a number of fronts. The first was did we want "rent a cops" in the union. This wasn't hard to overcome. The second question revolved around the NLRA rule that on its face makes it sound like security officers can't be in "mixed unions"—meaning unions that represent security and non-security workers. It isn't illegal. The board won't conduct elections or certify mixed unions. But if you are strong enough to force recognition and a contract, it is a freestanding agreement that is enforceable. The industrial argument won out—security workers were in the same buildings as janitors often working for the same companies as janitors.

The building owners initially went crazy saying there was no way they would allow unionized janitors and security in the same building. We beat Securitas relatively quickly based on pressure from the Swedish Transport Union. We also won Minnesota because the biggest cleaning contractor, Marsden, also was the biggest security contractor. In addition to global pressure, pressure on unionized building owners and pension pressure campaign was built around Civil Rights themes: black workers had been left behind. In LA demonstrations and actions were built around "I am a Man" [the slogan of the 1968 Memphis sanitation strike] with heavy support and leadership from black clergy and civil rights groups.

JM: How did you begin to widen your horizons, moving beyond building services and J4J before your departure from SEIU? What impact did the Great Recession have on your thinking?

SL: This idea of understanding where building owners get their capital and developing ways to use that for leverage was central to J4J. All of our work was based on going up the financial tree. Private equity companies started buying buildings and cleaning/security companies, putting them on our radar. For example, Blackstone bought the biggest office building company in the country—Equity Office. When we started looking at private equity companies we realized that they owned everything—buildings, nursing homes, hospitals, etc., and they got their capital from public employee pension funds. Building owners tried to claim they weren't responsible for cleaning contractors—saying the latter were "independent." Private equity made the same claim about the companies they own (portfolio companies). So the fight was similar—forcing the company at the top to take responsibility for companies they controlled. In private equity, we were trying to get ahead of a growing trend which was PE buyouts of companies and PE playing a bigger and bigger role in the economy. It offered an opportunity to have a fight at the highest level for hundreds of thousands of workers, versus the weakness of J4J, where we had fights with huge entities for relatively few workers.

Over time [we] realized that we were having huge fights with giant corporations for a very small amount of their work. It led us to think about going after the full portfolio of their workers. Our thinking was let's not just have a fight with Blackstone over janitors—let's have a fight with them about all their workers. This led us to security, then to private equity and bank workers. Andy Stern proposed doing a private equity campaign. He recognized that these companies were playing an increasingly important role in the economy. But he wanted to find a way to leverage private equity companies to be union through pension and other leverage, without organizing their workers. He thought there could be a grand deal with the industry that didn't require organizing workers.

Our thinking about banks grew out of a similar theory. In all our janitor campaigns we ran into banks as players in the real estate industry. Our theory was let's try a new sector/industry by focusing on the folks at the top. In addition, banks were key bad guys on consumer and other public issues. Globally, we had built a relationship with unions around the world in security and janitorial organizing. Banks are unionized in most of the world except the US. These bank workers' unions, led by the Brazilian bank workers, asked us to partner with them in organizing the bank sector in the US.

I was transferred out of my position as the Property Service Division Director prior to the Great Recession and continued to work on Private Equity and Banks while still serving in an elected position on the executive board. The Great Recession coincided with Stern leaving SEIU,[17] [and] lots of other factors from internal politics to the Great Recession all happened at the same time. There was a leadership change when Mary Kay [Henry] got elected President.[18] I argued that with the crash of the economy, the union needed to focus on finance, financialization, and a more fundamental challenge to how capitalism operates. But I lost that fight and left the union in 2011.

JM: Looking back, what key lessons did you draw from your experience with Justice for Janitors that have guided your work since?

SL: There are so many lessons from J4J. I dealt with some of these in an article for *The Nation* that Jono Shaffer and I wrote on the 25th anniversary of the Century City strike.[19] The overarching lesson is that there is no silver bullet—no one secret trick to winning. We developed a comprehensive strategy that played out differently depending on local and national conditions.

Central to the strategy was understanding how the industry worked—which early on led us to the conclusion that building owners and their financing had to be the target versus the cleaning contractor who was the "legal employer." From the beginning we realized the economy had reorganized and we couldn't organize by going through the NLRB and trying to win elections with cleaning contractors who were really just payroll agents for the building owners who had the money and power.

We realized that the very thing that made it hard to organize and maintain a union of janitors—contractors worked on 30-day cancelation clauses, which allowed building owners to quickly de-unionize by firing unionized cleaning contractors—also offered the opportunity to pressure building owners to fire nonunion contractors who mistreated workers. Nonunion contractors came to see that fighting the union could cost them work, which gave us great leverage in getting them to recognize the union when building owners were willing to put additional money into contracts to pay janitors more.

On the one hand, we did deep research and identified multiple levels of leverage on the employers. On the other, we organized janitors at work and in their neighborhoods. Leverage is insufficient without real deep worker support and actions. It is mass worker activity, strikes and disruption, civil disobedience, that creates the environment where financial and other leverage can work.

The lesson I've carried forward into all of our work is: workers organizing alone is insufficient to win on scale and leverage alone is insufficient. It is the *combination* that make[s it] possible to build citywide, regional, and national and global campaigns.

Two other things I would add. The first is that we were always based on forcing industry-wide bargaining—taking wages out of competition. Folks have recently rediscovered sectoral bargaining—J4J was always based on forcing sectoral bargaining.

The other is that we need a grand and inspiring vision to move workers that isn't just about getting more money. The union has to [have] been seen as the vehicle for uplift and liberation—married to a plan and strategy that gives workers the confidence to take risks to fight for that vision. The union is about coming out of the shadows, winning legalization and getting paid better for immigrants. And for security officers the union is about getting paid more and fighting structural racism that black workers face.

JM: As we look across the labor movement today, it seems that alumni of Justice for Janitors have gone on to play important roles in a whole range of activities. How do you see the legacy of J4J living on in their work?

SL: A couple years ago Randy Shaw wrote a book called *Beyond the Fields*[20] that followed many of the people that started off with the United Farm Workers union. He chronicled how that experience led them to lead all sort of different movements later. We have a similar situation in J4J. The folks who worked on J4J have gone on to be key leaders in all sort of ways. Cecile Richards, who went on to lead Planned Parenthood, helped lead the LA J4J campaign. The key leaders in United for Respect[21]—Andrea Dehlendorf, Eddie Iny, and Dan Schlademan—all came out of J4J. Lauren Jacobs, who is now the Executive Director of Powerswitch Action, worked for years on J4J. Jill Hurst, who helped set up the Athena campaign that is focused on organizing Amazon,[22] comes out of J4J. It would actually be an interesting project to build out the fuller list of J4J veterans who have gone on to play key roles in launching industry-wide campaigns, leverage strategies and new kinds of workers activism in the same way Randy did in his book.

JM: I'm also curious as to how you see the legacy of J4J living on in your own work. In recent years, you have been involved with a number of interesting initiatives, but of these I think the most significant is Bargaining for the Common Good [BCG]. What is BCG? And do you see some of the insights you gained through the J for J experience reflected in BCG's work?

SL: In addition to the stuff I described above about understanding the economy, and combining worker power with corporate leverage, we learned in J4J that we have to go way beyond the question of how workers are paid and treated at work. If you are harassed by police because of your race, that is a critical issue. If you're undocumented, that is part of the campaign. If you can't afford housing. J4J was about building a movement that is about transforming society to create hope and opportunity for the poorest workers. The bank worker campaign, BCG, the work in Puerto Rico, are all based on mass-organizing to challenge inequality, Wall Street and financialization.

J4J demonstrated in the US and globally that workers could win. It helped drive the labor movement to support undocumented workers, and it helped lead to John Sweeny becoming AFL-CIO president. It reestablished occupations and civil disobedience as central tactics for the labor movement. J4J also led in arguing that we shouldn't depend on the labor law to protect workers. It showed that sectoral organizing and bargaining can win and showed with the right strategy that workers in Florida and Texas could win. These are all lessons that continue to apply in the 2020s.

JM: In 1996, early in Sweeney's tenure as AFL-CIO president, you wrote an essay in the Boston Review called "Reviving Unions" in which you sounded an alarm. "We are now a movement in opposition," you wrote. "Hindered and hurt by our country's laws, we face a life and death struggle with the very corporations, politicians, and government with whom we've spent a lifetime building relationships." You called for militant action and you said that labor had to "move beyond wages and working conditions to lead a broad-based movement for economic and social justice." If anything, labor's crisis is deeper now than it was 25 years ago. How should labor respond?[23]

SL: What is most striking to me is how much of what has happened to workers and unions over the last 50 years was foretold by so many different people, going back at least to Sol Barkin.[24] Labor's density in the private sector peaked in the 1950s at 35 percent and has been in decline ever since. Countless books and articles have been written about the decline of the US labor movement. In 1993, I spoke at a meeting of the Food and Allied Trades department of the AFL-CIO before the 1993 AFL-CIO convention opened in San Francisco. I was told there was no media in the room and I should speak candidly, and so I did. The opening day of the AFL-CIO convention, the *San Francisco Chronicle*'s opening quote was me saying "we're dying." "Stephen Lerner, an organizer for the Service Employees International Union, warned earlier this week. 'We are at the abyss where we can disappear into something worse. Which is irrelevance.'"[25] John Sweeney called me, furious about the quote in the paper. After explaining I didn't know there was media in the room, I asked what was wrong with what I said? He said it undermined the labor movement to say we were dying in public. I remember saying to him that everybody but the labor movement talks about unions dying. A couple years later when Sweeney ran for president he said, "The labor movement faces something worse than death, the abyss of irrelevance."

I think the job is both harder and easier now. It is harder in the sense that unions are weaker and have less resources than twenty-five years ago. And some of the key points of leverage we used in "bargaining to organize" where we leveraged our strength in union contracts to win bargaining rights for non-union workers, is far harder now because density has dropped so much. On the other hand, there is a much deeper understanding and anger about economic concentration now then there was twenty-five years ago. Back then some folks in AFT [the American Federation of Teachers] attacked us for the bridge blockings saying we were destroying the image of the labor movement. Now teachers are engaging in illegal strikes and blocking streets.[26]

I think there is an opening, a possibility and potential to combine the lessons we've learned from past campaigns, with new and emerging strategies to rebuild and revive unions as part of a broader movement whose goal is to win fundamental and transformational economic and political change. When you combine the work to fight austerity and cancel the debt in Puerto Rico, with the explosion of Bargaining for Common Good work, with the Athena Amazon organizing campaign, with renewed efforts to leverage trillions in pension dollars, [with] the growing use of civil disobedience and occupations [. . .], we can start to see the contours of a winning movement. The power that the superrich and giant corporations have used to weaken unions, their success in gutting workers' living standards and imposing austerity around the country have created the conditions to birth a new movement. Our challenge is to seize this moment.

Notes

1. Stephen Lerner is a labor and community organizer who has spent more than three decades organizing hundreds of thousands of janitors, farm workers, garment workers, and other low-wage workers into unions, resulting in increased wages, first-time health benefits, paid sick days, and other improvements on the job. He was the Director of SEIU's Property Service Division, served on SEIU's International Executive Board, and was architect of the Justice for Janitors campaign. Lerner currently works with unions and community groups across the country to break the stranglehold Wall Street and big banks have had on our economy and democracy. In his previous role as director of SEIU's private equity project, Lerner launched a multi-year campaign to expose the overleveraged, unregulated, and unsustainable feeding frenzy of private equity firms during the boom years and the economic disaster that would follow once the bubble burst. Lerner has published numerous articles charting a path for a 21st century labor movement focused on growth and meeting the challenges of a global economy. In 2014 he helped launch the Bargaining for the Common Good network. Today he is a Senior Fellow at Georgetown University's Kalmanovitz Initiative for Labor & the Working Poor in Washington, D.C.

2. This interview was conducted in a series of exchanges in January and February 2020.

3. During the "Great Textile Strike" of 1934, governors of several states mobilized the state militia to suppress protests.

4. In February 2000, the AFL-CIO Executive Council unanimously adopted a resolution calling for amnesty for undocumented workers.

5. The Taft-Hartley Act of 1947 allowed U.S. unions to negotiate for the creation of multi-employer benefit funds in specific sectors. Unionized employers paid into these funds to cover health and retirement benefits. These funds were often invested in real estate.

6. Even the legendary Rep. John Lewis crossed a Justice for Janitors picket line during the protests. *Atlanta Constitution*, July 18, 1988, p. 41.

7. In 1999, SEIU President Andy Stern appointed a committee to outline the New Strength Unity Program, an effort to prepare the union for a major organizing push. A major feature of the program was a dues increase to fund new organizing in each of the union's divisions.

8. Saskia Sassen, *The Global City: New York, London, Tokyo* (Princeton: Princeton University Press, 2001).

9. See the introductory chapter to this book for a discussion of the uses of trusteeships to build the national union.

10. Stephen Lerner, "Global Unions, A Solution to Labor's Worldwide Decline," *New Labor Forum* 16:1 (2007): 23–37.

11. Lerner's memo read: "We all have a strange Schizophrenia about local 32BJ. We are in awe of its size, power and contracts. It is easy to rationalize and ignore the

dictatorial way it is run and the obscenity and embarrassment of Gus Bevona's salary. We excuse the local's refusal to support the most basic kinds of progressive politics and trade union activity. While repulsed by Bevona's racism and abusive treatment of people, we are silenced and seduced by his power." Memo available at: https://georgetown.box.com/s/oigmo8l1y2qdqodzk2gtvpan4m8ylanw.

12. The memo continued: "To ignore, fail to address, or hope that the Divisions internal problems and contradiction's will just go away is to make a decision to accept stagnation and eventual decline. It is a decision to throw away the incredible opportunities that the hard choices and work of the past eight years have made possible."

13. In 1997 the AFL-CIO came to the aid of the United Farm Workers in an unsuccessful effort to organize strawberry workers.

14. Stephen Lerner, "Global Corporations, Global Unions," *Contexts* 6:3 (2007): 16–22.

15. Mike Fishman was installed as trustee of Local 32BJ in 1999.

16. For more on Miami, see Stephen Lerner, Jill Hurst, and Glenn Adler, "The Gloves Off Economy," in *The Gloves Off Economy: Workplace Standards at the Bottom of America's Labor Market*, eds. Annette Bernhardt, Heather Boushey, Laura Dresser, Chris Tilly (Champaign, Ill.: Labor and Employment Relations Association, 2008): 243–268.

17. Stern resigned from SEIU's presidency in April 2010.

18. In May 2010, the 73-member SEIU executive board elected Henry to fill the vacancy created by Stern's resignation.

19. Stephen Lerner and Jono Shaffer, "25 Years Later: Lessons from the Organizers of Justice for Janitors," *The Nation*, June 26, 2015, https://www.thenation.com/article/25-years-later-lessons-from-the-organizers-of-justice-for-janitors/.

20. Randy Shaw, *Beyond the Fields: Cesar Chavez, the UFW, and the Struggle for Justice in the 21st Century* (Berkeley: University of California Press, 2010).

21. The Organization United for Respect, a multiracial national nonprofit organization fighting to improve the lives of retail workers, had its origins in the United Food & Commercial Workers' OUR Walmart campaign. See: https://united4respect.org/.

22. On this campaign, see https://www.nytimes.com/2019/11/26/technology/amazon-grass-roots-activists.htm.

23. Stephen Lerner, "Reviving Unions," *Boston Review* 21:2 (April/May 1996).

24. In 1961, Solomon Barkin wrote, "'Crisis' is not too strong a word for the cessation of the trade union movement's expansion into new areas and its decline in numerical strength." Solomon Barkin, *The Decline of the Labor Movement—And What Can Be Done About It* (Santa Barbara: Center for the Study of Democratic Institutions, 1961), 62.

25. Aurelio Rojas and Benjamin Pimentel, "Crucial Meeting for AFL-CIO To Open in S.F. Biennial Convention Finds U.S. Labor at a Crossroads," *San Francisco Chronicle*, October 1, 1993, 1.

26. The Chicago Teachers Union used civil disobedience to block traffic during their October 2019 strike. https://chalkbeat.org/posts/chicago/2019/10/25/chicago-teachers-tired-but-resolute-as-strike-winds-down-second-week/.

Conclusion

The Future of SEIU and (Post-Neoliberal?) Labor

LUÍS LM AGUIAR AND JOSEPH A. MCCARTIN

This first book-length academic treatment of SEIU examined the union's origins, traced its growth in North America, and considered aspects of its expanding influence on the global stage. Its methodological approaches range from historical and archival to observation and interviews with key union personnel and activists describing their involvement in the evolution of SEIU, as well as its current campaigns and challenges. We have offered accounts of the union from its beginnings through its rebranding in the Andy Stern years, to some of its most recent campaigns development, illuminating the synergies that arose among SEIU, other unions or social movements, and activists possessing diverse organizing experiences.[1] Along the way contributors engaged with critics of the union, in some cases echoing their critiques, while in others disputing or complicating their arguments with new research data and fresh case studies. Taken together these treatments help place the union in perspective, allowing us to evaluate its successes and failures in the context of ascendant neoliberalism, whose rise shaped the era within which SEIU emerged as arguably the most successful union in North America, and one of the most influential in the world.[2]

In the wake of rising rightwing populism and a global pandemic, neoliberalism is itself in crisis. Through campaigns like the Fight for $15, Andy Stern's successor, Mary Kay Henry, has attempted to place the union in a position to respond to the vulnerabilities neoliberal capitalism generates by intensifying the exploitation of low-wage service workers—the bread and butter of potential

SEIU members.[3] Henry aligned her union with the Occupy movement, immigration reform, Black Lives Matter, and critiques of meritocracy and inequality; yet whether SEIU can take advantage of neoliberalism's crisis to expand its size and influence is unclear. The union's success at meeting the challenges it now faces will depend in part on how it responds to developments within the United States and are discussed in various chapters in this volume and further identified below. As well, it remains to be seen how the union responds to changes beyond the US including changes to SEIU Canada that began under Stern, the resistance by presidents of Canadian union locals, and the remnants of the Canadianizing of the national labor movement.[4] Ascertaining the extent of innovative organizing strategies in a Canadian context of "favorable" labor legislation to unionizing workers certainly merits the attention of future researchers.[5]

Much remains to be discovered about the development of SEIU during the years covered by this volume. Among the questions future researchers should address are those generated by the union's growing diversity in membership and leadership. How has the process of diversifying the union's leadership cadre unfolded over time? What resistance has it generated and what roadblocks has it encountered? What institutional reorganizing was necessitated by the effort to create a leadership that more fully reflects the union's membership? What role did increasingly visible women and minorities themselves play in this reorganizing? As several SEIU local leaders were fired or forced to resign in 2017 in response to allegations of sexual harassment or misconduct, and as the union sided strongly with calls for thoroughgoing police reform in 2020, how was SEIU impacted by the #MeToo or Black Lives Matter movements?[6] These are among the timeliest questions researchers must answer to understand the evolving structural dynamic of the union.

Also on the agenda of future scholars must be deeper research into SEIU's recent campaigns, from the Fight for $15, to the contributions that SEIU locals in Los Angeles, San Diego, Oregon, Connecticut, and other settings have played in shaping the Bargaining for the Common Good model, which has gathered a growing number of public sector union adherents since the 2012 Chicago teachers strike.[7] In such efforts SEIU has continued to demonstrate movement unionism and showcase its capacity to galvanize into action large numbers of workers and supporters across various geographies in the United States.

The Fight for $15 will especially require further study. Although the fast-food workers lack structural or associational power, SEIU managed to stitch together supporting coalitions for the purpose of shaming employers for paying poverty wages and badly treating the most vulnerable workers in the economy. The union created moral power by mobilizing supporters and communities of allies to publicly perform "social dramas" on the mistreatment, stagnant or depressed wages, and social injustices endured by workers serving food to Americans. The point of this campaign is to pressure employers to recognize and legitimate workers' issues and their wish to unionize.[8] The Fight for $15 has shown that the union has lost none of the energy to innovate and mobilize large segments of the working class for progressive economic change. This is refreshing, but whether it is an indication of labor emerging from neoliberal's grip and constructing a model capable of building long-term worker power has yet to be determined and will require future investigations and analysis. We especially encourage research on the Fight for $15 that centers the voices of the workers, relating their experiences in both the workplace and the campaign. Such research might illuminate how this campaign has helped workers imagine what Kate Andrias calls "an aspirational labor law" that looks beyond reform of outdated and antiunion labor legislation toward a "new labor regime" capable of tackling "platform capitalism," overcoming the limitations of worksite organizing, transcending the employee-employer dyad of traditional collective bargaining, and moving toward broader and deeper forms of social bargaining.[9]

As the essays in this volume suggest, SEIU's story points us increasingly beyond the national context, and this too must be a focus of future research. Whether the globalization of capital since the late twentieth-century has given rise to its potential global grave-diggers is yet to be determined. SEIU's trajectory clearly demonstrates the extent to which labor has developed initiatives, partnerships, and campaigns across borders to fight capital flight, resist global competitiveness initiatives, geographical whipsawing, and capital's exploitation of space to accumulate globally. As SEIU's story also shows, the labor movement has replaced an older transnational labor movement of moribund international institutions espousing reactionary ideological politics with a new transnationalism focused on collaborating across borders to build organizational strength to resist capital's dominance.[10] And, like this developing international movement, SEIU too has shifted its international relations with other unions from spontaneous delegations of solidarity or unionists' exchange visits into formal partnerships and institutional infrastructures dedicated to globalizing labor solidarity.[11]

While the case studies in this volume demonstrate SEIU's work mobilizing the organizing model across borders and the utility of the Justice for Janitors campaign as a vehicle for working with ideologically compatible unions in organizing low wage workers, they also illuminate the challenges of coordinating and participating in organizing activities across diverse labor relations systems and local histories of organizing. SEIU has brought new ideas on organizing and a wealth of resources to bear on international campaigns. Yet the union, its ideas, and its leaders have struggled to overcome the outsider status that inevitably shadows a large U.S.-based union's activities in other nations. Future researchers will have much to examine in the many partnerships SEIU has generated with other unions, particularly in Latin America, a region with a long history of interference by U.S. unions.[12] SEIU's work in Brazil, its "Brillando con Justicia" campaign to organize cleaners in México City, and the role of Mexican-American union members in moving the union to organize their compatriots in their homeland are among the subjects that deserve deeper examination.

Finally, future scholars will have to grapple with the impact on SEIU of the COVID-19 pandemic and the election to the U.S. presidency of Joseph R. Biden, whom the union enthusiastically endorsed after remaining neutral during the 2020 Democratic party primaries. While the pandemic generated societal goodwill toward front-line workers, including the cleaners, health care, and service workers organized by SEIU, it also hit the union's membership hard. The pandemic's long-term impact will likely take years to assess—as will the union's alliance with President Biden, whose defeat of Donald Trump the pandemic helped seal.

How SEIU will fare in the 2020s is yet unclear. But, if its recent history is any indication, the union will spare no effort to make the pandemic crisis and Trump's ouster a turning point for workers. And one thing seems certain: the degree to which this enormous, ambitious, and complicated union succeeds in that effort will go a long way toward defining the future of the labor movement in a (we hope) post-neoliberal order.[13]

Notes

1. Jane McAlevey describes her experience in the environmental movement before joining SEIU and after Sweeney's tenure. See Jane McAlevey, *Raising Expectations and Raising Hell: My Decade Fighting for the Labor Movement* (New York: Verso, 2012). For a discussion of the influence of social movements on American union innovative strategies see, among many others, Jane McAlevey, "The Crisis of New Labor and Alinsky's Legacy: Revisiting the Roles of the Organic Grassroots Leaders in Building Powerful Organizations and Movements," *Politics & Society* 43 (3): 415–441; Kim Voss, "Same as It Ever Was? New Labor, the CIO Organizing Model, and the Future of American Unions," *Politics & Society* 43 (3): 453–457; and Dan Clawson, *The Next Upsurge: Labor and the New Social Movements* (Ithaca, NY: ILR, 2003).

2. Greg Albo, "The Crisis of Neoliberalism and the Impasse of the Union Movement," http://www.yorku.ca/albo/docs/2009/relay26_albo.pdf; David Camfield, "Renewal in Canadian Public Sector Unions: Neoliberalism and Union Praxis," *Relations Industrielles/*

Industrial Relations 62 (2): 282–304; Todd E. Vachon, Michael Wallace, and Allen Hyde, "Union Decline in a Neoliberal Age: Globalization, Financialization, European Integration, and Union Density in 18 Affluent Democracies," *Socius: Sociological Research for a Dynamic World* 2 (2016): 1–22; and Kim Moody, *US Labor in Trouble and Transition: The Failure of Reform from Above, the Promise of Revival from Below* (New York: Verso, 2007).

3. Kim Moody, *New Terrain: How Capital Is Reshaping the Battleground of Class War* (New York: Haymarket Books, 2017); Isabel Lorey, *State of Insecurity: Government of the Precarious* (New York: Verso, 2015); and Zygmunt Bauman, *Collateral Damage: Social Inequalities in a Global Age* (Malden, MA: Polity, 2011).

4. In 1960, 72% of Canadian union members belonged to US unions. By 2015, only 25% did so. The former number is in Dan Glenday, "Off the Ropes? New Challenges and Strengths Facing Trade Unions in Canada," in *Canadian Society: Meeting the Challenges of the Twenty-First Century*, ed. Dan Glenday and Ann Duffy (Toronto, ON: Oxford University Press, 2001) 18, table 1.2. The 25% figure is in https://www.canada.ca/en/employment-social-development/services/collective-bargaining-data/reports/union-coverage.html#chart1.

5. SEIU Healthcare represents 60,000 members in Ontario alone. https://seiuhealthcare.ca/. Another 12,000 Canadian workers are members of SEIU Local 2. http://seiulocal2.ca/our-union-a.

6. Mike Elk, "SEIU Manager Sexually Assaulted Staffer Then Was Rehired at Another SEIU Local," *Payday Report*, November 16, 2017, https://paydayreport.com/seiu-manager-sexually-assaulted-staffer-rehired-another-seiu-local/.

7. On Bargaining for the Common Good, see Joseph A. McCartin, "Bargaining for the Common Good," *Dissent* 63, no. 2 (Spring 2016): 128–135; Patrick M. Dixon, *Fixing LA and Remaking Public Sector Bargaining*, Kalmanovitz Initiative for Labor and the Working Poor, Georgetown University, July 13, 2016, https://lwp.georgetown.edu/publications/fixing-la-and-remaking-public-sector-bargaining/#; Joseph A. McCartin, "Public Sector Unionism under Assault: How to Combat the Scapegoating of Organized Labor," *New Labor Forum* 22, no. 3 (September 2013): 54–62; "Labor-based Coalition Urges Lamont, Lawmakers to Tax Wealthy to Fund 'People's Recovery' from Pandemic," http://www.seiu1199ne.org/2021/01/04/labor-based-coalition-urges-lamont-lawmakers-to-tax-wealthy-to-fund-peoples-recovery-from-pandemic/.

8. On public social dramas as workers' performance for change, see Jennifer Jihye Chun, *Organizing at the Margins: The Symbolic Politics of Labor in South Korea and the United States* (Ithaca, NY: ILR Press, 2009).

9. See Kate Andrias, "Constructing a New Labor Law for the Post–New Deal Era," in *Capitalism Contested: The New Deal and Its Legacies*, eds. Romain Huret, Nelson Lichtenstein, and Jean-Christian Vinel (Philadelphia, PA: University of Pennsylvania Press, 2020), 240–256.

10. Kim Moody, *Workers in a Lean World: Unions in the International Economy* (New York: Verso 1997); Dimitris Stevis and Terry Boswell, *Globalization & Labor: Democratizing Global Governance* (Lanham, MD: Rowman & Littlefield Publishers, 2008); and Kate

Bronfenbrenner, ed., *Global Unions: Challenging Transnational Capital through Cross-Border Campaigns* (Ithaca, NY: ILR Press, 2007).

11. Shaun Ryan and Andrew Herod, "Restructuring the Architecture of State Regulation in the Australian and Aotearoa/New Zealand Cleaning Industries and the Growth of Precarious Employment," in *The Dirty Work of Neoliberalism: Cleaners in the Global Economy*, eds. Luís LM Aguiar and Andrew Herod (Malden, MA: Blackwell Publishing), 60–80; Jaime McCallum, *Global Unions, Local Power: The New Spirit of Transnational Labor Organizing* (Ithaca, NY: IRL, 2013); and Jeremy Anderson, "Labor's Lines of Flight: Rethinking the Vulnerabilities of Transnational Capital." *Geoforum* 40 (2009): 959–968.

12. See Beth Sims, *Workers of the World Undermined: American Labor's Role in U.S. Foreign Policy* (Boston, MA: South End Press, 1992); Kim Scipes, *AFL-CIO's Secret War against Developing Country Workers: Solidarity or Sabotage?* (Lanham, MD: Lexington Books, 2010); and Eduardo Galeano, *Open Veins of Latin America: Five Centuries of the Pillage of a Continent* (New York: Monthly Review Press, 1997).

13. https://www.globenewswire.com/news-release/2020/05/12/2032161/0/en/SEIU-Local-2-Launches-Nationwide-Effort-to-Unionize-Essential-Workers.html.

Contributors

LUÍS LM AGUIAR is an associate professor in sociology at the University of British Columbia. He has been researching and publishing on cleaners across various geographies for more than twenty-five years. He edited (with Andrew Herod) *The Dirty Work of Neoliberalism: Cleaners in the Global Economy* (Blackwell 2006). In addition, he writes on unions, the tourism industry, urban inequalities, whiteness, and the changing political economy of the Okanagan Valley in the southern interior of British Columbia, Canada. A book on the *Fantasies of Whiteness in the Okanagan Valley* is forthcoming in 2021 from UBC Press.

ADRIENNE E. EATON is dean of the School of Management and Labor Relations, Rutgers University, and distinguished professor of labor studies and employment relations. Her research focuses on labor-management partnerships, union organizing, and the impact of unionization on various types of workers. She has been published in *Industrial and Labor Relations Review*, *Industrial Relations*, and other leading journals. She is coauthor of the book *Healing Together: The Labor-Management Partnership at Kaiser Permanente* and coeditor of the volume *Informal Workers and Collective Action: A Global Perspective*. She is a past president of the Rutgers AAUP-AFT, the union of faculty and graduate student employees at Rutgers.

JANICE FINE holds a PhD from MIT in political science and is professor of labor studies and employment relations at the School of Management and Labor

Relations, Rutgers University, where she teaches and writes about low-wage immigrant labor in the United States, historical and contemporary debates regarding federal immigration policy, dilemmas of labor standards enforcement, and innovative union and community organizing strategies. Fine serves as faculty coordinator of the Program on Immigration and Democracy at the Eagleton Institute of Politics and is a member of the graduate faculty in political science as well as the Department of Latino and Hispanic Caribbean Studies at Rutgers. She is author of the groundbreaking book *Worker Centers: Organizing Communities at the Edge of the Dream*. Her recent articles have appeared in the journals *International Migration Review*, *Labor Studies Journal*, *Politics & Society*, *Studies in American Political Development*, and *New Labor Forum*. Prior to coming to Rutgers in 2005, Fine worked as a community, labor, and electoral organizer for more than twenty-five years.

EUAN GIBB is based in São Paulo, Brazil. He works as the regional assistant for Interamerica in the global union Public Services International. Euan completed a master's degree with the Global Labour University in Berlin, Germany, and another in labour studies at McMaster University in Hamilton, Canada.

LAURENCE HAMEL-ROY is currently pursuing a PhD in humanities at Concordia University in Montreal on the transformation and gender bias of the Canadian unemployment insurance system. She holds a master's degree in sociology from the Université de Montréal, for which she studied the home support services sector in Quebec. Since 2016, she has been collaborating with Action travail des femmes (ATF) as an independent researcher promoting women's work in nontraditional employment sectors.

ALYSSA MAY KUCHINSKI is a PhD candidate in the History Department at Duke University. Born and raised in a working-class community in Holmes County, Ohio, she received her BA in history and government from Georgetown University in 2017. Her coauthored chapter featured in this collection emerged from her undergraduate thesis. She is currently working on her dissertation, which focuses on how local and state economic development policies affected working-class people throughout the twentieth-century United States.

TASHLIN LAKHANI is assistant professor of management and organizations at Cornell University's School of Hotel Administration in the SC Johnson College of Business. Her research focuses on understanding how ownership structures influence firms' human resource strategies and, in turn, employee and organizational outcomes. Her current work examines human resource practices and performance in franchise businesses in the hotel and restaurant industries.

She has also studied human resource management in global networks and the outcomes of different labor union strategies. Her research has been published in academic journals such as *Industrial & Labor Relations Review* and the *British Journal of Industrial Relations*, book chapters, and industry reports. She teaches courses on human resource management, labor relations, and franchising.

JOSEPH A. MCCARTIN is professor of history and executive director of the Kalmanovitz Initiative for Labor and the Working Poor at Georgetown University. His work examines the intersection of U.S. labor, social, and political history. His most recent books include *Collision Course: Ronald Reagan, the Air Traffic Controllers, and the Strike that Changed America*, and (coauthored with Melvyn Dubofsky) *Labor in America: A History* (9th edition), and he is the author of more than sixty articles and chapters in both scholarly and popular publications.

YANICK NOISEUX is associate professor of sociology at the Université de Montreal. His work focuses on union's renewal and nonstandard work, labor transformation, and social policies in the context of globalization. Principal investigator for the Interdisciplinary and Inter-university Research Group on Employment, Poverty and Social Protection (GIREPS in its French acronym, www.gireps.org), he's currently conducting research on collective organization on peripheral labor markets in Canada, Argentina, and India.

BENJAMIN L. PETERSON is a visiting assistant professor of political science and history at Alma College. He received his PhD in history from the University of Illinois at Chicago in 2016 and is currently working on a book project that explores the early evolution of SEIU in Chicago.

ALLISON PORTER is a senior partner in the Alvarez Porter Group, whose mission is to ignite social justice leaders and transform organizations. Allison was an organizer for ten years before working at and directing the AFL-CIO Organizing Institute, where she helped recruit and train a generation of union organizers. She has a master's degree in organization development from American University/NTL/NLC and is certified as an executive coach. Allison has three grown children and lives with her husband and small dog in Brooklyn, New York.

MAITE TAPIA is an associate professor at the School of Human Resources and Labor Relations at Michigan State University. Her research revolves around organizing strategies of trade unions and community organizations in the United States and Europe, as well as work, migration, and the concept of intersectionality. She has published some of her work in *Industrial Relations*, the *British Journal of Industrial Relations*, *Socio-Economic Review*, the *International Journal of*

Human Resource Management, and the *Journal of Industrial Relations* and is coeditor of the 2014 Cornell University Press book *Mobilizing against Inequality: Unions, Immigrant Workers, and the Crisis of Capitalism.*

VERONICA TERRIQUEZ is a tenured professor in the Chicana/o and Central American Studies Department and Urban Planning Department at UCLA. She received her PhD in sociology at UCLA, her master's degree in education at UC Berkeley, and her BA in sociology at Harvard University. Her research focuses on social inequality, civic engagement, and immigrant integration. Informed by over two decades of connections to social justice movements in California, much of her research has implications for local and regional policies affecting Latinx, immigrant, and other low-income communities. Her research has been published in *American Sociological Review, Social Problems, Social Science & Medicine, Community Development, Education Policy*, and other journals. Additionally, Dr. Terriquez has coauthored with colleagues and students more than forty widely disseminated research reports on labor, community, and youth organizing.

KYOUNG-HEE YU is associate professor at UTS Business School in Sydney, Australia. Kyoung-Hee's research has focused on institutional and organizational change processes affecting work and employment. Her recent work has examined the role of collective action and politics in institutional change, the international mobility of workers and issues of inclusion, and the future of work and workers' voice. Kyoung-Hee's work has been published in *Organization Studies*, the *British Journal of Industrial Relations, Human Relations*, and *Work, Employment & Society*. She earned her doctorate from MIT's Sloan School of Management.

Index

THE WORKING CLASS IN AMERICAN HISTORY

Worker City, Company Town: Iron and Cotton-Worker Protest
in Troy and Cohoes, New York, 1855–84 *Daniel J. Walkowitz*

Life, Work, and Rebellion in the Coal Fields: The Southern West Virginia
Miners, 1880–1922 *David Alan Corbin*

Women and American Socialism, 1870–1920 *Mari Jo Buhle*

Lives of Their Own: Blacks, Italians, and Poles in Pittsburgh, 1900–1960
John Bodnar, Roger Simon, and Michael P. Weber

Working-Class America: Essays on Labor, Community, and American Society
Edited by Michael H. Frisch and Daniel J. Walkowitz

Eugene V. Debs: Citizen and Socialist *Nick Salvatore*

American Labor and Immigration History, 1877–1920s: Recent European Research
Edited by Dirk Hoerder

Workingmen's Democracy: The Knights of Labor and American Politics *Leon Fink*

The Electrical Workers: A History of Labor at General Electric
and Westinghouse, 1923–60 *Ronald W. Schatz*

The Mechanics of Baltimore: Workers and Politics in the Age of Revolution, 1763–1812
Charles G. Steffen

The Practice of Solidarity: American Hat Finishers in the Nineteenth Century
David Bensman

The Labor History Reader *Edited by Daniel J. Leab*

Solidarity and Fragmentation: Working People and Class Consciousness
in Detroit, 1875–1900 *Richard Oestreicher*

Counter Cultures: Saleswomen, Managers, and Customers in American
Department Stores, 1890–1940 *Susan Porter Benson*

The New England Working Class and the New Labor History
Edited by Herbert G. Gutman and Donald H. Bell

Labor Leaders in America *Edited by Melvyn Dubofsky and Warren Van Tine*

Barons of Labor: The San Francisco Building Trades and Union Power
in the Progressive Era *Michael Kazin*

Gender at Work: The Dynamics of Job Segregation by Sex during World War II
Ruth Milkman

Once a Cigar Maker: Men, Women, and Work Culture in American
Cigar Factories, 1900–1919 *Patricia A. Cooper*

A Generation of Boomers: The Pattern of Railroad Labor Conflict
in Nineteenth-Century America *Shelton Stromquist*

Work and Community in the Jungle: Chicago's Packinghouse Workers, 1894–1922
James R. Barrett

Workers, Managers, and Welfare Capitalism: The Shoeworkers and Tanners
of Endicott Johnson, 1890–1950 *Gerald Zahavi*

Men, Women, and Work: Class, Gender, and Protest in the New England
Shoe Industry, 1780–1910 *Mary Blewett*

Workers on the Waterfront: Seamen, Longshoremen, and Unionism in the 1930s
Bruce Nelson

German Workers in Chicago: A Documentary History of Working-Class Culture from 1850 to World War I *Edited by Hartmut Keil and John B. Jentz*

On the Line: Essays in the History of Auto Work *Edited by Nelson Lichtenstein and Stephen Meyer III*

Labor's Flaming Youth: Telephone Operators and Worker Militancy, 1878–1923 *Stephen H. Norwood*

Another Civil War: Labor, Capital, and the State in the Anthracite Regions of Pennsylvania, 1840–68 *Grace Palladino*

Coal, Class, and Color: Blacks in Southern West Virginia, 1915–32 *Joe William Trotter Jr.*

For Democracy, Workers, and God: Labor Song-Poems and Labor Protest, 1865–95 *Clark D. Halker*

Dishing It Out: Waitresses and Their Unions in the Twentieth Century *Dorothy Sue Cobble*

The Spirit of 1848: German Immigrants, Labor Conflict, and the Coming of the Civil War *Bruce Levine*

Working Women of Collar City: Gender, Class, and Community in Troy, New York, 1864–86 *Carole Turbin*

Southern Labor and Black Civil Rights: Organizing Memphis Workers *Michael K. Honey*

Radicals of the Worst Sort: Laboring Women in Lawrence, Massachusetts, 1860–1912 *Ardis Cameron*

Producers, Proletarians, and Politicians: Workers and Party Politics in Evansville and New Albany, Indiana, 1850–87 *Lawrence M. Lipin*

The New Left and Labor in the 1960s *Peter B. Levy*

The Making of Western Labor Radicalism: Denver's Organized Workers, 1878–1905 *David Brundage*

In Search of the Working Class: Essays in American Labor History and Political Culture *Leon Fink*

Lawyers against Labor: From Individual Rights to Corporate Liberalism *Daniel R. Ernst*

"We Are All Leaders": The Alternative Unionism of the Early 1930s *Edited by Staughton Lynd*

The Female Economy: The Millinery and Dressmaking Trades, 1860–1930 *Wendy Gamber*

"Negro and White, Unite and Fight!": A Social History of Industrial Unionism in Meatpacking, 1930–90 *Roger Horowitz*

Power at Odds: The 1922 National Railroad Shopmen's Strike *Colin J. Davis*

The Common Ground of Womanhood: Class, Gender, and Working Girls' Clubs, 1884–1928 *Priscilla Murolo*

Marching Together: Women of the Brotherhood of Sleeping Car Porters *Melinda Chateauvert*

Down on the Killing Floor: Black and White Workers in Chicago's Packinghouses, 1904–54 *Rick Halpern*

Labor and Urban Politics: Class Conflict and the Origins of Modern Liberalism in Chicago, 1864–97 *Richard Schneirov*

All That Glitters: Class, Conflict, and Community in Cripple Creek *Elizabeth Jameson*

Waterfront Workers: New Perspectives on Race and Class *Edited by Calvin Winslow*

Labor Histories: Class, Politics, and the Working-Class Experience
Edited by Eric Arnesen, Julie Greene, and Bruce Laurie

The Pullman Strike and the Crisis of the 1890s: Essays on Labor and Politics
Edited by Richard Schneirov, Shelton Stromquist, and Nick Salvatore

AlabamaNorth: African-American Migrants, Community, and Working-Class Activism in Cleveland, 1914–45 *Kimberley L. Phillips*

Imagining Internationalism in American and British Labor, 1939–49 *Victor Silverman*

William Z. Foster and the Tragedy of American Radicalism *James R. Barrett*

Colliers across the Sea: A Comparative Study of Class Formation in Scotland and the American Midwest, 1830–1924 *John H. M. Laslett*

"Rights, Not Roses": Unions and the Rise of Working-Class Feminism, 1945–80
Dennis A. Deslippe

Testing the New Deal: The General Textile Strike of 1934 in the American South
Janet Irons

Hard Work: The Making of Labor History *Melvyn Dubofsky*

Southern Workers and the Search for Community: Spartanburg County, South Carolina
G. C. Waldrep III

We Shall Be All: A History of the Industrial Workers of the World (abridged edition)
Melvyn Dubofsky, ed. Joseph A. McCartin

Race, Class, and Power in the Alabama Coalfields, 1908–21 *Brian Kelly*

Duquesne and the Rise of Steel Unionism *James D. Rose*

Anaconda: Labor, Community, and Culture in Montana's Smelter City *Laurie Mercier*

Bridgeport's Socialist New Deal, 1915–36 *Cecelia Bucki*

Indispensable Outcasts: Hobo Workers and Community in the American Midwest, 1880–1930 *Frank Tobias Higbie*

After the Strike: A Century of Labor Struggle at Pullman *Susan Eleanor Hirsch*

Corruption and Reform in the Teamsters Union *David Witwer*

Waterfront Revolts: New York and London Dockworkers, 1946–61 *Colin J. Davis*

Black Workers' Struggle for Equality in Birmingham
Horace Huntley and David Montgomery

The Tribe of Black Ulysses: African American Men in the Industrial South
William P. Jones

City of Clerks: Office and Sales Workers in Philadelphia, 1870–1920 *Jerome P. Bjelopera*

Reinventing "The People": The Progressive Movement, the Class Problem, and the Origins of Modern Liberalism *Shelton Stromquist*

Radical Unionism in the Midwest, 1900–1950 *Rosemary Feurer*

Gendering Labor History *Alice Kessler-Harris*

James P. Cannon and the Origins of the American Revolutionary Left, 1890–1928
Bryan D. Palmer

Glass Towns: Industry, Labor, and Political Economy in Appalachia, 1890–1930s
Ken Fones-Wolf

Workers and the Wild: Conservation, Consumerism, and Labor in Oregon, 1910–30
Lawrence M. Lipin

Wobblies on the Waterfront: Interracial Unionism in Progressive-Era Philadelphia *Peter Cole*

Red Chicago: American Communism at Its Grassroots, 1928–35 *Randi Storch*

Labor's Cold War: Local Politics in a Global Context *Edited by Shelton Stromquist*

Bessie Abramowitz Hillman and the Making of the Amalgamated Clothing Workers of America *Karen Pastorello*

The Great Strikes of 1877 *Edited by David O. Stowell*

Union-Free America: Workers and Antiunion Culture *Lawrence Richards*

Race against Liberalism: Black Workers and the UAW in Detroit *David M. Lewis-Colman*

Teachers and Reform: Chicago Public Education, 1929–70 *John F. Lyons*

Upheaval in the Quiet Zone: 1199/SEIU and the Politics of Healthcare Unionism *Leon Fink and Brian Greenberg*

Shadow of the Racketeer: Scandal in Organized Labor *David Witwer*

Sweet Tyranny: Migrant Labor, Industrial Agriculture, and Imperial Politics *Kathleen Mapes*

Staley: The Fight for a New American Labor Movement *Steven K. Ashby and C. J. Hawking*

On the Ground: Labor Struggles in the American Airline Industry *Liesl Miller Orenic*

NAFTA and Labor in North America *Norman Caulfield*

Making Capitalism Safe: Work Safety and Health Regulation in America, 1880–1940 *Donald W. Rogers*

Good, Reliable, White Men: Railroad Brotherhoods, 1877–1917 *Paul Michel Taillon*

Spirit of Rebellion: Labor and Religion in the New Cotton South *Jarod Roll*

The Labor Question in America: Economic Democracy in the Gilded Age *Rosanne Currarino*

Banded Together: Economic Democratization in the Brass Valley *Jeremy Brecher*

The Gospel of the Working Class: Labor's Southern Prophets in New Deal America *Erik Gellman and Jarod Roll*

Guest Workers and Resistance to U.S. Corporate Despotism *Immanuel Ness*

Gleanings of Freedom: Free and Slave Labor along the Mason-Dixon Line, 1790–1860 *Max Grivno*

Chicago in the Age of Capital: Class, Politics, and Democracy during the Civil War and Reconstruction *John B. Jentz and Richard Schneirov*

Child Care in Black and White: Working Parents and the History of Orphanages *Jessie B. Ramey*

The Haymarket Conspiracy: Transatlantic Anarchist Networks *Timothy Messer-Kruse*

Detroit's Cold War: The Origins of Postwar Conservatism *Colleen Doody*

A Renegade Union: Interracial Organizing and Labor Radicalism *Lisa Phillips*

Palomino: Clinton Jencks and Mexican-American Unionism in the American Southwest *James J. Lorence*

Latin American Migrations to the U.S. Heartland: Changing Cultural Landscapes in Middle America *Edited by Linda Allegro and Andrew Grant Wood*

Man of Fire: Selected Writings *Ernesto Galarza, ed. Armando Ibarra and Rodolfo D. Torres*

A Contest of Ideas: Capital, Politics, and Labor *Nelson Lichtenstein*

Making the World Safe for Workers: Labor, the Left, and Wilsonian Internationalism
Elizabeth McKillen
The Rise of the Chicago Police Department: Class and Conflict, 1850–1894
Sam Mitrani
Workers in Hard Times: A Long View of Economic Crises
Edited by Leon Fink, Joseph A. McCartin, and Joan Sangster
Redeeming Time: Protestantism and Chicago's Eight-Hour Movement, 1866–1912
William A. Mirola
Struggle for the Soul of the Postwar South: White Evangelical Protestants and Operation Dixie *Elizabeth Fones-Wolf and Ken Fones-Wolf*
Free Labor: The Civil War and the Making of an American Working Class
Mark A. Lause
Death and Dying in the Working Class, 1865–1920 *Michael K. Rosenow*
Immigrants against the State: Yiddish and Italian Anarchism in America
Kenyon Zimmer
Fighting for Total Person Unionism: Harold Gibbons, Ernest Calloway, and Working-Class Citizenship *Robert Bussel*
Smokestacks in the Hills: Rural-Industrial Workers in West Virginia *Louis Martin*
Disaster Citizenship: Survivors, Solidarity, and Power in the Progressive Era
Jacob A. C. Remes
The Pew and the Picket Line: Christianity and the American Working Class
Edited by Christopher D. Cantwell, Heath W. Carter, and Janine Giordano Drake
Conservative Counterrevolution: Challenging Liberalism in 1950s Milwaukee
Tula A. Connell
Manhood on the Line: Working-Class Masculinities in the American Heartland
Steve Meyer
On Gender, Labor, and Inequality *Ruth Milkman*
The Making of Working-Class Religion *Matthew Pehl*
Civic Labors: Scholar Activism and Working-Class Studies *Edited by Dennis Deslippe, Eric Fure-Slocum, and John W. McKerley*
Victor Arnautoff and the Politics of Art *Robert W. Cherny*
Against Labor: How U.S. Employers Organized to Defeat Union Activism
Edited by Rosemary Feurer and Chad Pearson
Teacher Strike! Public Education and the Making of a New American Political Order
Jon Shelton
Hillbilly Hellraisers: Federal Power and Populist Defiance in the Ozarks *J. Blake Perkins*
Sewing the Fabric of Statehood: Garment Unions, American Labor, and the Establishment of the State of Israel *Adam Howard*
Labor and Justice across the America *Edited by Leon Fink and Juan Manuel Palacio*
Frontiers of Labor: Comparative Histories of the United States and Australia
Edited by Greg Patmore and Shelton Stromquist
Women Have Always Worked: A Concise History, Second Edition *Alice Kessler-Harris*
Remembering Lattimer: Labor, Migration, and Race in Pennsylvania Anthracite Country *Paul A. Shackel*

Disruption in Detroit: Autoworkers and the Elusive Postwar Boom *Daniel J. Clark*
To Live Here, You Have to Fight: How Women Led Appalachian Movements for Social Justice *Jessica Wilkerson*
Dockworker Power: Race and Activism in Durban and the San Francisco Bay Area *Peter Cole*
Labor's Mind: A History of Working-Class Intellectual Life *Tobias Higbie*
The World in a City: Multiethnic Radicalism in Early Twentieth-Century Los Angeles *David M. Struthers*
Death to Fascism: Louis Adamic's Fight for Democracy *John P. Enyeart*
Upon the Altar of Work: Child Labor and the Rise of a New American Sectionalism *Betsy Wood*
Workers against the City: The Fight for Free Speech in *Hague v. CIO* *Donald W. Rogers*
Union Renegades: Miners, Capitalism, and Organizing in the Gilded Age *Dana M. Caldemeyer*
The Labor Board Crew: Remaking Worker-Employer Relations from Pearl Harbor to the Reagan Era *Ronald W. Schatz*
Grand Army of Labor: Workers, Veterans, and the Meaning of the Civil War *Matthew E. Stanley*
A Matter of Moral Justice: Black Women Laundry Workers and the Fight for Justice *Jenny Carson*
Labor's End: How the Promise of Automation Degraded Work *Jason Resnikoff*
Toward a Cooperative Commonwealth: The Transplanted Roots of Farmer-Labor Radicalism in Texas *Thomas Alter II*
Working in the Magic City: Moral Economy in Early Twentieth-Century Miami *Thomas A. Castillo*
Where Are the Workers? Labor's Stories at Museums and Historic Sites *Edited by Robert Forrant and Mary Anne Trasciatti*
Labor's Outcasts: Migrant Farmworkers and Unions in North America, 1934–1966 *Andrew J. Hazelton*
Fraying Fabric: How Trade Policy and Industrial Decline Transformed America *James C. Benton*
Harry Bridges: Labor Radical, Labor Legend *Robert W. Cherny*
Strong Winds and Widow Makers: Workers, Nature, and Environmental Conflict in Pacific Northwest Timber Country *Steven C. Beda*
Purple Power: The History and Global Impact of SEIU *Edited by Luís LM Aguiar and Joseph A. McCartin*

The University of Illinois Press
is a founding member of the
Association of University Presses.

University of Illinois Press
1325 South Oak Street
Champaign, IL 61820-6903
www.press.uillinois.edu